This modern text is designed to prepare you for your future professional career. While theories, ideas, techniques, and data are dynamic, the information contained in this volume will provide you a quick and useful reference as well as a guide for future learning for many years to come. Your familiarity with the contents of this book will make it an important volume in your professional library.

EX LIBRIS

SALES FORCE MANAGEMENT
Text and Cases

SALES FORCE MANAGEMENT

Text and Cases

Derek A. Newton
Elis and Signe Olsson Professor
of Business Administration
Colgate Darden Graduate
School of Business Administration
University of Virginia

1982

BUSINESS PUBLICATIONS, INC.

Plano, Texas   75075

209-225
DYNAMIC
MASSONE

Case material of the Harvard Graduate School of
Business Administration and of the Colgate Darden
Graduate School of Business Administration is made
possible by the cooperation of business firms who may
wish to remain anonymous by having names, quantities,
and other identifying details disguised while basic
relationships are maintained. Cases are prepared as the
basis for class discussion rather than to illustrate either
effective or ineffective handling of administrative
situations.

ISBN 0-256-02755-2
Library of Congress Catalog Card No. 81–71750

Printed in the United States of America

1 2 3 4 5 6 7 8 9 MP 9 8 7 6 5 4 3 2

Dedicated to
Pete

Acknowledgments

Of the many people to whom I wish to express my gratitude, the most important are the several hundred busy practitioners of the marketing art who gave their names and experience so generously to the development of the material in this book. Were it not for the cooperation of these businessmen, and the countless others who have contributed case material in other areas of business administration, the case method of instruction would lose its effectiveness as a teaching vehicle.

Many of my colleagues have contributed to the material in this book. Specific acknowledgment is made within these covers to case authors or others who have made substantial contributions to the development of individual cases. At the risk of leaving someone out, I would like also to mention specifically the contributions of two of my colleagues who have made substantial intellectual contributions to me and to this book: Neil H. Borden, Jr., and Lawrence J. Ring. I am also deeply in debt to Beverly Seng for her many helpful suggestions and many hours of editorial assistance. Finally, I would like to thank my friend, Martin V. Marshall of the Harvard Business School, who taught me all I know about case writing.

Without the support and encouragement of The Colgate Darden Graduate Business School, University of Virginia, as personified by Dean Robert W. Haigh and Dean Emeritus C. Stewart Sheppard, and the financial support of the Darden School Sponsors, this book would never have appeared.

Contents

Part Four   The Marketing Executive   **209**

Marketing and Corporate Strategy. Customer Behavior. Market Segmentation. Product Positioning. Stimulating Demand: *Product Policy. Distribution Policy. Pricing Policy. Advertising Policy.*

Introduction

The purpose of this book is to provide students and practitioners with a framework for analyzing sales force management problems. A secondary purpose is to give them practice in recognizing some of the major issues in managing a sales force, with a view toward helping them become more effective decision makers.

This book is divided into four parts, corresponding to the four primary levels of sales force decision-making responsibility: salesman,[1] field sales manager or supervisor, sales executive, and marketing executive. Starting with the salesman at the ground level, so to speak, allows readers to identify the issues in the less complex situations. This understanding can later be applied to problems in more complex marketing situations.

Each part contains basic text material that gives background information, a modicum of technical information, and selected frameworks for solving problems commonly encountered at each level of decision-making responsibility.

Each part also contains several case situations. These cases are "verbal photographs" of actual business decisions. In some instances the names of the companies and individuals have been disguised. In most instances certain data have been disguised. While these steps have been taken to protect proprietary and confidential information, the data given in the cases are relevant for analysis and discussion.

The case situations include problems in marketing both consumer and industrial goods and services, but they exclude sales problems of retailing organizations. These cases are not designed to illustrate either effective or ineffective handling of administrative situations. Rather, they are to provide examples of the kind of information that is available to company executives in these situations, thereby giving the reader practice in developing the understanding and the decision-making skills needed to build and maintain an effective sales organization.

---

[1] For simplicity's sake, I will use the term *salesman* throughout this book to refer to both male and female professionals, rather than using the awkward androgynous *salesperson*. Since many female professionals of my acquaintance call themselves *salesmen*, I feel that this usage need not offend anyone.

THE SALESMAN

Part One of text and cases is designed to increase the reader's awareness of the multiple roles played by salesmen within various firms' marketing strategies. Starting with a close look at individual sales activities is important because personal selling activities differ considerably according to the role that a company assigns to its sales force. For example, some sales forces work with their companies' channels of distribution, such as wholesalers and retailers, to make these firms more effective resellers. Some sales forces act as "missionaries," calling on users or specifiers to persuade them to buy from the company's direct customers. Other sales forces sell directly to users. Obviously, these various selling situations require quite different activities and skills.

This section also discusses the elements of an effective sales presentation, stressing the consultative nature of modern professional selling. It is not the purpose of this book to teach someone how to become an expert salesman. Nevertheless, most readers will gain confidence in their ability to sell once they understand better the nature of professional salesmanship. The purpose of this section, however, is to present a senior manager's perspective on what constitutes effective selling within the context of the firm's strategic activities.

THE FIELD SALES MANAGER

Part Two of text and cases is designed to increase understanding of the importance of personal supervision in sales force management, and of the problems encountered in directing sales force activities in the field. Again, the objective of the case material is not to teach someone how to be a good supervisor per se, but to provide a top manager's perspective on what constitutes good supervision. This section raises such issues as, How do selling skills differ from managerial skills? Do the best salespeople make the best managers? What is the appropriate role for the field sales manager in the firm's marketing strategy? How can the field sales manager translate this understanding of the firm's marketing strategy into effective managerial behavior? What managerial behaviors and activities are most appropriate for influencing sales force behavior? How can sales management policies be designed to support the activities of field sales managers? The case material brings these issues into focus by describing the activities performed by typical field sales managers at the district or branch level.

THE SALES EXECUTIVE

Part Three of this book comprises text and cases designed to increase skill in analyzing and planning effective selling strategy, and in selecting and implementing policies to foster the achievement of marketing objectives. The cases help readers deal with questions such as these: What skills and attributes do our salespeople need? How should our salespeople be organized and deployed? What kind of and how much training do they need? What kind of direction and control do they need? What sort of compensation system would best influence their behavior? What is the best way to evaluate their performance, both individually and collectively?

THE MARKETING EXECUTIVE

The final section of this book, Part Four, comprises text and cases which explore the relationships among the sales force and the several elements of marketing strategy—most notably, product policy, pricing, distribution, and advertising.

This material is based on an examination of the marketplace, covering consumers' reactions, both as individuals and in the aggregate, the nature of competition and the structure of the industry, and the opportunities and risks inherent in a given marketing program. Both sales and marketing executives need to be highly skilled in assessing the probabilities of favorably influencing demand through effective use of the sales force. This skill is particularly critical when trade-offs must be made. For example, executives may need to decide whether the incremental dollar is better spent on advertising or on the sales force. Even when a trade-off is not the key consideration the major issue often is: Will an incremental dollar spent on advertising make our sales force more effective?

Both sales and marketing executives must be alert to an even more important consideration: namely, the continuing changes in the business environment. The consumer and the competition—separately or in concert—continually force a company to reassess its strategy. As a company modifies its strategy to protect itself or to take advantage of changes in the marketplace, it must also reassess the role played by its sales force. Unless the activities of the sales force correspond to the changed marketing strategy, vitrification of the total marketing activity will soon set in.

A CONCEPTUAL FRAMEWORK

Although the material in this book proceeds from the bottom up, the reader is encouraged to develop the ability to think from the top down. The ability to conceptualize at the highest level and translate this conceptualization into an action program at the lowest level is the critical skill of any executive—sales, manufacturing, or financial. Furthermore, the complexities of sales force management problems require the ability to understand the consequences of one's decisions on several organizational layers. To diagram these relationships, and to provide a conceptual framework for improv-

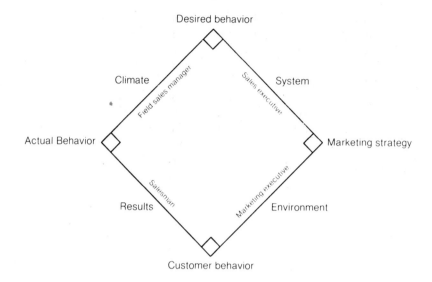

ing skills in building and maintaining an effective sales force, a baseball diamond will be used as a model.

Home plate is the alpha and omega of baseball. No runs are scored unless all four bases are touched. The behavior of the customer is the alpha and omega of business. For the marketer, no sale is made until all four bases are touched. Beginning with an analysis of customer behavior, the marketing executive atttempts to match his or her available resources to the risks, opportunities, and constraints in the competitive environment. This matching process results in a marketing strategy, a decision to create customers in a way unique to that company. The firm gets to first base when the marketing executive has developed a sound marketing strategy.

Working within the marketing strategy developed for the firm, the sales executive defines the role to be played by the sales force and creates a management system to support that role. The role is the desired behavior (what the executive would do if he or she were the *sole* salesman); the system is the combination of policies and practices selected to encourage the salesmen to behave in a particular manner (as the executive would behave if he or she were the sole salesman). The firm gets to second base when the sales executive has clearly defined the desired behavior of the sales force and has choosen that combination of policies and practices (selection, training, compensation, and so forth) that best encourages that behavior.

Working from an understanding of the desired sales force behavior, the field sales manager creates that supervisory climate that best encourages conformity between actual behavior (what the salesman does) and desired behavior (what the company wants him or her to do). The firm gets to third base if the field sales manager ensures that the actual behavior of the sales force is congruent with the desired behavior.

In baseball, only runs count, and the only way to score runs is to cross home plate. Similarly, the old cliché in business is, "Nothing happens until the sale is made." The firm crosses home plate as often as the actual behavior of the salesman produces the desired customer behavior.

Clearly, the most effective organizations touch all of the bases. To achieve this goal, many people must perform their jobs well. The salesman must be good at persuading the customer to buy. The field sales manager must be good at teaching and encouraging the salesmen to perform well. The sales executive must be good at defining the role of the sales force in the company's marketing mix, and good at creating a set of management policies and practices to encourage fulfillment of that role. The marketing executive and staff personnel must create an effective overall strategy within which the sales force operates. After all, the best sales force in the world would find it difficult to sell a product that was poorly distributed, poorly priced, and poorly promoted.

By analyzing the cases in this book, readers will increase their understanding of the sales force and marketing functions and of the relationships between them. To ease their analysis of these cases, readers should keep in mind the following questions:

1. What is the company's overall marketing strategy for the product?
2. What is the role of personal selling within that strategy?
3. What policies and practices has management developed to ensure effective direction of and control over personal selling activities?
4. How well are these policies and practices being implemented?
5. What are their effects on sales force behavior?

Part One
The Salesman

Managers make a serious mistake when they refer to what salesmen do as merely selling, as though the salesman's personality alone brings in the sale. Rather, the modern professional salesman relies as much on analytic skills as on charm and aggressiveness. And getting the order is just the final stage of a complex set of activities involving many people—within his own firm as well as within the customer's organization. Thus, to direct and supervise the sales force, managers must first understand in detail both the consultative nature of modern selling behavior and the complexity of the tasks that salesmen may perform.

THE EVOLUTION OF SELLING BEHAVIOR

Stage I: The Music Man

The concept of what constitutes good selling behavior has changed over the years. Back in the days before World War I (these dates are approximate and vary widely with the sophistication of individual firms), success in personal selling was regarded as a function of a salesman's personality, his or her ability to charm customers. The prevalent mythology was that "Good salesmen are born, not made." Consequently, few firms gave salesmen any training or supervision. Little attention was given to performance evaluation. Straight commission plans were relied on to weed out the unfit. Many of the general public's notions about salesmen stem from the sales practices of this era, as dramatized by several playwrights. Willie Loman of Arthur Miller's *Death of a Salesman* is a failure because he can no longer impress his customers; Harold Hill of *The Music Man* is so popular and entertaining that he can persuade anyone to buy almost anything.

Stage II: The Animated Catalog

After World War I, increased industrialization and competition caused many prospective buyers to pay closer attention to product performance. In response, sellers began to train their sales forces in product features. The

7

prevalent mythology was that "a good salesman is someone who knows his product." Although this stage was a vast improvement over the reliance on sheer personality, sales presentations tended to become mechanical repetitions of product information that could have easily been transmitted through a good product brochure. The "canned presentation" or "product pitch" produced a generation of salesmen who were little more than animated catalogs.

Stage III: The Magic Formula

During the 30s, as competition became more intense and sales forces got larger with influxes of young, inexperienced salesmen, sellers' training activities began to include attention to buyers' needs. Salesmen were trained to make canned sales presentations designed (1) to manipulate buyers' reactions and (2) to give salesmen confidence in their ability to sell by providing them with a "road map of the sale"—a series of steps through which they were to lead the cutomer. A prime example of this approach was AIDA: Attention—Interest—Desire—Action. Success in personal selling was considered a function of how well a salesman could communicate the benefits of the product line as opposed to the characteristics of the product line. The tactic was to "sell the sizzle instead of the steak."

The prevalent mythology was that "a good salesman controls the sale." Again, this stage was a vast improvement over the animated catalog. It acknowledged the presence of a customer and the legitimacy of his or her needs. But it produced a generation of salesmen who equated selling with outwitting the customer through a "magic formula."

Stage IV: The Problem Solver

During the 50s it became apparent to many sales executives not only that sophisticated buyers were becoming familiar with all these probing and closing techniques but also that customers' thought processes seldom followed the salesman's road map. Furthermore, buyers were demanding more professionalism from salesmen, asking them to take more of an advisory role. "Let me make up my own mind," was becoming a common buyers' plea. In response, sellers' training activities began to stress the salesman's role as a consultant. The sale became a two-step process: (1) to determine and articulate for the customer the real problem he or she faced and (2) to present the product's benefits as a partial or complete solution to that problem. This kind of selling forced the salesman to become more analytical and more sensitive to the wide range of factors affecting a buyer's decision. The salesman became less manipulative and more responsive. Success in personal selling was considered a function of how well a salesman could help customers determine the criteria for choosing among alternative products, as well as how skillful he was in demonstrating how his products satisfied these criteria. In this fashion, a good salesman literally "allowed the customer to buy." By helping customers to define their own needs, the salesman entered the sale at the very beginning and, in this way, could often place his products at a considerable competitive advantage. The sale itself was the final segment in a decision process that the salesman had helped the customer work through in its entirety. The prevalent mythology now refers to "consultative selling." Customers are more responsive to this new breed of professionals, and salesmen themselves feel more proud about what they do for a living. A new generation of salesmen is growing up as business problem solvers.

Obviously, these four stages did not fully replace one another, but have evolved to complement one another. It takes personal acceptability, technical competence, and flair for "selling the sizzle" to be an effective problem solver. However, a salesman who cannot handle this last stage, a role similar to that of a management consultant, will become increasingly beleaguered as customers come to expect this kind of professional activity. Indeed, there may be no alternative to stage IV. Increases in the efficiency of alternate methods of delivering a sales message—advertising, cable television, videophones, etc.—and a tendency to automate and computerize purchasing decisions, may sound the death knell for all but the most sophisticated and professional sales forces.

THE TASKS OF CONSULTATIVE SELLING

Having seen the consultative nature of modern personal selling, we are now in a better position to understand in detail the activities salesmen perform, activities that vary according to the firm's customers and to its overall marketing strategy. The examples that follow illustrate four main types of selling tasks: trade, missionary, technical, and entrepreneurial.[1] These categories are not exhaustive. For example, retail selling (behind-the-counter) and delivery (route) selling are not included, as these are outside the scope of this book. The attributes and skills required to carry out the four main selling tasks vary considerably. The managerial policies and the amount and kinds of supervision appropriate to each of these tasks also differ.

Trade Selling

The primary responsibility of the trade sales force is to build sales volume by providing the firm's customers with promotional assistance, thereby making the firm's resellers more effective. The trade sales force therefore *sells through* rather than *sells to* its customers. Trade selling is common in many industries, but it predominates in consumer durables and nondurables, such as furniture, apparel, textiles, and food, as well as in wholesaling firms. Since many consumer products tend to be mature and are promoted directly to the

---

[1] I am indebted to Robert N. McMurry, whose *Harvard Business Review* article "The Mystique of Super-Salesmanship," March–April 1961, suggested these categories to me.

user, a firm's trade selling is often less critical to marketing success than are its advertising and promotion.

The trade selling described below is that of a prominent firm that markets housewares though department stores, specialty stores, and discount houses. The brand is heavily advertised and the firm's products are well known for their quality.

The salesman sells the product line to wholesale distributors in an assigned geographical area, and to the major retail stores serviced by those distributors. The salesman typically devotes 80 percent of the time to distributor contacts and 20 percent to retail contacts. The salesman's territory may contain as few as 5 or as many as 15 wholesale distributors to be called on regularly. The call frequency varies from once a week to once a month, depending on the sales volume involved.

Each salesman is assigned a quota from headquarters. The salesman, in turn, prepares individual product quotas for each distributor and then tries to motivate the distributors to achieve or exceed these quotas. To accomplish the latter goal, the salesman works with each distributor, studying historic performance with each of the firm's product classes. The salesman assesses the distributor's present inventories and then, using rate-of-sale data to work out economic order quantities for each item, draws up orders for goods already stocked by the distributor. The salesman may also present new products and explain current or future promotions. Another of the salesman's key jobs is to counsel distributors to strengthen their performance with products that are not selling well.

Because a distributor may have 50 important product lines and 100 or so other lines, it is difficult to get 100 percent attention for any one firm's product line. Thus, in addition to advising the distributor's executives, the salesman may spend considerable time in sales meetings with the distributor's salespeople. These sales meetings generally are held on a Friday night or Saturday morning, quite often in a hotel suite. During these meetings, which may include dinner or breakfast, the salesman may make a formal product presentation. These presentations are designed to influence the distributor's sales personnel to sell the firm's products in the most effective and efficient manner.

In addition to calling on distributors and working with their sales personnel, the salesman keeps in frequent contact with key department store accounts and makes periodic calls on such retail firms as hardware, gift, and jewelry stores. These calls help the salesman to understand the markets served by all types of distribution channels. Calling on important retail accounts usually involves creating effective desplays for the retailer, improving the number and location of such displays, checking stock levels, holding sales meetings with retail salesclerks to show them how to sell, checking on the service provided by the distributors' sales personnel, introducing new products to the retailer, and handling credits for breakage.

As this example shows, if the professional trade salesman is to help distributors and retailers, he must thoroughly understand how the customer runs his business. Aggressiveness is probably less important than maturity, and technical competence is probably less important than "wearing well" with customers. Cases in this book that illustrate trade selling include Battlefield Group, Inc. (Case 4), Dynamic Products Corporation (Case 15), and Masonne Furniture Company (Case 18).

Missionary Selling

The missionary sells force builds sales volume by persuading second-order or indirect consumers to order from the firm's direct customers, which are its wholesalers and other channels of distribution. Thus, the missionary sales force *sells for* its direct customers, whereas the trade sales force *sells through* them. Missionary selling is common in the chemical, transportation, wholesaling, and pharmaceutical industries.

Within the pharmaceutical industry, for example, products are commonly classified as either ethical or proprietary, depending on the manufacturer's marketing method. Ethical products are marketed to the medical profession. The marketing program's objective is to persuade physicians to recommend or prescribe the product to the ultimate consumer, the patient. The industry further subdivides ethical products into two categories. Products available only by prescription are called prescription drugs; products that may be purchased without a prescription are called over-the-counter (OTC) drugs. Although consumers can legally purchase an OTC item without a prescription, physicians sometimes write prescriptions for OTC products, particularly if these products are manufactured by a firm which specializes in prescription pharmaceuticals.

Proprietary products, sometimes referred to as advertised remedies, or less accurately as patent medicines, are marketed directly to the final consumer. The manufacturers of proprietary products typically engage in heavy consumer advertising and extensive in-store displays. In comparison to proprietary products, OTC products usually are promoted only through point-of-sale displays.

Most firms that manufacture and market prescription pharmaceuticals depend heavily on missionary selling directed toward physicians and hospitals. These salesmen (or *detailers*, as they are known in the industry) are professional representatives who call regularly on physicians in their offices to give them up-to-date information on pharmaceutical products. While detailers usually focus on introducing new products, they also describe new applications for drugs already in use. To support their claim about their products, detailers usually make available to physicians drug samples, product literature, and reprints of medical journal articles. In many pharmaceutical companies, detailers are also given responsibility for calling on druggists to check inventories, to take care of returns, to answer questions, and to assist the druggist in ordering pharmaceuticals from the drug wholesaler. In some companies, detailers may also call on wholesalers. In these instances, the detailers serve as direct salesmen.

This description of their activities illustrates that detailers do not generally sell directly to doctors. Their task is essentially to provide physicians with enough information and reassurance about the products so that the physicians will prescribe them. Though not doctors themselves, detailers typically have pharmaceutical or medical training. They keep informed on current medical topics by reading company bulletins and medical journals. They are, of course, expected to have a thorough knowledge of their companies' products, including such information as technical and laboratory specifications, recommended dosages, and contraindications (conditions under which the drug should not be used).

Detailing has been criticized by many sources, both within and without the pharmaceutical industry and the medical profession, as an expensive form of promotion. Nevertheless, many physicians consider the work of the detailer essential to their keeping up with the latest developments in the pharmaceutical treatment of disease. The degree to which a particular physician relies on the detailer depends largely on the detailer's knowledge and dependability, and on the general reputation of the company he or she represents. The physician's reliance on the detailer also depends on the amount and kind of *other* sources of information available to the particular physician, such as medical journal articles, advice from colleagues, and personal experience with the pharmaceutical in question or the pharmaceutical manufacturer. It should also be recognized that the visit of a detailer in a physician's office interrupts, albeit for only 10 or 15 minutes, a heavy schedule of treating patients. The detailer's skill and tact must make the interruption seem welcome and necessary.

Many studies have been undertaken with a view to determining the relative influence of medical journal articles, journal advertising, professional colleagues, direct mail, drug product samples, and detailers in the physician's choice of what drug to prescribe. Most of these studies rank the detailer high in influence, usually after the influence of colleagues and journal articles.

As the description of the pharmaceutical detailer indicates, the professional missionary salesman may not need to be particularly aggressive. Good coverage of the market, efficiency in sales calls, and the ability to make a succinct yet persuasive presentation of product benefits are perhaps the most important skills. Cases in this book that illustrate missionary selling include Kramer Pharmaceuticals, (A) and (B) (Cases 8 and 9) and Fortress Rubber Company (Case 10).

Technical Selling

The primary responsibility of the technical sales force is to increase sales volume by providing the firm's customers with technical advice and assistance. Unlike the trade or missionary salesman, the technical salesman *sells directly to* the user or buyer. Technical selling is common in the chemical, machinery, office products, and heavy machinery industries. The industrial products salesman who sells investment casting to the customer's purchasing agents is a good example of this type of salesman.

Investment casting involves building a mold around a wax or plastic replica of the desired part and then melting out the replica to leave a precise cavity. Although investment casting is usually more expensive than other processes, it offers a number of advantages, including flexibility in the choice of configuration and material, reproduction of fine detail, and reduction of tooling setup, machining, and assembly operations.

The typical salesman employed by a firm in the investment casting industry calls on customers within a territory ranging from a few counties in some heavily industrialized areas to several states in less-industrialized areas. Salesmen are familiar not only with the products and manufacturing operations of their customers but also with the customers' personnel. This knowledge is necessary if the salesman is to be alert for possible applications for investment castings. When a salesman uncovers a potential application in a prospect's manufacturing process, the next step typically is to approach the firm's purchasing agent, or perhaps a design engineer.

To stimulate interest in investment casting, the salesman may, for example, select one of the customer's parts and say, "If we investment-cast this part I think we can save you money" or "We can make a superior product at the same cost you now have." The appeal need not be cost-oriented however. The salesman may say, "You can increase your production capacity by subcontracting what you now machine" or "We can cast this in a metal that you can't machine" or "We can cast in one piece what you are now assembling." Whatever the appeal, the salesman is not yet in a position to make commitments about the feasibility or cost of casting the part. Instead, the salesman's job is to prescreen potential applications. When a suggested application seems feasible, the customer is asked to submit a blueprint for analysis.

Blueprints received by the investment casting firm are sent to a sales engineering department where they are examined for investment-casting feasibility. Occasionally, the cost of casting is not competitive with prices charged for similar parts manufactured using other techniques. More often, manufacture is turned down because the particular alloy specified is not suitable for investment casting. If casting the part gains the approval of the sales engineers, the specifications are then submitted to cost engineers. Here, too, the order may be rejected because of certain blueprint specifications. If the cost engineers agree that all specifications are feasible, they quote a price for the salesman to relay to the customer, basing the figure on estimated production cost.

The salesmen are usually required to follow up on the rejected blueprints, to explain to the customer the reasons for rejection and to try to work out a compromise. For example, if the quotation is too high, the salesman may suggest that the price could be lowered if the customer were to make design changes. These follow-up calls may lead to a part's being costed as many as four times. Of course, not all calls on potential customers result in orders or even prospects. Some calls are made simply to inform the potential customer about the process, with the hope that the customer may discover some possible applications.

As this example shows, the technical salesman—compared to the trade or missionary salesman—is more likely to need technical and analytical skills to enable him or her to identify and solve customers' problems. But the technical salesman must also have the interpersonal skills required for the other selling tasks. He or she must be able to persuade customers that the products can solve their problems. In calling on both sorts of skills, the technical salesman resembles a management consultant. Cases in this book that illustrate technical selling include Lawford Electric Company (Case 1), Continental Can Company (Case 3), and Austin Fibre Corporation (Case 14).

Entrepreneurial Selling

The primary responsibility of the entrepreneurial sales force is to obtain new accounts for its company. Converting a total stranger into a customer is the critical task. This kind of selling is variously called canvassing, bird-dogging, and cold calling. Like technical selling, it is *selling to* customers. Unlike technical selling, it may require a great deal of aggressiveness and the capacity to withstand feelings of rejection when customers say no. Entrepreneurial selling is common in almost all industries. The salesman for a regional paint manufacturer is a good example of an entrepreneurial salesman.

Although the largest company in the industry is Sherwin-Williams, which accounts for better than 25 percent of the total paint market, at the other end of the scale are many small regional paint manufacturers. This independent segment of the industry is one of the major areas in U.S. manufacturing still open to the small entrepreneur. The smaller companies sell paint to three types of customers: painting contractors, independent retail stores (usually combined hardware and paint stores), and large industrial users, such as factories, schools, and institutions.

Painting contractors usually are former painters who, with a small investment, have created independent firms ranging in size from those with one or two painters working side by side with the owner-contractor to those with a force of several hundred painters. Contractors' employees are often, but not always, unionized. The painting contractor is very difficult for the salesman to contact, being available for sales calls only in the late afternoon and evening at home. In choosing paint, contractors are concerned primarily with its spreading quality and appearance, and with the technical services provided by the manufacturer. Price is typically not a determining factor in the contractor's purchase decision. Contractors are quite willing to try new products in their search for better quality and service, but they tend to form opinions about total product lines on the basis of one sample. As a result, contractor's image of the company is important to his or her purchase decision.

The typical paint store carries three or four brands of paint, of which one or two first-line brands are nationally advertised and one or two brands are not. The unadvertised paints are priced somewhat lower than the advertised brands. Because virtually all retail stores already carry several brands of paint, retailers are reluctant to give shelf space to any new brand. This reluctance is even more pronounced regarding a nonadvertised brand. When the retailer does decide to add a new line of paint, he or she is usually interested primarily in shelf space and stock turnover. In most cases, a paint salesman is able to get shelf space in a new account only at the expense of an existing brand, usually the store's unadvertised second line.

Purchasing agents for the large industrial users typically order paint directly from the paint salesman. These customers usually use an in-house group of painters, to be supplemented during the summer by independent painting contractors. Selling paint to industrial customers requires both adequate-quality paint and a low price. Most sales are conducted through bids. Once the salesman gets his or her firm on the list of approved bidders, price is the determining factor. Getting on the approved list generally requires convincing purchasing agents that one's paint is of acceptable quality. On some industrial projects the architect, rather than the purchasing agent, makes the decision concerning acceptability. Architects often list a number of approved paint brands on their drawings or blueprints, the final choice being made on the basis of price. Getting on an approved list is often quite difficult, since architects are most reluctant to spend time talking with paint salesmen, believing that four or five approved brands are sufficient.

A typical day selling paint starts with an early visit (between 7 and 8 A.M.) to several retail paint stores. Because the early morning hours find many painting contractors picking up paint for that day at their local paint stores, a paint salesman may combine a call on retail store operators with calls on local painters. The remainder of the morning is usually spent calling on architects or retail stores to discuss the merits of one's paint. Lunch is often eaten on location where contractors and their painting crews are working. In the afternoon, a salesman may return to the factory to review the orders phoned into the plant during the day. It is not unusual for customers to phone the plant to request that paint be delivered that same day. For large-volume customers, the salesman often delivers the paint personally. In the late afternoon or early evening the salesman may call on painting contractors at home, office, or if the contractor was working overtime, on the job. It is also not unusual for a salesman to spend every evening on the telephone just saying hello to customers and occasionally obtaining orders from them.

As this example shows, the entrepreneurial salesman needs to be an aggressive self-starter who can balance the all-too-infrequent exhilaration of making the sale with the all-too-frequent deflation that comes with the polite—or sometimes brutal—rejection. Cases in this book that illustrate entrepreneurial selling include Gateway Corporation (Case 12) and Avon Products, Inc. (Case 17).

Hybrid Sales Forces

To some extent, almost every sales organization is a hybrid of two or more of these four types of sales forces. Many sales jobs require new-business development in addition to trade, missionary, or technical selling. Many sales jobs require missionary work in addition to trade or technical selling.

Top managers must recognize that no two selling jobs are alike, even in firms competing in the same industry. Each firm will have a different marketing strategy, each strategy requiring different behavior from the sales force. It is important, therefore, that all parties involved—salesman, field manager, sales executive, and marketing executive—understand in detail the desired sales force behavior. The salesman can then do his or her job as it should be done; the field manager can appropriately direct and coach the sales force; the sales executive can formulate policies and procedures to encourage the salesman to do the job; and the marketing executive can design marketing strategies that maximize the efficiency and effectiveness of the sales force.

Case 1
Lawford Electric Company

On February 2, 1979, Mr. Robert Allen, a field sales engineer for the Systems and Controls Division of the Lawford Electric Company, was notified by a letter from Bayfield Milling Company that Bayfield had decided to purchase the drive system for a new shearing line from one of Lawford's competitors. The news was a bitter disappointment to Mr. Allen. This sale, which he had been working on for over a year, would have been a $871,000 order for him. He decided to review his call reports to see whether his failure to secure the order was caused by any flaw in his sales presentation to Bayfield personnel. He was sure that the Lawford equipment was equivalent, if not superior, to that manufactured by his competitors, AG Corporation, Kennedy Electric, and Hamilton Electric. He was just as certain that Bayfield personnel had been scrupulously fair in their decision.

BACKGROUND INFORMATION

Lawford was one of the oldest, largest, and most respected firms in the electrical equipment industry. It manufactured a broad line of electric motors, generating equipment, and control devices. Its products and service backup were widely regarded for quality and reliability. Lawford's sales volume in 1978 was in excess of $200 million, second only to Kennedy Electric in this segment of the electrical equipment industry.

Lawford sales executives considered Mr. Allen an above-average sales engineer. His background was similar to that of most of Lawford's 37 field sales engineers. He held a bachelor's degree in electrical engineering and was working on his master's degree in a night program at a local university. He had joined Lawford directly after college graduation in 1968 as an assistant sales engineer, handling routine telephone sales inquiries, and processing and following up on customer orders. He had been promoted to his present position in 1970. A lifelong resident of Buffalo, Mr. Allen considered himself fortunate to be assigned to the Buffalo sales territory, the site of his company's headquarters. He was married, had two young children, and was active in community affairs—Junior Chamber of Commerce, Rotary Club, and the local chapter of the Institute of Electrical and Electronic Engineers.

The Bayfield Milling Company was located in upstate New York, not far from the Lawford headquarters in Buffalo. Bayfield converted strip steel purchased from large steel producers into a variety of forms, for sale to steel supply houses and end users. The company also engaged in a limited steel supply business of its own. Bayfield sales in 1978 were in excess of $80 million.

Mr. Allen had been calling on Bayfield regularly during the past eight years. Given the size of his territory, which included the metropolitan areas of Albany, Syracuse, and Rochester, and the importance of Bayfield, whose annual purchases from Lawford occasionally totaled as much as $50,000, Mr. Allen attempted to call on Bayfield at least once a month. During this eight-year period Mr. Allen had formed close business friendships with Bayfield's purchasing agent, Mr. George Gibson, and with several of the company's engineers and operations personnel.

The shearing line recently ordered by Bayfield from Magna Machinery Corporation would add a new capability to Bayfield's mill operation, enabling the firm to convert rolled strips of steel into steel sheet of various dimensions. The shearing line would unroll strips of steel at high speed. Because the new equipment could control the speed and tension of the strip at several points along the line, it could trim, flatten, and shear the strip into sheets of precise dimensions. The machinery could then convey the finished sheets to a stacking device and ultimately to a pallet for transfer to warehouse, truck, or flatcar. The cost of the mechanicals—including uncoiling rolls, pinch rolls, and drag rolls to control tension, plus side trimmers, shears, and conveyors—was about $2 million. The drive system would be about another $900,000.

ALLEN'S SALES ACTIVITY

From his call reports Mr. Allen reconstructed his activities during the period between January 13, 1978, when he learned of Bayfield's need for the new drive system, and February 2, 1979, when he learned that he had lost the sale.

January 13, 1978

Called on Gibson. Learned from him that Bayfield was soliciting bids on a drive system for a new shearing line. The line was to be purchased from Magna Machinery Corporation for delivery and installation in January 1980. Preliminary bids on the drive system for the line were due on July 14, 1978. Final bids were due on December 29, 1978, the award to be announced on February 2, 1979. Gibson got very businesslike with me and said that *no* supplier sales personnel—including staff and management—were to contact Bayfield engineering personnel to discuss product specifications ("specs"). He said that the operations vice president did not want the engineering people bothered, since they would be too busy working on other problems connected with the new shearing line. Instead, all supplier personnel were to work through Gibson, although contact was to be permitted with operations personnel. Gibson gave me the name of the Magna engineer to contact for details of the new line. Gibson said that, judging from the preliminary bids, he would choose four or five suppliers to submit final bids. The final decision would be a joint one made by Gibson, purchasing; Lorenz, chief engineer; Mainwaring, plant superintendent; and Vogel, operations vice president—also not to be contacted in person. Gibson suggested that Lawford would be a cinch to be one of the finalists, but that Vogel and Lorenz would be "pretty hard-nosed" about the final decision. I took this to mean that cost would be an important factor.

Returned to the office and wrote the Magna engineer in Cleveland for the specs on the shearing line. Wrote to Albany Fabricators for a testimonial letter about the drive system I sold them last year for their slitting line. Told the boss (Fred Webster, Lawford regional sales manager) about the situation. "Anything I can do to help . . . ," he said. Took home for review our general specifications on various Lawford drive components.

January 23, 1978

Received specs from Magna (see Exhibit 1). Took them to Pollack (Lawford's systems design engineer) and asked him to put together a tentative system for the Magna line. Called Mainwaring at Bayfield and made a luncheon date for next week.

February 2, 1978

Spent all morning with Gibson. Found out that operations and engineering are in a bad hassle over the drive system specs, but Gibson didn't understand the technicalities of the dispute. Showed him Pollack's tentative ideas. He seemed impressed. Spent about an hour going over the features of our variable voltage speed drives, stressing our static regulators for accurate speed control and our portable control panels. Left him a mountain of literature, including the Albany Fabricators' testimonial letter.

Spent $30 on lunch with Mainwaring and his assistant, Hughes. Told Hughes about a good place to buy a boat. Mainwaring denied that his people and engineering were having a hassle; the problem seemed to be that nobody had a clear understanding of what was needed. He added that "maybe the preliminary specs will give us a few ideas." He seemed to feel that engineering would draw up specs with whatever features his operations people wanted. Made a mental note to concentrate my sales efforts on Mainwaring.

After lunch I went over the same ground with Mainwaring and Hughes that I covered with Gibson, only in more detail. They both seemed concerned with reliability: "down-time kills you." I reminded them that Lawford, being a neighbor, so to speak, was in the best position to provide prompt and regular service. They agreed. Left them with the testimonial letter, a mountain of literature, and a copy of Pollack's proposal.

At home that evening I formulated my strategy. Decided to concentrate on Mainwaring at first, emphasizing our service capability and product reliability. After Lawford had passed the preliminary-bid stage, I would shift my major effort to Lorenz in order to get a crack at influencing the final specs. Gibson would be "kept on board" throughout. *overly self confident*

February 17, 1978

Stopped by to check progress with Gibson. Nothing new from him, so I spent some time talking about our mutual activities in Rotary. Arranged a lunch with him, Lorenz, Mainwaring, and my boss, Fred Webster, for the middle of next month.

Went to see Mainwaring, but he was out for the day. Hughes and I discussed some developments in systems design that improve reliability. Spent about an hour with the foreman on the cutting floor. He seemed to want a line that would allow fine tolerances in cutting accuracy. Talked to him about the advantages of the Lawford regulator systems as aids in controlling tolerances, due to their high-speed response capabilities. Discovered that two of their four slitting lines are powered by Lawford drive systems, one by a Kennedy system, and one by an AG. The two Lawford systems were the oldest and the newest. Checked with several operators and they were unanimous in their praise of the Lawford machinery, although one man liked the AG because of the case steel motor enclosure. When I pointed out that this feature made the motor bulky and harder to secure access for service, he remarked that he didn't have to service it but he "sure liked a big, heavy motor." Bought him a Coke and we parted friends.

March 14, 1978

Webster bought us all—Lorenz, Mainwaring, Gibson, Hughes, and myself—a magnificent lunch at the country club and made a great pitch about Lawford quality and service. This was the first time that I had met Lorenz— he joined Bayfield less than six months ago. He seemed a sour individual, but he loosened up after the second martini. After lunch I got Gibson aside and asked him about new developments. He now believed, as Mainwaring had previously indicated, that the difficulty seemed to center on uncertainty as to what was needed in the drive system, and not on a dispute about features. He indicated that engineering had stopped working on the specs until after Bayfield had had a chance to look over the preliminary bids.

April 10, 1978

Spent the morning with Mainwaring discussing the trade-off between the inertia in a heavy machine, which can provide for an even feed, and the speed of response in a light machine, which allows more precise cutting tolerances. Left him with some additional literature describing Lawford's latest developments in regulator systems, and a paperweight (a scale model of an experimental automobile powered by a Lawford electric motor). Stopped by to see Gibson and closed a $2,500 order for circuit breakers.

May 19, 1978

Spent the day with Pollack working out the details of our tentative bid. His idea, based on my input, was a complete drive system that would include DC adjustable voltage drive motors and control equipment, AC motors, a static DC constant potential power supply, and a static master regulator system. All components would be Lawford-made—a servicing advantage to Bayfield—and would include a one-year warranty and a service contract. Judging by the Magna-line specs, I thought that the system offered a perfect compromise between even feed and cutting precision. Webster approved the pricing of $895,000, and I mailed out the bid later that week.

May 30, 1978

Checked with Gibson, who grinned when I asked him how our bid looked. He said not to bother him until after July 17. We both laughed and I left for a brief visit on the cutting floor with the foreman. Found him grumbling about the regulatory instability on the older Lawford slitting-line drive system. Good-naturedly reminded him that regulators are temperature-sensitive and that a drive system of that age deserves congratulations, not criticism. He laughed and said that maybe we should replace it with another. I said that if he meant that Bayfield should replace it with another Lawford, I would take it up immediately with Mainwaring. He laughed again and said that the machine was OK; he was only pulling my leg. On the way out I saw my old friend, the AG booster, and I bought him another Coke.

July 17, 1978

Gibson telephoned and said that a letter was in the mail inviting Lawford to bid on the final specifications. The other firms invited to bid are Kennedy, AG, and Hamilton. I dug up price lists and specs on our competitors' systems and took them home to study that evening.

The Kennedy product line is almost identical to Lawford's. Felt that Kennedy's has about a 5 percent price advantage over Lawford, item for item. But, on the other hand, their reputation for quality and service is not as good as Lawford's. Unlike both Kennedy and Lawford, AG and Hamilton don't manufacture all their own components. Lacking unit responsibility, neither of these two companies can offer an extensively field-tested, integrated package. AG could offer more capacity in its regulator system than any of the other companies. This incremental capacity, however, would come at considerable additional cost to Bayfield. I felt that Bayfield would need add-on benefits only if they found themselves in the unlikely circumstance of buying another shearing line. Hamilton equipment I consider over-priced.

July 19, 1978

Stopped by to see Gibson. He suggested that our tentative bid was "a little high." Assured him that Lawford would be "rock bottom" once we had the final specs to bid on. Asked him about the committee's thinking on regulator capacity, and he told me to go see Lorenz, but reminded me that supplier personnel could not bother anyone else in the engineering section. Lorenz was free, and I spent about an hour with him talking about our components. He did not seem as concerned about add-on capacity in the regulator system as he did about the system's stability. He said that the operating people were concerned about temperature sensitivity. Since this feature is one of Lawford's strong points, I went into considerable detail with him about our temperature stability. Left him some additional highly technical literature to supplement the literature I had left with Gibson and Mainwaring, which apparently had found its way to Lorenz's desk.

August 2, 1978

Gibson told me over the phone that the committee had made no progress on the specs, nor did he expect any progress during August because of vacation schedules. He suggested that I check back after Labor Day.

September 12, 1978

Had lunch with Gibson and Lorenz. Both men agreed now that the committee had been in a bind over the specs. From the considerable experience that Bayfield personnel had had with drive systems for smaller lines, such as the slitters, the committee had proceeded on the belief that this experience would be transferable and would therefore make a decision about a drive system for the shearing line relatively easy, despite the increased size and complexity of the operation.

Apparently the problem had been a lack of criteria upon which the specs could be developed. Mainwaring had finally recognized this fact after the tentative bids had been opened. Implicit in all the tentative proposals were assumptions about criteria that were, in turn, manifested in a variety of specs. Accordingly, Mainwaring had requested technical assistance from

Magna engineers to develop criteria for Bayfield's installation. Mainwaring had just made a two-day visit to Magna headquarters, and had brought these criteria back with him. Bayfield operating and engineering personnel were just beginning to study them. Lorenz expected the final specs to be ready by early November.

This news elated me, because I felt that I was now in a position to go to work on Lorenz. I wanted to make sure that the specs included certain features standard with our constant potential power supply and our control panels. Incorporating these features into the final specs would, I felt, give Lawford a big price advantage in the bidding. Since Lorenz was busy that afternoon, I made an appointment to see him the following week.

September 20, 1978

Had lunch with Lorenz and spent two more hours with him that afternoon. Covered thoroughly all aspects of our system, with heavy emphasis on standard features in our power supply sets and control panels that reduce the incidence of generator breakdown and control component failure. He listened attentively throughout and asked very few additional questions. He seemed sold on the Lawford benefits.

October 4, 1978

Had lunch with Hughes, who told me that Mainwaring had left Bayfield for another job and that he had been promoted to Mainwaring's former position as plant superintendent. Neither Hughes nor Gibson, with whom I talked later that afternoon, cared to go into details. Discussed with Hughes the reliability features that I had discussed with Lorenz, only this time I stressed the benefits from the user's point of view, instead of the cost savings. Over dessert and coffee we discussed the merits of our respective boats. After lunch Gibson and I talked price, but he managed to talk a lot without telling me much. Got the feeling that the operations vice president, Vogel, was upset about "some of the trimmings" that the engineers wanted to write into the specs.

November 6, 1978

Received final specs for the drive system in the mail from Gibson. Also got an invitation to make a formal presentation on our bid to Vogel, Lorenz, Hughes, and Gibson on December 27. The specs were a surprise. Bayfield has gone along with our power supply and control features, but is also specifying some special wiring, which is no problem, and a significant amount of additional capacity in the master regulator—which could be a problem. I put Pollack to work drawing up the final proposal and arranged for him and Webster to participate in the formal presentation.

November 8, 1978

Called Gibson on the phone to verify the December 27 presentation date. Lawford is to be given one hour for a presentation, as are our three competitors. The alphabet gives us a break; ours will be the last presentation on that day. All four suppliers are expected to hand in their bids at the conclusion of their respective presentations. Asked him a few questions about the specs, and he suggested that I see Lorenz.

November 13, 1978

Spent two hours in the morning going over specs with Lorenz, who, it turned out, was a stickler for attention to small details. Gave him a brief pitch on every detail, and he seemed satisfied with my assurances that Lawford could deliver on all its promises. Stopped by to see Hughes, who was quite busy, so I left after 10 minutes. Neither he, Gibson, nor Lorenz was available for lunch.

December 27, 1978

Our presentation went very well. Webster did a great job on Lawford's reliability and service. Pollack covered thoroughly the technical aspects of our proposed drive system, matching them with all Bayfield's specifications. I concluded with a summary and handed the sealed bid to Vogel. The bid, which Pollack, Webster, and I had agonized over for hours, was a rock-bottom $871,000.

February 2, 1979

After opening Gibson's letter and learning that AG had won the bid, I called Gibson on the phone. He said that all bids had been in the "plus or minus $10,000 range" and that AG had just edged out Lawford. I asked him on what basis. He replied that Vogel, Lorenz, and Hughes had felt the AG system "fitted in better" with the new shearing operation, but each gave different reasons for thinking so. He strongly suggested that holding a post-mortem with the three men, either individually or collectively, would be a waste of time, since all Bayfield personnel concerned in the purchase were relieved that the decision was over and done with. He congratulated me on Lawford's showing and said that he hoped that I did not feel too bad about "coming in second."

Exhibit 1
General Description of Magna Shearing Line Drive Machinery Requirements

Entry System consists of:

Processor uncoiler, 100 kw., to operate as a drag generator. It is powered from a current-regulated static power supply. The motor field is controlled by a CEMF* regulator. The combination of the two regulator systems will ensure constant horsepower control over the full range of coil diameter.

Processor, 500 HP motor powered from a voltage-regulated static power supply.

The No. 1 Loop regulator controls processor speed.

No. 1 Pinch Roll, two 30 HP motors powered from a current-regulated static power supply.

Side Trimmer, 250 HP motor, and side trimmer Pinch Roll. 30 HP, powered from a voltage-regulated static power supply.

No. 2 Pinch Roll, two 30 HP motors powered from a voltage-regulated static power supply.

The No. 2 Loop regulator controls the side trimmer and No. 2 Loop Pinch Roll speed.

Temper Mill System consists of:

The No. 1 Bridle, three 120 HP and one 200 HP motor to be powered from a current-regulated static power supply. These motors are to operate as drag generators, with tachometer generator for speed indication.

Temper Mill, Top—600 HP, Bottom—600 HP, powered from a speed-regulated static power supply. One tachometer generator for speed indication and another for speed regulation.

No. 2 Bridle, one 200 HP, one 120 HP, two 250 HP, powered from a static power supply which will be current-regulated if the temper mill is used, and speed-regulated when the temper mill is not used. A tachometer generator will provide the speed signal for regulation.

A voltage-regulated static power supply will be used to power No. 3 Loop Pinch Roll, two 20 HP motors when shearing. It will also be used to power a deflector roll, 7.5 HP, and an oiling machine, 20 HP, when the line is run for coiling.

The No. 3 Loop regulator, used only when shearing, controls the entire mill system speed.

The No. 1 Bridle is always used whether shearing or recoiling, and is current-regulated for tension control.

The temper mill may be open or closed when either recoiling or shearing. If mill is closed, the No. 2 Bridle is current-regulated. If mill is open, the rolls will not touch the strip and the No. 2 Bridle is speed-regulated.

If the mill is closed, it sets the speed of the mill system. If open, the No. 2 Bridle sets mill system speed.

Tension Reel—Hallden Shear System consists of:

Tension Reel, 500 HP motor, powered from a current-regulated static power supply. The motor field is controlled by a CEMF Regulator. The two-regulator combination will regulate for constant HP through the entire coil buildup.

Hallden Shear, 400 HP motor, powered from the same static power supply as the tension reel, except that now it will be voltage-regulated. The speed signal provided by a tachometer generator, driven by the shear leveler, will be the reference to the conveyor section.

---

*Counter electromotive force.

Exhibit 1 *(continued)*

The maximum line of speed when shearing is 350 FPM† at a rated voltage.

When recoiling, the system's line speed can be increased by field weakening on some of the drives from 500 FPM to 1,000 FPM, as outlined earlier. A selector switch on the main desk can preset the speed at 500 FPM or 1,000 FPM. Interlocking will be provided to prevent change while the line is running.

When shearing, the Hallden Shear is the keynoter for the section beyond the shear. However, the line reference for the line as either a recoiling or shearing up to and through the shear is provided by the line reference motor-operated rheostat.

Conveyor and Leveler System consists of:

The drives beyond the shear through Prime Pinch Roll (excluding the leveler), as shown on the single line, powered from a voltage-regulated semiconverter static power supply.

The strip leveler, 400 HP motor, powered from a speed-regulated static power supply.

This section will have a fixed minimum speed of 75 FPM.

The drives are geared at 400 FPM, with field weakening to 450 FPM on all those drives beyond the McKay Leveler.

---

† Feet per minute.

Case 2
Jim Steiner

Jim Steiner, 35, is a sales representative for a large medical supply company. This case is the transcript of an interview, made in September 1979, in which Jim Steiner talked about his job, his career prospects and aspirations, and his company's management policies.

EMPLOYMENT HISTORY AND PRESENT POSITION

"I was selling business machines in late 1968 and living in Memphis, Tennessee. I wanted a more responsible sales position. I heard from a friend that his company's Clinical Division was looking for someone to cover Florida, Georgia, and Alabama. They wanted the person to relocate to Tampa. I had just gotten married and had no children at the time; the money sounded right, the potential sounded right, and, most of all, the job sounded interesting—selling to hospitals and to clinical labs. I went to work for them and stayed in Tampa for five years. I became the top sales rep in the division.

"In 1973 I was offered a 'promotion' to sales training manager. I went for straight salary. I lost my company car, lost the benefits of an expense account, and moved to company headquarters in Minneapolis. I was the entire sales training department. I was the first sales training manager in the division, so I had the chance to develop some initial programs and work on some of the packaged selling skill programs, such as Xerox's.

"Clinical prided itself at that time, and still does, on hiring high-quality sales representatives. But they had very few guys with quality medical experience. They seemed to go heavily to the IBM, Xerox, Exxon, and Standard Oil type of guys. The reps would have all the rudimentary sales skills, but not in medical sales. So I found myself spending a lot of time teaching them basic medical terminology, the ins and outs of hospital sales, who to see and who to avoid (there's politics in hospitals—just as much as there is at company headquarters).

Copyright © 1980 by The Colgate Darden Graduate Business School Sponsors, University of Virginia. Reproduced by permission. This case was prepared in collaboration with Timothy A. Hill.

"But basically what I did was leave a \$32,000-a-year position in 1973, when \$32,000 meant more than it does today, and go for a straight salary of about \$16,200. And housing conditions weren't any better then. I was seeing the new guys coming in at a base salary of \$10,000 to \$13,000 and then going out, after I taught them everything I knew—and then six months later not only were they making the base salary, which was what I was making, but they were driving a company car and getting a commission check for \$5,000. I really found that frustrating. I know I come on like I'm really dollar-motivated, but I'd like to say that I'm not. I could probably be making more money than I am right now, in fact, but I'm happy in what I'm doing. It did get to me, though, when I couldn't afford the vacation that my neighbors would be taking when the snow was up to here. By the time I left, my salary was up to \$20,000, but still that was not commensurate with what I could have been making in the field.

"I was probably two and one-half years on that job. I found it interesting, but it didn't lead anywhere. And although I enjoyed it personally, I must admit that my wife was unhappy about the weather and the house. I feel very strongly that my family should come before my job. I can see where perhaps I was taking some of the frustrations of the job out on her, and so it came to 'Let's look around and see what's available both inside and outside the company.' I had an opportunity to go with the Serum Testing Division out in California, but quite frankly, a quick flight out there to look at the housing market in Orange County proved that I would be going from the frying pan into the fire. I thought about the International Division, but there's one negative thing about that job, and that's the traveling. I did make one trip with the International Division. For about a month I visited Europe and met with some of the Clinical European sales people in France, Germany, Switzerland, Belgium, and England.

"Then I heard about an opening here with the Pacemaker Division. It was splitting away from the Prosthetics Division and might one day, hopefully in the not too distant future, become a division of its own. That has, to a degree, happened, as you know. When I first started with this division just three short years ago, we had a sales manager, but he reported to a gentleman who had general prosthetic responsibilities. About a year ago, the division added a director of marketing. We now have a director of marketing, a national sales manager, and slots for four district managers. So really right now, Pacemaker has developed more than Clinical had in 1969. I have been here three years and am now the top producer. I look back and say, 'Well, at least for whatever it is worth, I was the top sales rep for Clinical and now the top sales rep for Pacemaker.

"I guess my track record has shown that I am not a guy to quit, although I guess I have gone through three completely different jobs within the company. Two of them have been careers of my choice. With the second job I was younger, and the promotion, the office, and the title sounded good. After I tried that for a while, however, I went to where I wanted to live.

THE SELLING JOB

The Product Line

"I look at this job I have now as one of the headier positions in the company. I do think (we have to pat ourselves on the back because no one else will do it) that the Pacemaker sales force has more responsibility than the other sales entities in the organization. By that I mean, let's say you were with the Clinical Division and a test doesn't work. So what? There's going to be somebody mad at you, but you've only lost some time. If you were with the Kidney Division and a kidney coil ruptures, so what? Perhaps a little bit more of a problem, but the patient isn't going to die. Perhaps he's going to lose a little blood and may have to have a transfusion and have the inconvenience of being dialyzed again.

"But with what we're selling, a pacemaker, the patient is totally dependent from a life-support standpoint on what we sell. If it malfunctions, he's dead. So there's that pressure at our end of the selling. And there's that pressure at the decision end for the doctor. If he has a system that is working for him now, he's going to be leery of trying somebody else's system just because a sales rep comes in and says that it is better. The rep may or may not have some documentation to prove that. So there are some very interesting technical sales problems. In fact, sometimes I think that our guys get lost in that. Maybe they should get back to the basics a little bit more. But I am very happy with what I am doing today.

"I think one thing is necessary for this type of selling. We need a senior sales rep, we need someone who is willing to give three to five years to the job. Like I have been and am doing. You're not going to get a producer—I don't care how good a salesman he is—in, say, six months in this business. Until you feel comfortable with the product, I don't think you can be a good sales rep.

The Territory

"I have about the same size territory now as I had when I joined Clinical. But the thing that's different in this division is that our calls are determined by our product mix. We only have products for hospitals doing open-heart surgery. And even though it is a very glamorous thing, the number of hospitals doing open-heart surgery is still quite limited. I have three and one half states, but I only have 28 hospitals that I can conceivably call on. Outside of this city, where I have 6 of those 28 hospitals, each major city may have 2 major hospitals. It may be 150 miles to the next major city that would have an open-heart surgery program. With Clinical, I can't say that we called on every individual hospital, but we certainly found ourselves calling on the smaller hospitals in the in-between towns, like Ocala.

"So all of a sudden, you have to learn time and territorial management.

You can't just start in the car and get out of the airport and think, Where am I going tomorrow? Am I going to X, or maybe the weather is nicer up in Y? You may not be able to get airline reservations or a ticket, and you would be completely spinning your wheels.

The Customers

"In our selling situation, we deal with a very unique customer. It's the doctor who does the surgery. He is usually very wealthy. Most of the doctors I call on are millionaires. If they are not, a year or two later they will be. So, you're not going to impress them by entertainment. Just coming in and buying them a steak is not going to cut it. You impress them by being friendly with them, and if you've got some tickets to a sold-out ballgame or to a concert for their wives, with you and your wife, they're going to love this. But they're going to look at the product very critically.

"The better you get to know your accounts, the less likely they are to buy away from you. I pride myself on accounts that I've developed. I know the doctors. I know their wives. And they know me. We get together socially; we get together professionally, too. And I think the more I get to know an account, the harder it's going to be for competition to come in and take away part or all of my business.

"There are a few accounts that you'll never convert. Any sales manager or marketing person will agree that, for various psychological reasons in the medical field, there are still a lot of rabbit's feet that people hang on to. There are some people who hate the company. There are some people whose toes the company stepped on in the past and they are not going to let me forget that. I have a couple of accounts like that. I have other accounts where the competition is in deep. It's very hard for me to get to first base, if you will.

"Also, our product isn't something that lets you walk in and say, 'Here's our pacemaker, it's $925. It's solid, it works.' You can tell them that, but you've got to start coming around three or four times to show them that when you tell them you'll be there, you're there. If you tell them you'll be there at 6:30 in the morning, you're there at 6:15 waiting for them. They appreciate that. And so that's why I hope management will realize that we're selling a life-support system, not a test tube or a Band-Aid.

Territory Management

"This is a typical week. Tomorrow I'm calling on a big out-of-town hospital. What I'll do is fly there in the morning, rent a car, call on the one hospital that does open-heart surgery, and talk to the doctors. Tomorrow afternoon or tomorrow evening I'll drive for a couple of hours down to another big city and spend the evening and Wednesday calling on the four hospitals there that do open-heart surgery. Spend Wednesday night there, too. Thursday morning I will get up and drive down to a third city to meet a doctor for lunch. Then I'll fly back home Thursday afternoon.

"I find that now I am out generally two or three nights a week. I did a survey for myself. I pulled my expense reports and added up the nights out. I've been averaging about two and a half nights. I've been doing my best to try to route myself to get that down to no more than two nights by going out on a Tuesday and coming back and being home by Thursday night.

"As I said earlier, my family is getting more and more important to me as I get older. I don't know if that is natural or not. But my little girl is in the second grade and my little boy is now in preschool. Other guys on the road tell me that their kid is in the second grade, and then all of a sudden he's graduating from college, and they were making sales calls in the interim. That's not going to happen in my family.

"I have an office in the basement of my house, which is necessary because I have a fair amount of paperwork. I have a file cabinet and a desk and telephone down there. I maintain a 24-hour answering service that the company pays for. The office in my house actually comes down to a very nice income tax deduction at the end of the year—a very legal one. If I need to spend an administrative day cleaning up some paperwork and directing some letters to customers, I can do it in the house. If I'm there, I can take a break or have lunch with my wife, which is sort of a trade-off for being out on the road the next three nights. And by being home you can be there when the kids get home from school and say hello.

"All the mail comes to the house. Most of my calls come in on my answering service, although everyone in the company has my home phone number and can call me at home. But chances are better to get me through the answering service. I left the house this morning around 7:25 and I won't be back home until about 8 Thursday night. My wife doesn't work and has a lot of neighborhood activities, so chances of catching her home during the day are 50-50. The answering service works out very nicely because it's 24-hour pickup, and I can call in and check my messages any time I need to.

MANAGEMENT ASPIRATIONS

"In April, I was happy with what I was doing. My boss, Don Boze, had indicated to me that he was going to be in this position for two to five years. If I have made the commitment to stay here (which I pretty well have) that blocked any opportunity for a district manager's position for me—here, at least—and I resigned myself to be very happy in my sales position. I still am. I must make that perfectly clear.

"But now the situation has changed. Don called me on July 28th and said that he was leaving. With Don's resignation, there is a lot more opportunity for upward mobility, and I want to be part of it. If I'm not, I have to look at the fact that the company is telling me something very indirectly: 'Hey, you've been around for 10 years as the top salesman, but we still don't have room for you.' They would be telling me either that I could be a sales rep here for the rest of my life as long as I produce, or else that there is no room for me down the road. I could be their 55-year-old guy with my detail bag if I wanted to. But I guess my thinking has changed dramatically to the point of 'Hey, let's face it. I want this district manager job right now very badly and I feel that I could do a very good job.'

"I have seen some managers that I feel like I could do at least as well as, if not a lot better. Here in this job I don't feel that I've been ready until now, as far as my knowledge of the market. You've got to know the ins and outs, and what makes the surgeons tick, and what makes the pacemaker work. And I think my skill at managing accounts can be applied to managing people. If you can control an account that is going to buy your product, which is more expensive and more difficult to run, then you can certainly motivate a guy to go out and make $35,000 a year. I think that would be easy.

"Just as the company can give me no promise or guarantees, I can give them no promises or guarantees. Six months down the road I may hate it and say, 'I either want my job back or I'm leaving.'

"But I don't think that would happen. I pride myself on the fact that the president calls me by my first name when he sees me, because we worked on a couple of projects together at headquarters and we happened to take a plane flight one time together. When he sees me he makes a point of saying, 'Hey, Jim, how's it going?' I think that I have been around enough of the top guys in the company that a little bit of their charisma has rubbed off on me somewhere. Not too much or I wouldn't be here in a sales job. But to a degree it's where I want to be.

"Some of my peers are fighting tooth and nail for this district manager's position. They are pulling out all of the political stops and I'm not. We'll see. Maybe it works—maybe it doesn't. I've just done that job that I think is required and, well, I don't have to belabor that point.

"I know that all along there have been guys that have been just upward-oriented. I am amazed at these guys because I know that in the Clinical Division most promotional opportunities, unless there are some unusual circumstances, are not likely to come for three to four years. If a guy is not going to accept that fact, then it would be better for him not to come into a field job. I see these guys with their Brooks Brothers suits saying, 'I was the number one region producer at Xerox and I'm coming here because I want to be the national sales manager. I'll do the right kind of job in a year and I'll have it.'

"I sit back and say, 'Well, you can do that kind of a job, but you won't have it in a year.'

"I rationalized that the district manager job wasn't open so there was no chance for me and I was happy. Today it's open. I want it. I am even ready to make the personal commitment that if I don't get it, then I should look elsewhere, if that's what I want. But I'm not sure that's what I want. And I realize, too, that there are very few opportunities in sales management in the medical field. Unless there is somebody being promoted or leaving or dying along the way, there is no opening.

"Generally, to stay at the level you are now, you have to make a lateral transfer. As a sales rep, I could possibly get a sales job with another company. If I were a district manager, I could get a district manager's job in another company. But if you want to go up a step, it is hard unless you are willing to go down a step in the size and scope of the company.

"I had a couple of offers for district manager jobs for very small companies, and I talked openly about them to Don before he left. The grass looks greener on the other side of the fence. But it also scared the hell out of me, too, because these small companies are undercapitalized. In one case the product wasn't even FDA-approved yet. So you get back to whether you want to stay on the sales force for the rest of your life or not, again I don't think that I do.

"I'd still like to have a challenge somewhere within the company. I look at it like it's the company's responsibility to come to me—not mine to go begging to the company. Still, I don't want to go back to Minneapolis. If they called me right now and offered me any type of staff position in Minneapolis up to $35,000, I'd probably say no. Thirty-five would be the break-even point, because that's what I'm making now plus the company car. It would cost me to duplicate my house in Minneapolis. If I say I don't want to go to Minneapolis, I wonder what I'm even doing with this company—because what will I do after the DM's job if I'm selected for it? There are really no marketing opportunities in this city with this company.

CAREER PATHS IN THE COMPANY

"A guy from Personnel came down last week and told me that I had some of the rudiments of managing, but that no one had ever bothered to develop them. If he's right, and I have to agree with him on this, my previous managers let me down.

"For so long, I thought that the only avenue of promotion would be sales rep to district manager to national sales manager to director of marketing. The other opportunities within the company have never really been explained. We're almost like minority employees with our rights being violated in the field because we have no access to what's available in Minneapolis. There are a lot of promotional opportunities within the company that would be better filled by a dedicated guy already working here, even though he doesn't have an MBA, rather than a guy off the street. Certainly there are product manager jobs, which, of course, I am familiar with and am not interested in. But there is international marketing, too.

"And maybe the guy doesn't even have to stay in marketing. What's to prevent a guy from going to Personnel to interview people for sales positions? A guy like me would know what is necessary rather than some guy from a head-hunter's shop, and maybe some guys in the field would like a job like that. It would give them, number one, promotion, and I guess that's the big thing for a lot of guys. Number two, it would give them a chance to broaden their responsibilities. They have already proved that they can sell. I've proved that. I want a challenge now. This isn't much of a challenge any more. I enjoyed doing it and I do it well. I don't mean to boast. You can look on my IBM sheets and my income record.

"I think that we should develop some training programs for guys like me. I have to admit I am bitter that they have not spent one penny on any development for me. If you've got the guys in the field, let's develop them. Maybe he's got the skills, maybe he doesn't. If he does, let's make this guy a manager candidate or find out that he isn't, rather than promoting according to crisis: 'We've got a slot; we've got a guy who's producing; he's our DM.'

"We should have a program where we could make a guy available for a week's training in management. It would be good for the company because they'd find out what the guy's made of, and it would be good for the guy because if he didn't get a shot with our company, he could use that expertise somewhere else. I've never had that opportunity. I've never been to any type of management training seminar in my life. I think that I know what management is, but basically I guess I don't. If I were a district manager and had good men under me (which I would hope to have, because that is one way in which a good manager is marked), I would push to have some training programs developed, or push to have more avenues of promotion developed.

THE COMPANY'S MANAGERS AND MANAGEMENT POLICIES

"In 10 years with this company I worked with a variety of district managers. It seems like when they were with me they were just interested in getting the sale. If you've got a key account and they can help in any way, they'll say, 'Let's make a joint sales call, team style. Let's go give them the old one-two. You hit 'em high. I'll hit 'em low. And we'll get the order.'

"But they are completely negligent with any other development. The average district manager is untrained for his job, is not equipped for it, and is probably not a very good manager. He was a tremendous salesman at one point or other. The company has a responsibility if they want good management. They better start developing it and not just telling the guy to go out and sell, sell, sell, and then all of a sudden one day just walk in and say, 'You don't sell anymore, you're a DM. Now you manage. Look it up in the dictionary.'

"If you go out and spend a couple of days with some of our managers, you're going to find these guys are basically salesmen in DMs' clothing. They know how to conduct a sales call; they know how to manage a territory; they probably have a little bit better savvy, if you will, than the average guy. If they've done a good job and their sales have been the best, they've been chosen. So, it's a very sales-oriented position.

"I know of no one who has been promoted and then complained about being ill-equipped to manage. But I've known a lot who have left. In retrospect I can look back and see a lot of guys who did make that step to district manager and really weren't qualified immediately to make it. One of the most immediate functions the district manager is asked to do is to hire somebody to take his place. For example, if I do get the call to be the new manager, obviously one of my first responsibilities is to find somebody to take my sales position here. I've had no training whatsoever in interviewing candidates—questions to ask, what have you. I know that there are courses available on interviewing sales candidates, but I haven't been offered them and I doubt if any of our sales people have before becoming managers. The most important function of the DM is to hire the right guy. It would be my responsibility to find the person, do the initial interviews. He would be subjected to a battery of interviews in Minneapolis by our sales manager, the director of marketing, and various other people in the home office; but obviously I would have to make the initial contacts in the field, working through either recruiters or referrals of one kind or another.

"I can't really rate Don's management abilities, except one thing that might not have been in his favor: he was very frank and very honest. It probably didn't win him a lot of points. He would never have survived in Minneapolis. He probably made a good career decision to leave, because he was the kind of guy to call a spade a spade. He actually had close to violent arguments when he felt something wasn't right. He defended his people in the field. I'd have to say that. He'd go to bat for you. I think that's a sign of a good manager, too. One of my philosophies is that you work harder for someone you respect for sure and like a little bit. I wouldn't work my rear end off completely for someone I hated. And I don't see how I could respect somebody that I hated. It's a little give and take.

"But a manager also has to motivate his guys. Don might have been lacking in that area. Guys in the field with any company, and its not necessarily just the medical industry, can make more money doing what I'm doing, living where they want to live, than they can back in the 'home office,' whether its Buffalo, Poughkeepsie, or Minneapolis. So the guys in the office say it's not fair, and I have to agree with them in a way. But in the field it's not fair either, because you're so fat and happy and contented. What I need is someone to give me a swift kick in the butt. I don't know from a management standpoint how that can be done. They can try to fire me, but so what? I can get a higher paying job tomorrow. They could add more incentives to the program. But I've got all my basic material wants. Not a jet plane or a Winnebago, but I'm not too much into either of those. The travel contest I really find myself involved in. My wife and I got to go to Europe last year for 10 days. It was fantastic: first class, all expenses paid, Paris, Monte Carlo. Again, we could have paid for it if we had wanted to plan for it next summer. We would have the dollars to do it, but it's something you don't normally really do. All of a sudden in this contest the company provided us with the possibility, so I found myself excited about that. I'm not excited about a whip over my head or some guy saying, "Well, I won't accept any excuses.' That doesn't really motivate me too much. I think it might motivate younger guys or it might motivate guys in other situations. But when you get a group of senior sales reps and they're doing well and making good money, they don't need to put up with bullshit. So again, I don't know what motivates me.

"I guess I didn't realize it at the time, but I didn't see Don for extended periods of time. I attributed that to the fact that I was doing well. We have some guys in the district that he was spending more time with, along with an administrative job comes a lot of paperwork too, one or two days a week. So Don was staying busy. But in retrospect, I think the reason was that Don was getting sales from me. We were both benefiting by the fact that our commission checks were enhanced. Don himself spent no time with me; it was probably not his fault.

"Maybe they're under pressure to produce, so they look to their better producing guys and say, 'Hey, don't worry about this or that. Just get me 50 more pacemakers or $100,000 more from this account and you get a bigger commission check and the heat's off.'

"If I didn't have a calendar in front of me, I could tell you at least a week to 10 days before the end of the fourth quarter, because I start getting calls from my district manager saying, 'We realize that you are doing all that you can, but we really have a commitment to make here and we need interest in this product area,' or, 'We need orders,' or as district says, 'I need 50 more pacemakers this month from somewhere. Can I count on you?'

"So, good old Jim goes out and gets him 42 of them. All I get for it is my commission, not even a thank you. So I call this pressure to produce.

"That's all that Don wanted. That's all that they all wanted. Dollar sales. They could care less really about me as an individual or me as a developing manager, or developing as a benefit to the company. Just as long as I could get the sales. If the territory burned down I wonder what really would happen to you. My Clinical territory had pretty well peaked out, and I saw that coming. I left. The guy that took my place had one good year and then he struggled, because there just weren't that many more cream-of-the-crop accounts. There are always accounts out there, but the easy ones were gone. I see the same thing happening here. When I came to Pacemakers, we had some business. I can't really say zero business, but our quarterly quota for pacemakers was 105. That means what was sold in the quarter that year. Last year my quarterly quota was 355. This year it will be over 500. That's a pretty good increase.

"If you produce here, you can make some money. But the district manager always sits down with a new guy and says, 'The sky is the limit. The base is low, but commission dollars are wide open.'

"I've grown mature enough to know that the sky is not the limit. There has got to be a book somewhere saying what a salesman will make and can make, and if he makes more than that in a year, several things will happen. Cut his territory; cut his commission; decrease the percent paid as his commission; raise his quota; keep the commission dollars in check. I don't know what that figure is. I know some guys get a little bit more than I. But when a rep starts making $20,000, I'm sure that somewhere somebody starts figuring out how to control that.

"But still, $35,000 or $40,000 doesn't feel that bad. And we have a nice security blanket with our base salary and benefits. If all else fails, if we have total product recall, until I could regroup or the company could regroup, I'd have something coming in. I'd have my expenses covered. I wouldn't have to worry about that coming out of my pocket. I'd have a company car to drive.

"There are other sales jobs where there is not that security blanket. And generally, the higher the income potential, the shorter the security blanket. In some open-end commission or straight-draw programs it is possible (and I know personally some guys who are doing this) to make $60,000, $70,000, close to a $100,000 a year. But that's a good year. There could be a recall year, or a disaster, or you could get sick or injured in some fashion, and then I wonder what commitment the company would really have to you.

"I wonder more and more what commitment the company has to me. That's become a real problem in my mind. I've given them my best for 10 years and now they're saying that's not enough. I prefer more of the benefits, but still with the commission you can make more money than you can in middle management. So they've made a career decision hard for me to handle. Do I want to leave this and go to Minneapolis in a staff job and put up with the eight-to-five office routine?

CONCLUSION

"You could describe me as sort of a low-profile person. My ego, on a scale of 1 to 10, is definitely not a 10. I can roll with the punches as long as I'm happy and my family is happy. I don't let frustrations bother me. I never get mad. I cast things off. If I don't like something I'll just ignore it. It will go away. I am not the type of person who is prone to heart attacks. I really don't get excited, although I find myself more and more getting that way. My frustrations are few and far between. I get some frustrations on the job when I can't sell an account. I get some frustrations with the company. Right now my frustrations are not significant. I'll let Minneapolis handle their hirings and firings and assignments and transfers and, as long as it doesn't hurt me, I don't get excited one way or the other.

"Several names have been mentioned as competition for the DM job. There's another sales type that lives up in Boston, who has done a very good job—not as good as mine in numbers, but that's not the only thing that they look at. And there's a couple of staff guys who would be very interested in it.

"Don Boze called me on the 28th of July and told me that he was leaving. Today is the 17th of September and they have not made a decision. They told me that they are not near a decision. Everybody and his brother is aware of it and gossiping and talking about it. It's almost like they've left it open so long that every Tom, Dick, and Harry has heard about it and wants it.

"Well, I don't know if I'll get the job or not. You can't tell what makes the decision factor. I'm getting a little tired of what I'm doing now. It takes no real initiative and I'm the kind of guy who does like work, who responds to something new, to something different. I've been here now for three years. I don't want to leave my home here, but I do want to do something different. Even if it's outside of the company, if that's the way it has to be.

"I'm so positive and success-oriented that the worst thing that could happen to me is if somebody said, 'You're out.' I may quit, but I guess that is my one main fear, that I'll be unsuccessful. I guess that's what's kept me from looking outside the company. Revealing my true inner soul now. I know I'm successful here, so why risk the outside?"

Case 3
Continental Can Company

Continental Can Company, Inc. (CCC), based in New York City, was in 1966 one of the largest companies in the packaging industry. The company was organized into three operating groups, corresponding to its product lines: Paper Products; Plastics, Closures, and Consumer Products; and Metal Products, the largest group and the focus of this case. (Exhibit 1 gives selected financial data from CCC's 1965 annual report.)

In the fall of 1966, senior executives of the Metal Products Group (MPG) met to review the MPG sales force operations. Although these executives had no immediate plans to change the current selling organization and incentive systems, they believed that frequent reviews were essential to maintain an effective organization.

Exhibit 1
Selected Financial Data ($ millions)

	1965	1964
Net sales and operating revenues:		
Metal and composite containers	$ 694.2	$ 660.4
Paper products and flexible packaging	386.9	361.1
Plastics, glass and closures	111.5	102.2
All other	30.0	29.0
	1,222.6	1,152.7
Other income	3.2	48.4*
Total income	1,225.8	1,201.1
Cost of goods and operating expenses	974.4	972.7
Selling, administration, and research	90.1	83.7
Depreciation and depletion	45.1	44.1
Interest	8.0	7.8
Total expenses	1,117.6	1,108.3
Earnings before taxes	105.0	92.8
Earnings after taxes	$ 59.2	$ 48.9

*Includes adjustment for sale of assets.
Source: 1965 annual report.

THE COMPANY'S ORGANIZATION

In addition to the three major product groups, the company's organization comprised International Operations, a Canadian subsidiary, and various corporate staff groups. Among these latter was the corporate marketing and planning group, which assisted the divisions within the various operating groups. The corporate marketing and planning group also coordinated the plans and activities of each operating group with those of the company as a whole. One corporate marketing executive noted the difficulty of this task:

> Most of our people have come up under the philosophy of beating our competitors out of a share point. Now, we believe, our business decisions have become more sophisticated. But you just don't wave a wand over a company with 48,000 employees and expect a new way of thinking to come about overnight.

The Metal Products Group was subdivided geographically into Eastern, Central, Pacific, and Southern divisions. (Exhibit 2 shows a simplified organizational chart, focusing on the Metal Products Group and one of its divisions.) The MPG *divisional general managers* spent about 35 percent of their time on manufacturing problems and 65 percent of their time on sales problems. In manufacturing, the divisional general manager tried to increase efficiency by monitoring material spoilage, quality control, overtime, equipment breakdowns, and warehousing. In sales, the divisional manager called on senior executives of major customers, coordinated sales and production, and oversaw the sales force. The divisional general manager received weekly sales activity reports, but most of his control over the sales force was exerted through daily contact with the divisional sales manager and monthly visits with the district sales managers. The divisional general managers believed that these contacts gave them sufficient control over the sales force. According to one general manager,

> One individual's lack of effort within one district can affect 5 percent of my sales. I try to investigate what led up to every large sale and every lost sale. I have a pretty good idea what's going on out in the field about three fourths of the time.

A *divisional sales manager* was the line boss of from five to nine district sales managers. Reporting to him in addition were three industry/product sales managers responsible for seeing that appropriate sales efforts were directed to certain key markets—namely, beer, soft drinks, oil, coffee, and meat. The divisional sales manager also made calls on top executives within major accounts and spent much of his time personally supervising the district sales managers.

A *district sales manager* usually supervised from four to eight salesmen and was in charge of his district sales office. A typical district sales manager spent about one third of his time calling on executives of customer firms, one third on direct supervision and field trips with his salesmen, and the remain-

Exhibit 2
Partial Organization Chart (emphasis on Metal Products Group)

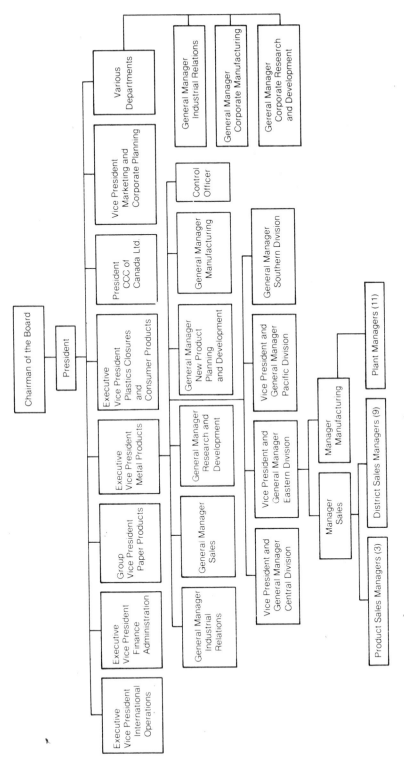

Source: Company records.

der on office administration, community affairs, and relations with can plants. All district sales managers had been promoted from the ranks of the sales force.

THE METAL CONTAINER MARKET

About 2,500 products from 160 industries were packaged in cans of more than 600 sizes, shapes, and styles. MPG manufactured beer cans, soft-drink cans, aerosol cans, motor oil cans, food cans, steel pails, and a variety of oblong cans. Over the past 10 years the metal container industry had grown steadily, in part because sales of beer, soft drinks, and aerosols had accelerated. In 1965 the brewing industry used over 12 billion cans and the soft-drink industry 5½ billion. Total production in 1965 was estimated to exceed 55 billion cans, and sales were expected to exceed $2.5 billion. CCC's corporate marketing and planning executives estimated that by 1971 sales in the metal can industry would approach 67 billion containers, or $3 billion.

The metal can industry was not without significant competition from manufacturers of glass, plastic, and composite containers. In recent years, plastics had won away the detergent can business and made inroads into the household and industrial products field, glass had encroached upon the market for fruit and vegetable containers, and composite cans had made large gains in motor oil containers. Furthermore, within the metal container market self-manufacture was threatening commercial manufacture. In 1965, CCC executives estimated that 20 percent of the market was supplied by self-manufacture. Of the commercial market, CCC executives estimated that their company and the American Can Company each held 35 percent market shares, the National Can Company held 10 percent, Crown Cork & Seal held 8 percent, and the remaining smaller companies shared the other 12 percent.

MPG executives presented the following data to illustrate the soft-drink segment's rapid growth from 1964 to 1965 and its expected future growth:

Industry Shipments (millions of base boxes; one base box = 500 cans)

	Total	Percent Increase from Previous Year
1965	7.8	39.3
1966 (estimate)	11.3	43.6
1967 (forecast)	14.4	28.0

Expanded product lines and heavy promotional efforts were expected to sustain growth in the soft-drink industry for the next few years. The changing population mix would also help to expand this market. The age group

push bev container
beer + soft drink
push team help.

that drank the most soft drinks (the 10- to 29-year-olds) was expected to grow during the late 1960s at an average annual rate of 3 percent—well above the rate projected for the overall population. According to MPG executives, this market growth would benefit the can more than other containers because of the can's convenience. Major beverage companies, which controlled the bulk of the soft-drink market, were aggressively promoting the can. One-way bottles, however, which had been caught in an industrywide capacity squeeze in 1966, were expected to provide increasing competition in the convenience market, increasing their share of the total soft-drink container market well above the 1965 level of 2.8 percent.

MPG SALES ACTIVITIES

The typical MPG sales representative was a college graduate who started selling in his middle 20s with little if any previous sales experience. Before being assigned to a territory, he had spent a year in a company training program, learning about the company, its policies, its product lines, its manufacturing techniques, and some general selling techniques. Each sales representative was expected to sell the complete product line of the metals group; that is, he was to sell vegetable cans to vegetable packers, oil cans to oil companies, beer cans to brewers, and soft-drink cans to beverage companies.

The number of accounts within a given geographic territory varied considerably. An MPG sales rep in New York City, for instance, could be assigned as few as 7 accounts, whereas a sales rep in Richmond, Virginia, might be responsible for as many as 75 accounts. Reps did very little prospecting for potential new can users; however, they did call on firms that used cans made by competitors, and expended considerable effort to increase the CCC share of split accounts.

The sales rep's most important task was to maintain current business. Very few customers gave all their can business to one supplier; most customers spread their business among two or three sources. It was considered difficult, under static circumstances, for a sales rep to alter his company's share of a customer's business significantly. If his competitor ran into problems with delivery, quality control, or pricing, the MPG sales rep might not always be able to step in, since his own firm was subject to similar problems. Customer's managerial changes or improved MPG products, however, often provided opportunity to shift customer's purchase patterns.

On the other hand, the sales reps themselves maintained that "hustle" paid off. One sales rep described his experience:

> I spent three and one half years in Boston. With some growth, some luck, and a lot of hustle, I was able to increase our business there from $2.5 million to $4 million.
>
> Next, I got transferred to New York City. The year I worked the hardest I fell 4 percent behind. When I got promoted at the end of that year, my succes-

sor came along and went 3.5 percent ahead. The reason was mainly due to a competitive development. We were a few months late with the tear-top coffee can. My successor got the business back because we came out with the same can bearing an improved lithograph technique.

Most of the selling to major national accounts was team selling: the sales representative dealt with local purchasing agents and executives, the district sales manager made calls at a higher executive level, and the divisional general manager called on top executives. These arrangements were flexible, however, and each account was assigned to a specific sales representative. There were no "house accounts."

Herbert Macon's success with one of his customers illustrates both hustle and teamwork. Macon, who had been an MPG salesman for about 11 years, had as one of his major customers a food company that purchased all its coffee cans from CCC. Over the years, Macon had gotten to know all the people in this customer's purchasing and packaging departments, as well as many of the firm's marketing and sales executives. Several years before, this company had purchased a smaller company that it continued to operate as a fairly autonomous subsidiary. CCC had never sold any cans to the subsidiary. Macon saw this situation as a challenge. He began to collect information on the type and quantity of cans the subsidiary used, and he drew up plans for a suitable substitute to be provided by CCC.

During his first sales presentation in August 1964 made to personnel in the purchasing department, Macon used a five-page brochure to support his recommendation—an open-top can with a clear plastic cover to replace the old-style can. The brochure included a complete pricing analysis that demonstrated that the CCC can could save the subsidiary $450,000 on an annual can volume of $2.5 million. Top executives of the subsidiary were brought into the negotiations during a second sales call. These executives were impressed with the dollar savings on the CCC can and with Macon's analysis, but they decided that the new can was not perfectly suited to their particular product. Nevertheless, Macon was asked to continue his efforts to find them a new kind of metal can.

In March 1965, Macon returned to this prospective customer with some newly developed CCC easy-open, tear-top cans. The subsidiary's top executives objected to certain minor features of these new designs, but, impressed with Macon's ingenuity, they offered to give CCC half their existing can business if CCC would meet the price of their current source. Macon returned to his office and asked CCC financial personnel to undertake an economic analysis of this offer. The resulting analysis indicated an excellent payback on the required investment but, at the same time, Macon was told by his research and development department that a new and improved can was on the drawing board. At this point, Macon reported to the prospect that his company would prefer to supply the firm with a superior container as soon as it was perfected.

In April 1966, the new can was ready and Macon presented it to the top executives of the subsidiary. This presentation was quite elaborate, involving flip charts, can samples, and supporting advertising and promotional material. The price saving on this particular can was only $100,000 per year, but the can fit the prospect's needs far better than the first can that Macon had recommended. The presentation met with immediate favorable response and, a week later, Macon brought in CCC engineering services personnel to show the customer how to make minor changes in can-handling equipment, to install some minor machinery for making the required plastic overcaps, and to make a complete survey of the customer's materials handling operation. This engineering service, Macon admitted, was over and above the requirement for the sale. The customer scheduled the new CCC cans into production in September 1966.

Macon's work illustrates the complexity of the selling process. In his words:

> On a sale like this, everybody gets into the act. All I did was to show a little initiative. The people who did the real selling on this job are the marketing people, the R&D people, and the engineering department. Without them we would never have gotten the business.
>
> My main job is keeping my ear to the ground in these large corporations. Buying is getting more rational. You can't count on their liking you any more; the world is too competitive. What this kind of selling takes is one hell of a lot of backup.

MPG'S SALES FORECASTS

Each year two separate forecasts were developed for the Metal Products Group, one prepared by each division and one by corporate marketing personnel. The two sets of figures were then adjusted against each other at corporate headquarters.

The Divisional Sales Forecasts

In August of each year, divisional marketing personnel began to collect data for the sales forecast for the following year. Each MPG sales rep submitted to his district sales manager an analysis of the expected volume of business for the following year, grouping the information by type of can, by supplying plant, and by major customer account (all accounts with yearly billing under $100,000 were grouped together). Exhibit 3 illustrates a part of one sales rep's customer analysis.

Each district sales manager collected, checked, and discussed these reports from his sales reps, totaled his district's estimates by plant, and forwarded these data to the divisional sales manager, who referred the data to the product managers. The product managers then combined these estimates by product groups, analyzed the data very carefully, and refined the estimates in terms of expected events in the marketplace, competitive activ-

Exhibit 3
Example of Salesman's Account Analysis (partial)

Account*	Supplying CCC Plant	1965 ($000)†	1966E ($000)	1967F ($000)‡	Remarks
Acme Cola, Inc.	A	780	300	1,500	Regain loss to American
	B	181	200	—	Handled out of A
	C	1,013	500	1,750	
Delta Beverage Co.	A	877	1,000	700	Loss to National
	B	821	1,000	1,000	
	D	157	200	250	
	E	182	550	400	
Gamma Bottling Co...........	F	337	400	1,000	
	B	203	350	—	Handled out of F
All accounts with annual can purchases of under $50,000		144	150	150	

* Disguised.

† Sales revenue to CCC for 100,000 soft-drink can order was approximately $3,500. A small customer might spend from $12,000 to $15,000 a year on cans; a major soft-drink bottler might spend as much as $8 or $10 million. Among the sales force, a $10,000 increase or a $10,000 new account was considered good; a $100,000 account gain was considered a coup.

‡ The 1967 figures represent the salesman's forecast of soft-drink can orders by major customers and CCC plant. The 1966 figures represent the salesman's latest adjustment of his previous year's forecast. The 1965 figures are actual for 1965.

ity, and other information generated by their marketing research. The data were then submitted to the divisional general manager, who considered the figures in relation to the estimates of divisional plant capacity forwarded by the plant managers. (Plant managers also conferred with divisional sales managers whenever they thought forecasts from the sales force were unrealistic.) From these forecasts, the divisional general manager had to determine whether any new equipment would be needed to produce the goods demanded by the sales plan. During 1965 and 1966, most of the soft-drink can lines in CCC plants throughout the country were operating at or near capacity. (Incremental equipment requests were generally made in terms of additional "can lines," each costing approximately $75,000.)

Using the knowledge of his territory gathered from high-level contact with the larger customers, the divisional general manager probed and questioned the division marketing staff in order to make the sales forecast as precise as possible. If the sales forecast was too low, the divisional general manager could not justify new equipment; if the forecast was too high, the division's performance against the forecast would be unfavorable. One divisional general manager remarked,

> I don't know the specific figure for the company's desired return on investment. I do know that additional equipment is easier to justify if I can show a loss in market share if I don't have it.

In September the final divisional sales forecast was released to the plant managers for preliminary scheduling of production runs. The forecast sent to the plant managers was quantified by product. Each plant received from each sales district its can production requirements by month and in the following detail: item number, size and style of can, dimensions, plate grade of body and lids, inside and outside lacquer, and packing instructions (number per case, etc.). This forecast was reviewed by district sales managers on a quarterly basis throughout the following year. Revisions were forwarded to plant personnel for production rescheduling every quarter, and more frequently when necessary. The divisional forecast was also submitted, with recommendations for additional equipment, for review by the corporate marketing and planning group.

The Corporate Forecasts

Separate sales forecasts for each division were made independently by the corporate marketing staff. The basis for the forecasts was a detailed analysis of growth rates in each market segment. Corporate marketing personnel also maintained personal contact with senior executives of MPG's major accounts. These contacts enabled them to forecast changes in major customers' demands and in CCC's share of these customers' business. Exhibit 4 shows a forecast prepared by corporate marketing staff for an MPG division in August 1966.

Just as the divisional personnel spent a great deal of time and effort to make their forecast precise enough for production planning and scheduling, corporate marketing personnel took similar pains to be precise, for other reasons. CCC had many investment opportunities, and one of the major responsibilities of the corporate marketing and planning group was to provide a corporate executive committee with forecasts from all the divisions in the company so that the committee would have better evidence on which to base their investment decisions. The data-gathering activity behind this long-range financial planning required a more extended time horizon than typically held by division marketing personnel.

The forecasts made by corporate marketing personnel by product line rarely varied more than two or three percentage points from actual. For many of the various metal can products, forecasting was relatively easy because sales of the items typically grew at an annual growth rate of 2 percent or 3 percent. In contrast, forecasting for the soft-drink market was more difficult because the annual growth rate of soft-drinks in cans in some areas was as high as 40 percent. A single decision by a major bottler, such as Coca-Cola, could cause a major shift in the demand for containers. Nevertheless, the corporate marketing group's forecasts of the company's share of the rapidly growing soft-drink market were as accurate as its forecasts in CCC's other markets.

Exhibit 4
Example of Corporate Staff Forecast for Division A

	Actual CCC Shipments (000 base boxes)		Actual Gross Sales ($000)		Estimated Market Growth (percent)	
	1964	1965	1964	1965	1965–66	1966–67
Total containers	8,218	8,4688	$152,235	$159,704		
Total cans	8,000	8,275	142,359	149,719	4.6	4.1
Fruits and fruit juices............	734	692	12,305	11,870	0.4	3.6
Vegetables and vegetable juices ...1,154		1,173	18,316	19,118	2.5	—
Evaporated and condensed milk...	—	—	—	—	2.7	−3.5
Other dairy products	66	56	1,348	1,054	−5.6	−1–5
Fish and seafood................	144	142	2,432	2,417	7.3	0.2
Lard and shortening.............	36	30	792	602	−6.8	−1–0
Meat and poultry	153	97	2,916	1,620	4.4	2.8
Coffee	430	419	7,517	7,372	2.4	0.7
Baby food	56	34	1,242	758	5.4	10.3
Miscellaneous food	506	519	7,844	8,522	2.7	1.8
Soft drinks	725	1,141	13,093	21,256	24.4	21.2
Beer.........................1,946		2,093	35,494	38,687	3.5	3.5
Paints, varnishes and products	186	170	3,903	3,693	1.5	0.2
Oil, open-top	787	740	10,729	9,859	2.5	0.6
Antifreeze.....................	42	44	742	794	—	−2.6
Pet food	297	238	4,198	3,454	5.1	2.2
Household and industrial.........	499	410	13,388	11,019	1.0	—
Aerosols	239	278	6,100	7,625	13.7	17.9
Miscellaneous metal items........	218	193	9,876	99,985		

Combining the Forecasts

During September the corporate marketing people met with the marketing staffs of each of the divisions. During a series of meetings between these two groups, differences between the corporate forecasts for the coming year and the division forecasts for the same period were, to quote one divisional general manager, "massaged." Corporate marketing personnel had to try to prove that the corporate forecast was the more accurate. Usually, divisional managers accepted the corporate forecast. One corporate marketing executive explained the divisions' compliance in this way:

> The division people can agree or not. They recognize, however, that they have little data on their market other than those built up by their own division people and the sales force. We seldom lost an argument.

The precision of the massaged forecasts is illustrated by the following statement made by a divisional marketing executive:

> Our final forecast generally comes within 0.5 percent. This is a real tribute to the corporate marketing people. Nevertheless, we do have our differences of opinion. Last year, they made us reduce our forecast by 1.6 percent. We ended up the year ahead 1.9 percent. If they hadn't asked for the reduction, we would have been within 0.3 percent. On the other hand, most of the time they are more accurate than we are.

MPG'S SALES BUDGET

Once the corporate and divisional people had agreed on the sales forecast, usually by November, divisional accounting personnel began to draw up their sales budget. Continuing cost analyses for each plant were used to determine the future gross margins on sales. Accounting personnel then developed a complete projected income statement for each division, based on historical and projected relationships between sales and expenses for each plant and sales office in the division. If additional facilities had been requested by the divisional general manager, the projections of additional sales and expenses were included in the division's income statement, subject to review and approval by an executive committee. The final budget for each division was submitted to this executive committee toward the end of November. Once approved, the budget became top management's yardstick for evaluating the performance of the division and its personnel. Occasionally, the executive committee adjusted divisional sales objectives and budgets in order to meet corporate sales or profit objectives. Usually, however, this readjustment was not necessary, because the divisional budgets reflected the best information available to the corporate marketing and planning group.

MPG'S QUOTA DEVELOPMENT

By the beginning of December, the executive budget and forecast committee had concluded its review. Corporate marketing personnel now began to develop sales quotas for each of the divisions. This activity was usually completed early in January. The divisional sales quota was the same as the division's forecasted dollar sales volume. Dollar sales volume was based on the projected growth rate, after adjustments for price changes, losses to self-manufacture and other competitive activity, business transferred to or from other divisions, and sales contingent upon new equipment.

The divisional marketing personnel took this quota from the corporate marketing people, broke it down by product group, and allocated it to the districts, taking into consideration the district's forecasted sales and the various adjustments for growth, price changes and so forth. Thus, each district received a dollar quota figure, reflecting its share of the division's quota.

The major difference between the sales quota for the district and the sales forecasted for the district was that the quota did not include expected competitive losses or gains that were incorporated in the forecast. These data were removed because competitive changes were considered within the control of the district personnel. Changes due to market growth, on the other hand, were retained in sales quotas, because sales representatives were expected to maintain normal market growth.

MPG'S INCENTIVE SYSTEM

Managers

All managers above the rank of district sales manager received, in addition to salary, the opportunity to earn income from the management incentive program (MIP). The MIP bonus was tied to the division's income, relative to the sales budget and to the company's overall profitability. In a good year, the MIP bonus could amount to more than 50 percent of a manager's annual salary. In a bad year, the bonus might be zero. The amounts paid to each manager were determined by a corporate executive committee.

A typical salary for a district sales manager was $1,500 a month, but this figure could be supplemented at the end of the year by one or both of two extra payments. The first was a sales incentive bonus based on the average bonus earned by the sales reps in the district. The second was an override tied to the profitability of the division. This bonus was a scaled down version of the MIP. On average, this bonus amounted to another 10 percent of the district sales manager's base salary.

Salespeople

A typical salary for a sales representative was $1,000 a month, supplemented at the end of the year by his share of the sales incentive bonus for the district. This total district bonus was calculated as follows: If the district as a whole made less than 85 percent of its quota, no bonus was paid. At 86 percent the district earned a bonus equal to 1 percent of the total of the salaries of the representatives in that district. At 87 percent this figure increased to 2 percent, and so on. Thus, if the district made 100 percent of its quota, the bonus would amount to 15 percent of the total of the representatives' salaries in that district. In addition, for each .4 of a percent of market share change gained by the Metal Products Group, an additional 1 percent of the salaries was added to all the district bonuses.

The distribution of the district bonus among the sales representatives was the responsibility of the district sales manager, who based his bonus allocations on his end-of-the-fiscal-year formal ratings of his salesmen. The end-of-the-year rating, when completed by the district sales manager and approved by the divisional general manager and divisional sales manager, was discussed with the individual appraised. Each sales rep was required to sign his rating form. An additional formal rating, conducted during the summer, was not tied to the bonus determination.

The district manager appraised each sales representative's work on the basis of 27 items, which are listed in Exhibit 5. The importance of each item was indicated by the number following the item. For example, the first item under "customer relations" was assigned a weight of 3. Four major rating categories ranging from "not satisfactory" to "superior" were set up, and point values assigned to each. To determine an individual's overall rating, the manager multiplied the weight of each item by the score he had given the representative on that item.

The maximum possible rating was 940, achievable only if an individual were rated superior-plus on all 27 factors. In a district with eight sales reps,

Exhibit 5
Items on Salesmen's Appraisal Form

	Not satisfactory 1 2	Satisfactory 3 4 5	Excellent 6 7 8	Superior 9 10

Item	Weighting × Grade = Points

I. CUSTOMER RELATIONS

1. Is he well thought of by his customers?	3
2. Does he frequently and effectively contact the management of customers and prospects?	2
3. Does he willingly devote extra time to his work when it is necessary?.....................	3
4. Does he willingly accept the more unpleasant assignments?	3
5. Does he handle complaints well?	2
6. Has he been accurate in estimating his customer's requirements?.....................	5
7. Has he secured the cooperation of his customers in revising estimates where necessary?	3
8. Is he tactful in handling customers?............	3
9. Is he aggressive?	4
10. Does he handle claims quickly and efficiently? ...	5

II. OFFICE PERFORMANCE

1. Is he well thought of by his associates in the Company?	2
2. Does he cooperate fully with others in the office?..	4
3. Does he cooperate with other salesmen?.........	3
4. Does he maintain sufficient and satisfactory records on his customers?	3
5. Does he have and follow a good call plan?	2
6. Does he keep management well informed of conditions and changes in his territory?...........	5
7. Are his correspondence and his reports complete concise, and accurate?	2
8. Are his expenses well controlled?................	4
9. Does he solve his own problems?...............	4

III. KNOWLEDGE AND INFORMATION

1. Does he have a good knowledge of our products?..	4
2. Does he have a good knowledge of our C.E.S. equipment and its uses?.......................	5
3. Is he well informed on the competitive situation in his territory?.................................	3

Exhibit 5 *(continued)*

---

4. Does he have a good knowledge of the credit
   situation in his territory?   3
5. Does he attempt to improve his knowledge of the
   Company, our customers, and prospects?   5

IV. HOW ENTHUSIASTIC IS HE ABOUT HIS JOB?
1. A salesman should have an active, loyal, and
   willing interest in his work.   4

V. DOES HE USE MATURE JUDGMENT IN
    ANALYZING PROBLEMS?
1. A salesman should be able to analyze problems
   factually, logically, and with common sense.   4

VI. IS HE IMAGINATIVE AND RESOURCEFUL
     IN HIS WORK?
1. We want a salesman to use initiative and his own
   head in his work.   4   _____
                                              TOTAL POINTS =

---

if the ratings varied from 470 (satisfactory-plus in all factors) to 750 (excellent to excellent-plus in all factors), a total point score for all eight sales reps would be in the vicinity of 4,800 points. This number would be divided into the district sales bonus to determine the dollar value of a point, and the resultant figure would be multiplied by each individual's point score to arrive at his share of the bonus.

Part Two
The Field Sales Manager

The primary responsibility of the field sales manager is to encourage conformity between actual behavior (what the salesman does) and desired behavior (what the company wants him or her to do). But this important position is often the Achilles heel of the sales force. Good field sales management is made up of (1) a properly defined job which permits the manager to spend enough time performing appropriate field supervisory activities and (2) personal behaviors that meet the needs of subordinates and encourage them to high performance.

FIELD SUPERVISION

The lack of adequate field supervision is a common complaint among salesmen, their customers, and even senior managers. One reason for the lack of adequate field supervision is managers' beliefs that experienced salesmen do not need supervision or will not stand for it. "Salesmen should be treated as if they were in business for themselves," many managers assume. According to this view, mature salesmen—particularly those paid on straight commission—when left alone will act in their own self-interest and maximize their own and the company's sales volume. This view found its genesis in the *Music Man* stage of selling behavior, and it is still fairly widespread.

Nowadays, however, marketing strategies are too dynamic and complex to permit salesmen to act merely in their own self-interest. Most sales organizations require their personnel to perform many activities that fall outside a salesman's definition of his or her self-interest. Salesmen are seldom in business for themselves. They are hired to implement marketing strategy. Furthermore, lack of supervision is particularly damaging to high-performance salesmen, who often want to do even better and whose efforts are all too often taken for granted.

A second reason for inadequate field supervision is that companies often fail to define the sales manager's job properly. Field managers and senior managers alike often do not recognize that the field sales manager's keys tasks are observing actual sales force behavior and working to improve it *in the field.*

Instead of giving highest priority to supervisory tasks, some companies assign field sales managers customers of their own to handle—either because "it's good for them to keep their hands in" or because the size or importance of the accounts seem to warrant their receiving a manager's attention. This practice can cause managers to overemphasize selling at the expense of developing the skills of their salesmen—particularly if the managers' incomes and performance appraisals depend on their success with their own accounts.

Other firms, rather than seeing their managers as primarily salesmen, see them as primarily administrators. This attitude causes field sales managers to become bogged down with paperwork, report writing, and other duties often better left to staff specialists—activities such as recruiting and hiring new salesmen, reconciling expense accounts, or conducting customer surveys. Assigning any administrative task to a field sales manager should always be considered as a trade-off. Is this administrative task worth depriving a manager of time in the field to work with his or her salesmen?

Often newly promoted field sales managers are well aware that field supervision should be their first priority. Yet they may be uncertain *how* to supervise.

One reason for such uncertainty is their own lack of training. Many firms routinely promote their best salesmen without preparing them adequately for their new responsibilities. But success as a salesman does not guarantee success as a manager. Unless the selling job had a great deal of managerial content—such as a job in which planning, coordinating, and integrating the tasks of many people were critical to consummating the sale—most salesmen find that managing other people's activities requires different skills from asking a customer for an order. Indeed, in many sales organizations the supersalesman is often the least likely to be a good planner, a good organizer, and a good delegator. Furthermore, the supersalesman is often unaware of the reasons for his or her success and, thus, is unable to coach and direct the behavior of others.

A second reason for new managers' uncertainty is that senior managers may fail to communicate their objectives for the sales force. Not only must senior managers define for field sales managers the precise role of the sales force in the firm's marketing strategy, but they must also update that definition every time that changes in the competitive environment force changes in marketing strategy. If current desired behavior is not understood, field sales managers have no recourse but to direct their salesmen to perform as they always have—or, even worse, to perform as the managers performed when *they* were salesmen. Unless the activities of the sales force correspond to the desired behavior as determined by marketing strategy, the sales force will be doing one thing while senior executives will be expecting another. Once the field sales manager understands the sales force's role in the firm's marketing strategy, he or she can determine the kinds of supervision appropriate to this role and to the needs of individual salesmen.

Coaching. The manager's most important task is to teach his or her salesmen how to sell efficiently and effectively. Most coaching takes place one-on-one in the field; some of it takes place in small group training sessions. Working in the field allows the manager to make calls with a salesman and to observe, participate in, demonstrate, or take over the sale. *Observation* is the most common practice when making calls with experienced salesmen. "Sidewalk critiques" give the field sales manager the opportunity to compliment professional behavior and to correct unprofessional behavior. *Participation* in the sale can be an effective method of training salesmen in the finer points of such activities as answering questions, handling objections, and asking for the order. *Demonstration* is a tool for helping salesmen learn how to handle a module of the sale; for instance, how to make a new-product introduction. *Taking over* is a technique usually reserved for rescuing an important sale when it is obvious that the selling situation is beyond the salesman's control.

Counseling.   This activity requires a great deal of judgment on the part of the field sales manager. On the one hand, giving advice and direction in response to a salesman's request for career guidance is an important aspect of the manager's job. On the other hand, helping a salesman iron out marital or financial problems is seldom wise. Field sales managers cannot be expected to act as priests or psychiatrists. Nevertheless, listening in a nondirective, nonjudgmental fashion to a salesman's personal problems can be supportive and morale-building when the salesman's personal problems begin to affect job performance. Most experienced field sales managers, however, confine their prescriptive advice to pointing out the job-related consequences of a salesman's personal situation.

Controlling.   The responsibility for the performance of his or her salesmen ultimately rests with the field sales manager. An organizational climate that encourages high performance will be created largely through the field sales manager's personal style, but also affected by the pressures and expectations of superiors and subordinates. This man-in-the-middle position is a tough situation for the average field sales manager. Handling it requires a clear understanding of the job's authorities and responsibilities, as well as considerable insight into the motivations of other people. The appropriate amount of control is usually determined by the competence of the salesmen and the risks inherent in the selling situations. *Delegation* ("You take care of it") is usually a safe course with competent salesmen. *Direction* ("Take care of it *this* way") is more often required for less competent salesmen or in high-risk selling situations. *Doing* ("Let me take care of it") may be necessary when salesmen are unable or ill-equipped to take charge themselves.

Evaluating.   Not only must the field sales manager monitor and evaluate performance, he or she must communicate this evaluation to the individual salesmen. How to measure performance, how to identify areas for individual improvement, and how to communicate the evaluation in such a way that the salesman will be able to improve his or her performance are among the most demanding of the field sales manager's tasks. Experienced field sales managers find that performance appraisals can be powerful tools for improving results, when they adhere to the following rules: (1) Appraise performance along dimensions relevant to the job. (2) Avoid appraising personal attributes. (3) Appraise frequently. (4) Focus appraisal on future action plans, not on past peccadillos.

Administrating. A certain amount of administrative duties are required of most field sales managers. Determining sales territories and administering sales quotas are two of the more frequent ones.

Assigning Territories. Many field sales managers are required to assign accounts to their salesmen. This activity involves making judgments about workload, matching salesmens' characteristics to those of key customers, estimating sales potential, and, above all, trying to balance fairly an individual's workload against the potential sales volume within his or her territory.

Administering Sales Quotas. Field managers must communicate sales objectives to salesmen. Many companies use personal sales quotas to make these objectives clear. Some companies base quotas on historical sales performance, others on estimates of sales potential, and still others attempt to tailor the quota to the strengths and weaknesses of the individual salesman. Some companies view quotas as forecasts—they expect quotas to be met. Other companies view quotas as targets—they expect only the best salesmen to meet them. Still other companies use quotas as a basis for compensation. To administer quotas effectively, the field sales manager must understand their purpose and understand the influence that they exert on salesmen in various situations. For instance, quotas based on historical sales (often called ratchets when they are based on percent increases over the previous year's sales) tend to give the better salesmen the harder challenge, as they must get more and more sales from the same territory. And quotas based on potential sales tend to give the weaker salesmen the harder challenge, for the potential in their territories grows faster than their abilities. Quotas can be personalized to challenge strong and weak performers equally. But personalized quotas do not provide the sales forecasting that historical quotas do, nor the comparative evaluation possibilities of quotas based on potential.

LEADERSHIP BEHAVIOR

The manner in which a manager coaches, counsels, controls, evaluates, and administers may be described as his or her personal style of leadership. Effective sales managers are those whose style encourages and stimulates their salesmen to high achievement. A manager's personal style depends largely on his or her private definition of leadership, whether this definition is unconscious or articulated. This section will orient readers to various theories of leadership and to the theories' usefulness to managers trying to develop their own skills of leadership.

Traitist Definitions of Leadership

A traitist, in pure form, believes that leaders possess certain common personal traits that would enable them to become leaders in any situation. A typical list of such traits might well include courage, determination, mental adaptiveness, knowledge, and integrity. Some traitists added certain skills and techniques to their list of qualities, such as the ability to gain cooperation, to communicate, or to stimulate other people's ideas. These latter qualities seem less inherent and thus more learnable.

Unfortunately, efforts to establish any such list of universal qualities have not been convincing. Even if researchers were able to confirm such a list, the qualities therein would probably elude precise and practical definition. Nevertheless, a consensus exists, even among nontraitists, that leaders tend to exhibit greater than normal intelligence, drive or physical energy, and a quality roughly described as the "desire to lead." Managers trying to develop their own skills may find that descriptions of leadership traits help them to inventory their own qualities and to pinpoint skills that need work.

Situational Definitions of Leadership

Today, there are few pure traitists left. In retrospect, we may judge that this approach proved inadequate because leaders do not function in isolation. They must deal with followers within definite cultural, social, and physical contexts. As the traitists lost acceptance, new theorists began to shift their emphasis away from the leader as an entity toward the leader in a specific context. Pure situationists argued for abandoning any search for traits, believing that leadership was entirely a function of the situation. The distinguished British scientist and author C. P. Snow, for example, held that great leaders emerge from specific contexts to meet specific demands.

Despite Snow's belief, however, few situationists abandoned the search for significant characteristics among leaders. Instead, they tried to identify traits of leadership common among leaders acting in similar situations. For instance, among primitive tribes multiple leadership is common: food-gathering is lead by a hunter chosen for his ability to organize others to pursue the quarry; defense is lead by a warrior chosen for his skill and courage; tribal continuity is ensured by an chieftain chosen for his wisdom and charisma. Similarly, specific leadership characteristics may vary according to the stage of corporate development. Technical creativity and "dynamic salesmanship" may be the critical elements is guiding a company through its entrepreneurial stage; skills in organizing and communicating may be the critical elements in guiding a company through its stage of rapid growth; vision and the ability to develop a strong sense of cohesion among various managers and divisions may be the critical elements in maintaining the viability of the mature company.

Situational theories aid the managers by focusing his or her attention on specific supervisory tasks or contexts, such as evaluating or counseling salesmen, and on the specific behaviors most useful to leaders in each situation.

Human Relations Definitions of Leadership

The human relations definition of leadership, especially influential in the 1930s and 1940s but still influential today, developed as a reaction against the so-called scientific management ideas propounded by Taylor, Gilbreth, and others. The human relations school held that scientific management dehumanized people, by seeing them as mere resources to be used, ordered, and manipulated by their leaders. The human relations definitions are based on the assumption that people can be motivated to work more efficiently and productively if their psychological and social needs are understood and satisfied. Warren G. Bennis describes the founders of this new conception of leadership:

> Elton Mayo, with his emphasis on the significance of the human group and *affiliation* as the strongest human need; Kurt Lewin, who stressed the promise of democratic and group decision-making as well as the importance of *participation* in motivating people; J. L. Moreno, with his emphasis on *positive* feelings and liking as fundamentals in group action; and Carl Rogers, the founder of "non-directive therapy," who underscored the need for understanding, *empathy*, and self-realization. [1]

The work of these men and their associates provoked professional managers to acknowledge the importance of informal interpersonal relationships among workers. One of the basic tenets of the human relations school is that groups whose members help to set their own goals have higher morale and more commitment to the organization than do groups directed by authoritarian leaders. In the strict human relations approach, the interaction among group members is more important than the influence of the leader upon the group. Thus, leadership is seen as facilitation of group process—as execution rather than innovation; as task accomplishment rather than task definition.

Although this school did not consider leadership to be as important as group processes, the theorists' analyses of group processes do offer insights for professional managers. Managers studying these analyses may learn techniques of helping a group to solve problems and to accept decisions. Managers may also learn the importance of considering the group's real concerns and its intellectual and emotional characteristics.

Revisions and Definitions of Leadership

Although the human relations definitions of leadership are still much in evidence, they have come under criticism. Whereas the human relations school criticized scientific management as "organizations without people," a later group of theorists criticized the human relations school as "people without organizations." Some critics even said that the human relations school

---

[1] See Bennis' *Changing Organizations—Essays on the Development and Evolution of Human Organization* (New York: McGraw-Hill, 1966), chap. 4.

actually dehumanized the individual by minimizing his or her role and worth in relation to the group.

Bennis uses the term *revisionists* to classify a rather diverse group of thinkers who, since 1950 and increasingly since 1960, have been trying to reconcile and integrate concepts of leadership derived from traitists, situationalists, scientific managers, and various schools of organizational theory. About these authors, Bennis says:

> In general, they share a common concern for revising the naive, unsubstantiated, and unrealistic aspects of the human relations approach without sacrificing its radical departure from traditional theory.
>
> The revisionists recognize clearly that organizational theory must take into account such factors as purpose and goal, status and power differentials, and hierarchy. And, finally, they have come to know that leadership ultimately has to act in ways other than, or in addition to, leading a group discussion.[2]

Three prominent revisionists are Chris Argyris, Douglas M. McGregor, and Robert McMurray. Argyris concentrates on the relationship between the individual and the organization.[3] His main thesis is that the individual's needs and the formal organization's demands are basically incompatible. The organization's demands for task specialization, chain of command, unity of direction, and so on, make it impossible for the individual to reach "self-actualization" within an organization. The leader's first responsibility, then, is to debureaucratize the formal organization as much as possible, so that the structure provides "increasingly meaningful challenges and opportunity for responsibility."

McGregor, widely acknowledged as the behavioral scientist having had the greatest single influence on practicing executives, sees leadership as a collaborative relationship between superior and subordinate that takes full account of their interdependency.[4] The leader is a helper, trainer, consultant, and coordinator. He or she is principally concerned with creating an organizational climate in which employees can exercise increasing self-direction and self-control. McGregor called this type of leadership Theory Y management, contrasting it to dictatorial or Theory X management. Although McGregor's Theory Y placed him in the human relations camp, his later statements gave him a solid position among the revisionists. In *The Professional Manager*, published posthumously, he admitted the need for authoritarian leadership in situations wherein mutual commitment to objectives cannot be obtained. He also underscored the situational nature of leadership:

> Depending upon the particular situation in which he finds himself, a manager who holds the beliefs that I called Theory X could adopt a considerable array of strategies, some of which would be typically called "hard" and some of which would be called "soft." The same is true with respect to Theory Y.[5]

---

[2] Ibid.
[3] Chris Argyris, *Personality and Organization* (New York: Harper & Row, 1957).
[4] Douglas M. McGregor, *The Human Side of Enterprise* (New York: McGraw-Hill, 1960).
[5] Douglas McGregor, *The Professional Manager* (New York: McGraw-Hill, 1967), p. 79.

R. N. McMurray, a psychoanalyst, argues for "benevolent autocracy."[6] He claims that, while consultative management is theoretically preferable, it is not realistic or practical. Managers tend to be hard-driving people who basically do not believe in the human-relations approach. And furthermore, he argues, followers prefer regimentation. Benevolent autocracy, he believes, gets results through structure, routine, and control over supervisor/subordinate relationships.

CONCLUSION

My purpose in outlining these theories of leadership is to help managers to reflect upon their own styles of leadership and to recognize that in each particular supervisory situation one may choose how to behave. Such choices define one's personal style of leadership and establish an organizational climate that stimulates others to perform well—or poorly.

Of course, a manager is seldom completely free to behave—to adopt a leadership style—as the situation may call for. Personal styles are heavily influenced by corporate cultures, which recognize and reward certain kinds of behavior; by superiors, who act as role models for aspiring young managers; and by personal values, which preclude certain kinds of behavior.

Despite these and other constraints on behavior, the professional manager can exercise a great deal of flexibility in choosing his or her style. Compare the leadership exercised over two groups, a Marine Corps platoon and a research laboratory. The managerial tasks differ: ensuring instant obedience is poles apart from encouraging creative thinking. The people are different: young, healthy, relatively less-educated recruits have different wants and needs than do mature, highly educated technicians and scientists. Because of these differences, the climates that encourage top performance from these two groups will also differ. The marines will perform best within an organizational climate that they perceive as fostering structure, order, rewards for physical prowess, and intense interdependence and camaraderie. The scientists will perform best within an organizational climate perceived to foster freedom, creativity, rewards for intellectual accomplishment, and the free flow of ideas.

These two managerial situations are extreme cases. But they illustrate that an effective managerial style is one tailored to the organization's goals and to the needs of the people who are to accomplish those goals. A sales manager's style will be defined by his or her manner of coaching, counseling, evaluating, and so on, as well as by the relative emphasis he or she places on each of these supervisory tasks. Ideally, the resulting style of leadership will stimulate this particular set of salesmen to meet the specific goals that the firm's marketing strategy has decreed for the sales force.

---

[6]R. N. McMurray, "The Case for Benevolent Autocracy," *Harvard Business Review*, January–February 1958, pp. 82–90.

Case 4
Battlefield Group, Inc.

In January 1979, six months after joining the Battlefield Group, Inc. (BGI), a furniture manufacturer headquartered in Charlottesville, Virginia, Mr. Mark Rhoads, national sales manager, was wondering what actions to take regarding three problem salespeople. The first was Frank O'Brien, who was poorly servicing an oversized territory; the second was James Schmidt, a management trainee who was beginning to look like a hiring mistake; and the third was Frank Irons, who had failed to submit adequate reports of his activities for the last six months.

THE FURNITURE INDUSTRY

Over 1,200 furniture manufacturers operated more than 5,000 production facilities in the United States in 1977. Characteristic of the furniture industry was a wide dispersion of manufacturing capability: a large number of regional producers concentrated their production efforts in a limited number of styles, and their sales efforts in limited geographic areas. In this relatively low-capital-intensive industry, the largest firm had an approximate market share of 3 percent, from a total sales volume estimated at $6.3 billion. BGI, its 1978 sales volume in excess of $64 million, was among the 20 largest firms.

Total advertising expenditures by manufacturers were estimated to be less than 1 percent of sales. According to a recent survey by a prominent market research firm, fewer than 44 percent of the married couples interviewed could name one furniture manufacturer.

The retail furniture industry was also fragmented, made up chiefly of small firms earning low returns on investment. Industry estimates placed retail furniture volume, exclusive of bedding and furnishings, at nearly $13 billion. These sales were shared by some 50,000 retailers, ranging from full-line department stores and furniture stores to small neighborhood specialty shops. According to BGI executives, most manufacturers "sold pieces of furniture to as many accounts as they could reach."

BGI'S MARKETING AND SALES

In 1975 BGI had come under new management. At that time, the company was manufacturing and marketing high-quality "case goods" (non-upholstered pieces) in the medium price range. Its products were distributed through an extremely large number of dealers; average volume per dealer was low. Sales in 1975 were slightly over $40 million. By 1978, however, BGI had increased its sales by more than 16 percent annually—a rate more than double that of the industry—by reducing the number of its accounts significantly and by broadening its product line, both by expanding its case goods and by entering the contemporary upholstery market.

BGI executives described their new marketing strategy as one based on selective distribution and national advertising in shelter magazines. They chose the best dealers within each major marketing area, provided them with a wide line of high-quality, high-margin, special-order merchandise in tasteful, stylish contemporary designs, and assisted them with store layout, promotion, and clerk training. In return, the retailer provided floor space sufficient to display a representative sampling of the BGI line, local advertising support, and enthusiastic retail floor selling effort. For these activities the retailer received a profitable line relatively free from price promotion; the option of minimal investment in inventory; market segment with minimal competition; and some degree of consumer preselling, by virtue of BGI's national advertising. In 1978, BGI spent about $1.3 million in such magazines as *House Beautiful*.

Of the 53 people on the BGI sales force, all but six were independent agents. Each agent was assigned a geographic territory and paid his or her own expenses out of a 5 percent commission on sales. Only two of the agents represented other furniture manufacturers, and neither of them sold lines that competed with BGI products. Agents' earnings ranged from $36,000 to over $100,000 in 1978, with an average of $60,000. The six nonagent salespeople were considered management trainees. Each had been hired within the past two years and was paid a straight salary of $40,000 a year.

According to BGI executives, the major problem with the sales force was converting the agents—most of whom were over 40 years old and had been with BGI from 10 to 20 years—from "furniture peddlers" to retail consultants, the role called for by the new marketing strategy.

Each of the 53 BGI salespeople reported directly to Mark Rhoads, the national sales manager. Rhoads had spent seven years as a field sales engineer with an electrical equipment manufacturer before leaving that job to earn his MBA from a prominent university. He had been hired by BGI as national sales manager directly upon graduation. He was 34, was married and had two children, and he was a reserve officer in the Air Force.

THE PROBLEM OF THE OVERSIZED TERRITORY

Frank O'Brien had been a furniture salesman for almost 40 years. He had been an agent for BGI for more than 25 of those years, selling the BGI line to retailers in Florida, Alabama, and Georgia. In 1978, he produced $2.1 million in sales from 165 dealers, most of this revenue coming from Florida. In addition to his considerable income from BGI, O'Brien had a 40 percent interest in an automobile dealership run by his younger brother in Tampa. Rhoads estimated O'Brien's age as 68.

One of Rhoads's first steps upon assuming his national sales manager responsibilities had been to develop measures of potential sales volume for each territory, based on *Sales Management* magazine's *Index of Buying Power*. These data were adjusted to reflect the number of family units with incomes over $15,000 (BGI's target customers) and to accommodate a geographical "preference index" for contemporary furniture. Rhoads then advised each agent of the quota or share of potential sales assigned to his or her territory. According to Rhoads's calculations, O'Brien's territorial quota should have been $2.5 million, or $.4 million above the sales he had realized in 1978.

Rhoads was concerned that O'Brien did not seem to be working his territory to its full potential, and also that O'Brien had been reluctant to follow the new BGI strategy of "program selling" to selected accounts. According to Rhoads, O'Brien still preferred to sell "sticks of furniture to all his furniture dealer friends"—to firms whose images and business practices were inconsistent with BGI's policy of choosing only the best outlets to represent the firm.

Rhoads believed that the problems in O'Brien's territory should be considered in the context of another problem: the uneven distribution of accounts within a neighboring territory. The Carolinas were currently in the territory of Bob Milton, who also handled Virginia and was eager to concentrate on the latter state. Consequently, BGI's penetration and distribution were superficial in the Carolinas. (Virginia was home base not only for BGI but also for many other major furniture manufacturers.) Penetration and distribution were also spotty in Georgia and Alabama, states within O'Brien's territory.

Rhoads felt that creating a new sales territory would help resolve these difficulties. Georgia and Alabama could be split off from O'Brien's territory and joined to the Carolinas, from Milton's territory. Rhoads believed this grouping of states to be the most natural one, and he felt that current sales volume in those states could double under the new scheme. The territory would be assigned to a new agent, Arley Baldwin.

Rhoads's proposal met with the full agreement of the president of BGI, who had, in fact, hired Baldwin—a man of outstanding credentials, including 12 years of retail furniture store management experience. The president offered only this caveat:

> Take it easy with O'Brien. He is the oldest and most respected man on the sales force. He is practically idolized by many people in the industry. I don't want him feeling that we don't treat people right. Remember this, too: the only man on our sales force who produces more sales than Frank is a man Frank picked out for us himself.

Rhoads estimated that the loss of Georgia and Alabama would reduce O'Brien's sales volume by about $400,000 in 1979. Rhoads did not believe that the loss of income would upset O'Brien as much as the loss of prestige. He knew that O'Brien was sensitive about his age ("The only time you'll see me slow down is when I drop dead") and proud of the volume of business that he brought in ("If I were five years younger I'd still be number one").

During the remainder of 1978, Rhoads had had several meetings with O'Brien. He had spent two days with him on the road visiting some of his dealers, and he had dined with O'Brien's family (including eight grandchildren) at O'Brien's home in Tampa. Although Rhoads had never broached the subject of splitting the territory, O'Brien had sensed the possibility. On the last occasion that they had had drinks together, at a Christmas party at the Charlottesville plant, O'Brien had given Rhoads "a million reasons" for leaving him alone, including the observation that Baldwin, whom he had just met, "couldn't sell a bone to a hungry dog." O'Brien's parting comment had been: "I like you, young fella, but don't ever fool around with my wife or my territory—and not necessarily in that order."

Rhoads was now considering three alternatives:

1. Make the change. Inform O'Brien and place Baldwin in the territory.
2. Same as option 1. But ask O'Brien to "train" Baldwin and give him a 1 percent override on all Baldwin's sales in Georgia and Alabama for the next two years.
3. Do nothing until O'Brien retires.

THE PROBLEM OF THE "HIRING MISTAKE"

One of Rhoads's first assignments had been to hire an agent to fill a territory becoming vacant through the voluntary retirement of 66-year-old Frank Gorman. "Old Frank," as he was known to everyone, had been second only to Frank O'Brien in experience and company longevity. His territory, Texas and Oklahoma, included some 50 accounts and produced $800,000 in sales in 1977, approximately half the territory's potential sales, according to Rhoads's calculations. Gorman had given notice several months before Rhoads had joined BGI, stating that he desired to retire as soon as a replacement could be hired.

Late in September 1978, Rhoads had interviewed James Schmidt, a 28-year-old sales representative for a major manufacturer of drapery and upholstery fabrics. One of BGI's important customers on the West Coast had referred Schmidt to BGI's president and had suggested BGI to Schmidt as a company that offered a fine opportunity to advance into management. Although Schmidt was happy with his current employer, he agreed to consider a change. Subsequently, Rhoads, during his first business trip to San Francisco, had had dinner with Schmidt and had been so favorably impressed that he invited Schmidt to come to Charlottesville to meet the rest of the BGI management team.

A week later Schmidt made the trip to Charlottesville and had impressed everyone he met. He had an A.B. degree in marketing from a West Coast university where he had also played varsity football. His academic record was excellent. Like Rhoads, he was a Reserve officer in the Air Force. Rhoads talked Schmidt into leaving his present employer and accepting a position as a management trainee at $40,000 a year, $6,000 more than his current earnings.

The president of BGI concurred wholeheartedly with the decision to give Schmidt management trainee status. Schmidt appeared to fit perfectly into the president's plan to provide his fast-growing company with future executives. From Rhoads's point of view, Schmidt's four years of experience selling fabrics to department, furniture, and specialty stores offered BGI the perfect opportunity to improve distribution quality in one of the poorest performing territories, at a cost substantially below the 5 percent commission rate.

Schmidt, his wife, and two children found a house in Dallas, and Schmidt reported to Charlottesville for a two-week training period. He seemed to grasp the features of the BGI line rapidly, and he showed quick understanding and appreciation of the company's way of doing business.

On December 1, Schmidt took over the Texas-Oklahoma territory. One week later Rhoads received from Schmidt a lengthy memorandum, dated December 3, which contained a complete market analysis of Dallas. In this memo, Schmidt named the account that he believed BGI should be doing business with. Several days later Schmidt advised Rhoads by letter that he had "pitched" this account and that "they are all fired up about taking us on."

Rhoads became concerned at this point over (1) the reliability of a "market survey" conducted in two days and (2) Schmidt's violation of company policy in committing BGI to a prospective account without prior approval from the national sales manager.

Rhoads decided for the time being to say nothing to Schmidt that might curb his enthusiasm. He contented himself with sending Schmidt a list of the seven Dallas stores with which BGI was currently doing business. Schmidt was instructed to evaluate each of these stores, with a view to determining *jointly* with Rhoads the best distribution pattern. Furthermore, he instructed Schmidt to take no further action on the prospective account until the two men had decided which dealers to drop. Rhoads indicated that he would visit with Schmidt toward the end of the month. Schmidt sent no more memos, and Rhoads assumed that Schmidt was doing all right.

As he had promised, Rhoads made arrangements with Schmidt later that month and started off on a three-day trip through Texas, visiting dealers. During this trip Rhoads began to detect in Schmidt's business acumen and personality some basic problems that had previously escaped notice.

First, Schmidt's knowledge of the BGI product line was not as extensive as had appeared during the training period. His inability to handle dealer questions was obvious. Rhoads began to feel that perhaps he ought not to have assumed that an agent of Schmidt's age and background would not need extensive training—although no such training was available within the company's present programs.

Second, Rhoads now found Schmidt's sense of humor singularly inappropriate. One dealer was particularly offended by Schmidt's gratuitous impersonation of President Carter. What had seemed "easy going" in Charlottesville now struck Rhoads as flippant in Houston.

Third, Rhoads sensed a definite coolness toward Schmidt on the part of store personnel in BGI's major Houston account. The furniture buyer, one of the most respected men in the industry, seemed uncomfortable in Schmidt's presence. However, Rhoads was unable to get the buyer aside during the brief visit to discover what was amiss.

From Houston, the pair traveled to Dallas, where the distribution pattern was up for review. Rhoads and Schmidt discussed at length the seven current accounts, plus the account suggested by Schmidt. They began their Dallas visits by going to Schmidt's prospect. The store disappointed Rhoads. Unimpressive in appearance and located in a highway shopping center, the store offered furniture lines and conducted promotional practices (including "SALE" signs festooning the store's windows) that were not compatible with the BGI image. A 20-minute conversation with the store's buyer confirmed Rhoad's initial opinion, and Rhoads terminated the negotiations.

From there they proceeded to the one current account that Schmidt recommended keeping. This store was even worse. The account had been opened by Old Frank in 1977, and in Rhoads's opinion, approval should never have been granted. In a half-hour conversation with the buyer, Rhoads convinced her that the BGI line was not her kind of merchandise. The buyer agreed to stop buying the line, and the two parted with warm handshakes.

With a now very subdued Schmidt, Rhoads proceeded to Kluber's, generally recognized as the premier furniture store in the Southwest. Standing in the middle of the very elegant contemporary section of the store, Rhoads said to Schmidt, "Why didn't you recommend this store in your distribution plan?"

Schmidt replied, somewhat tentatively, "I thought this store was too rich for our blood. Besides, its growth rate has peaked out and it already carries a line competitive with ours."

Rhoads was now considering four alternatives:

1. Take Schmidt to dinner and afterward give him a stern lecture about his performance and what he would have to do to shape up.
2. Same as option 1, but place him on 90-day probation as well.

3. Recall him to Charlottesville for additional intensive training.
4. Terminate his services.

THE PROBLEM OF THE "MISSING SALESMAN"

Frank Irons had been a BGI agent for two and a half years. Before joining BGI, he had been a furniture buyer for a department store in Philadelphia. The president of BGI had asked him to leave this position to become BGI's agent in New England, a territory then producing almost no sales volume for BGI. Because of the extensive sales development work required in these six New England states, Irons was given a "guaranteed draw" of $3,000 a month against his commissions.

Irons was an exceptionally handsome man, and he had a reputation for "walking the straight and narrow path" and for being a very religious and family-centered man. He did not drink, smoke, or swear. He was 35 years old, a college graduate, and the father of five children.

Shortly after taking over as national sales manager in July 1978, Rhoads received a telephone call from Irons, whom he had not yet met. Irons said that marital difficulties were detracting from his job performance. Irons asked Rhoads to be patient for a few weeks until he could resolve some of his personal problems.

In late August, during a routine review of sales trends by accounts, Rhoads detected an alarming situation in Irons's largest account. This store, one of the largest and most prominent in New England, showed a steady decline in BGI sales during the past year. Rhoads's 1978 sales projection indicated a $100,000 decrease from actual 1977 sales volume.

In September Rhoads and Irons visited this store together and held a long discussion with the buyer about the BGI line. The buyer, Ken Smith, indicated that he was attempting to work his way out of an extremely heavy inventory position on some of his other lines, and that as soon as he had cleared up this problem he would renew his attention to the BGI line. Smith readily admitted that he had been letting floor display and retail training efforts on the BGI line go by the board while he concentrated on moving out his overstocked lines.

During this conversation with Smith, Rhoads sensed a very warm business relationship between Smith and Irons. On the other hand, he recognized that Irons had not been devoting enough time to this account. At the conclusion of the discussion, Rhoads expressed a desire to meet Sharon Pelham, the store's general manager. Smith said that Pelham was tied up for the day and that there was no real need to meet with her now, particularly in view of the accord reached among the three of them in regard to future sales activities in the BGI line.

That evening Rhoads and Irons dined together, and Irons talked about some of his personal problems. His wife had taken the children, moved back to Philadelphia, and was suing him for divorce. She had made a number of charges against his accounts at department and clothing stores, and, even though Irons had now closed these accounts, he was in serious financial difficulty. However, Rhoads uncovered the fact that despite Irons's marital and financial problems, he had enrolled in a body-building course in an expensive health club and was spending many hours each week in weight-lifting and similar activities. In addition, Rhoads noticed that Irons had had several drinks before and during dinner and that he had begun to use profanity. At this time Rhoads made no comment about Irons's behavior, nor did he offer any advice about his personal problems. Irons promised to follow Ken Smith's activities closely and to advice Rhoads of his progress.

Late in October, Rhoads received a letter from Ken Smith informing him that the store was dropping the BGI line and expanding its account with a competitive line. Rhoads was dismayed at what he believed to be Smith's duplicity. Not only was he annoyed with himself at having been taken in, but he was also upset that Irons apparently had also failed to grasp the situation. When contacted, Irons had no explanation and expressed similar shock and frustration.

During November, it became increasingly difficult to get hold of Irons. Memos went unanswered, telephone calls could not be completed, and telegrams were returned for no address. Irons had moved from his home in Marblehead, Massachusetts, and his telephone had been disconnected. Rhoads made occasional contact with Irons only after long and tedious persistence. When Rhoads complained, Irons indicated that the situation was temporary—he would soon find a permanent residence. In the meantime, he gave Rhoads a postal box number to which monthly checks could be mailed. Rhoads discovered when he tried to use the box as a channel of communication that Irons only used it at the beginning of the month for the explicit purpose noted.

In December, the situation deteriorated. The BGI controller received several calls from the New England Telephone Company inquiring about Irons's current address. It seemed that he owed over $500. A similar inquiry came from American Express, which was attempting to collect $900 from Irons. Two substantial BGI customers called Rhoads to find out why Irons had not visited them in over a month. A BGI agent ran across Irons in New York City during a weekend and called Rhoads to let him know that Irons was swearing and drinking, had given up religion completely, and was becoming increasingly infatuated with his physical appearance.

Throughout December, Rhoads continued to send memos to Irons, indicating his displeasure with the way Irons was servicing his territory and failing to maintain adequate communications. Many of these memos were unanswered. Rhoads was becoming more and more concerned. But, except for the complete loss of Irons' largest account, sales volume in Irons's territory was continuing to grow rapidly. It appeared to Rhoads that Irons's 1978 sales performance, despite the loss of his major account, would exceed his quota and, for the first time, enable him to cover his draw.

Irons did not show up at the BGI Christmas party, and Rhoads heard a rumor from another BGI agent that Irons had taken another job. During the first week in January, Rhoads flew to Boston to visit several of Irons's accounts by himself.

On his first call, upon a relatively new account that Irons had opened the previous March, Rhoads found good rapport between the buyer and Irons, as well as evidence that Irons' visits had been fairly frequent and regular. On his second and third calls, however, Rhoads discovered that while Irons' rapport was still excellent, neither buyer had seen him for six weeks. After visiting two more accounts in Hartford, Connecticut, Rhoads concluded that Irons was still working his territory, albeit less regularly, and that no evidence supported the accusation that Irons had taken another job.

In New Haven, Connecticut, while visiting the second customer whom he had planned to visit in that city and the last before returning to Charlottesville, Rhoads ran into Irons, who was flabbbergasted to see him. Rhoads and Irons made one more call together, took a dealer out to dinner, and then returned to Rhoads's motel room for a discussion. Irons made a lengthy plea for patience while he worked out his personal and financial problems, which were taking longer to straighten out than Irons had originally thought.

Rhoads was now considering the following alternatives:

1. Indicate complete support to Irons in his predicament and allow him to work out his personal problems at his own pace, as long as sales volume did not suffer in his territory.

2. Same as option 1, but offer advice on Irons's personal and financial problems as a way of underlining the company's concern for his well-being. One example that came readily to Rhoads's mind was Iron's need for a bank loan to consolidate his debts and allow him to stretch out his payments.

3. Place Irons on 90-day probation, with the condition that the frequency of account coverage would have to be increased, communication improved, and call reports submitted weekly on all sales activities.

4. Terminate his services.

Case 5
Immuno-Diagnostic Corporation

In October 1979, Mr. Fred Morton, national sales manager for the Immuno-Diagnostic Corporation (IDC) of Boston, Massachusetts, was deciding which of seven sales representatives should be promoted to the two new regional sales manager positions. IDC developed, manufactured, and marketed immuno-assay diagnostic test kits for use in hospitals and medical laboratories. The kits included vials of chemical reagents and trace elements. The chemicals, when mixed with substances from a patient's body fluids, became bonded to these substances. The diagnostician could then identify aberrant cells or foreign matter. Each kit was priced according to the number and types of tests that could be run from a single kit. A large hospital or lab might run 1500 tests in a week, paying about 50 cents per test. IDC's domestic sales volume in 1978 was $7.8 million, accounting for about 20 percent of the market of these kinds of testing devices.

THE EVOLUTION OF IDC'S SALES FORCE

When Mr. Morton joined the company in 1975 as a sales representative, he was expected to manage his territory as if it were his own business, without direct field supervision. The sales force then comprised six people, all of whom thought of themselves as independent entrepreneurs. Because of the technological sophistication of the product line, IDC sales representatives generally knew more about the product than did the doctor or lab technician on whom they were calling.

Sales volume in 1977 was up over 140 percent from 1976. At the beginning of 1978, Fred Morton was promoted to national sales manager and moved to Boston. The sales force now numbered 18. Senior executives, seeing the need for more direct management of the sales representatives,

Copyright © 1980 by The Colgate Darden Graduate Business School Sponsors, University of Virginia. Reproduced by permission. This case was prepared in collaboration with Timothy A. Hill.

empowered Morton to create a new level of field sales management. Accordingly, in mid-1978, Morton divided the country into three regions. The first promotion to regional manager was made on the West Coast. Arnold Nelson, the former senior sales representative there, had been with IDC for three years, had an excellent sales record, and had experience in management with his prior company. The Midwest and East Coast regions continued to be managed by Morton in his capacity as national sales manager throughout the remainder of 1978.

Sales volume in 1978 was up another 140 percent over 1977. At the beginning of 1979, the sales force numbered 24, equally divided among the three regions. The Midwest regional manager's position was filled by Carter Berg, another senior sales representative with an outstanding sales record and management experience in a prior company. Morton continued as East Coast regional manager as well as national sales manager.

Sales volume this far in 1979 was up 135 percent over the same period in 1978. On the basis of this growth rate, senior executives forecasted a sales force of 32 by the end of 1980. Because Morton believed that one to eight was the optimum span of control for field managers, he recommended creating a fourth regional manager position. Once the plan was approved, he split the East Coast territory into two regions, adding some territory from the Midwest region. He came up with four regions relatively balanced in terms of personnel, size, population, and sales potential. Morton now had two regional sales manager openings: one for the northeast region (from New England to the Virginia–Carolina border, and west to include Pennsylvania and West Virginia) and one for the southeast region (from North Carolina to Florida and west to include Tennessee, Arkansas, Oklahoma, and Texas).

Morton wanted the Northeast regional manager to be in a position to help him with national sales management duties. He asked Carter Berg, his Midwest regional manager, if he would move to the Boston area and take over the Northeast region. Berg, who was living in Cincinnati, agreed. He was originally from New York City and his wife from Massachusetts. This move left Morton with two regions empty: he had to replace Berg in the Midwest and replace himself in the Southeast.

Morton determined that the Southeast regional sales manager should be located in Atlanta, as it was the geographically central city. As Atlanta had no resident sales representative now, the promotion would require another relocation. He estimated the costs of relocating Berg to Boston, the new Southeast Manager to Atlanta, and the new Midwest manager to either Chicago or Cincinnati, at $6,000 for each move.

Compensation for the regional sales managers in 1980 was to be determined as follows:

1. Salary: $25,000 a year, revised annually.
2. Bonus A: 50 percent of salary paid at end of fiscal year if *all* four quarterly performance reviews are satisfactory or better.

3. Bonus B: an amount ranging to maximum of 75 percent of salary paid annually, based on the achievement of *company* sales objectives.

Company executives expected the average regional sales manager to earn a total of $50,000 in 1980, from the following sources: salary, $25,000; bonus A, $12,500; and bonus B, $12,500.

The compensation plan for sales representatives in 1979 was as follows:

1. Salary: $15,600.
2. Bonus A: Paid at end of each fiscal year from a pool based on a percentage of total *regional* sales and determined subjectively by the national sales manager according to each individual's contribution to the region's growth in sales, his or her experience with the company, and ratings on quarterly performance reviews.
3. Bonus B: Ten percent of the individual's sales growth over previous quarter, paid at the end of each quarter.

Company executives expected the average sales representative to earn a total of $32,600 in 1979, from the following sources: salary, $15,600; bonus A, $7,000; and bonus B, $10,000.

THE CANDIDATES FOR REGIONAL MANAGER

The current sales representatives had originally been selected because they were self-motivated, money-oriented, and experienced in selling. No sales representative had ever left the company voluntarily. Seven people seemed to have particularly promising managerial potential. All seven had excellent sales records and were projected to be among the top 10 representatives in sales volume in 1979. Morton's perceptions of these candidates appear below.

Ann Clifford

Ann Clifford had been with IDC for four years as a sales representative in Washington, D.C. She had moved there from Atlanta, where she had worked for seven years as a hospital laboratory technician and supervisor. Morton considered her technical knowledge to be the best on the sales force. She had quickly established an outstanding sales record in the mid-Atlantic territory. He considered her to be a strong self-starter, highly self-motivated, and very flexible. For both her and her husband it was a second marriage. She had two stepchildren. In 1978, she had ranked 10th in sales volume; currently, she ranked 8th. Morton estimated her 1979 earnings at about $41,000. She was 33 years old and held a BS degree in biochemistry from Georgia State University.

In 1978 Clifford had expressed a strong interest in a regional manager's position. When the position was filled, she was disappointed, stating that she didn't understand why she wasn't given more careful consideration. She had told Morton "the next time it comes around, I definitely want to be considered."

In the early months of 1979, Morton felt that Clifford was no longer interested in management. However, he explained later, "It turned out that I was misinterpreting the signals that I was receiving from her. She had decided to concentrate on selling. The objective that she set for herself in 1979 was to be the number 1 sales representative. If the management opportunity came along, fine. If it didn't, fine. I had misinterpreted her decision as a lack of interest in management. I found out after talking to her that she felt just as strongly as ever about a management position, and was willing to move if necessary to take such a position."

John Butler

John Butler had joined IDC at the beginning of 1978 and had been assigned to the Boston territory. He had extensive prior sales and management experience, including three and a half years as a diagnostic sales specialist with a leading scientific instruments company and two years as a director of operations for a company in which he was the principal stockholder. (This company had been successful; Butler had sold his interest to a major corporation.) Morton felt that Butler's special skill was high-level business negotiating. Butler was married and had no children. In 1978, he ranked fourth in sales volume; currently, he ranked seventh. Morton estimated that Butler would earn about $41,000 in 1979. He was 53 years old and held an MS degree in biochemistry from the University of Pittsburgh.

According to Morton, Butler was "A pro from the word go. He's been in the system a long time. He's been through it all and seen it all from a number of different perspectives. As a result, he's highly respected by the sales people here. He's very much a self-starter; money still turns him on even though he is rather well-off financially. Management in a sophisticated sales organization is the one thing he has not yet done. He wants it very badly as more or less his final thing."

Paul Teller

Paul Teller had been with the company for four years as the sales representative in Columbia, South Carolina. His prior experience included three years as a sales representative with a company in a related industry, and four years as the manager of a large hospital laboratory. He was the most senior person in tenure in his region, and Morton considered him to have excellent product knowledge and the ability to communicate that product knowledge to other people. Morton described him as "extremely helpful, one of the best recruiters we have in terms of finding good quality salespeople for our company."

Teller ranked 11th in sales volume in 1978; currently, he ranked 9th. Morton expected him to earn about $39,000 in 1979. He was a Vietnam veteran, 41 years old, married, with three children. He held a BA in chemistry from High Point College. In the summer of 1979, Morton discovered that Teller was having some personal problems that he was unwilling to disclose or discuss.

Martin Kinsman

Martin Kinsman was the IDC sales representative in Nashville. He had been with the company for two and a half years. Before that, Kinsman had spent three years as a technical sales representative for a scientific products manufacturer and two years as a supervisor in a hospital laboratory. He had developed an excellent reputation with his peers for total cooperation and unselfishness. Morton described him as "a very enthusiastic, supercharged person. He sells nine-tenths of what he sells on enthusiasm."

Mr. Kinsman had recently remarried. He had no children. Kinsman had expressed to Morton on an earlier occasion that his new wife was having some difficulty with the amount of travel his job entailed. When the subject of promotions came up, Kinsman had said, "I just don't know how my wife would take it." Morton had responded, "You know that the amount of traveling necessary as a regional manager is considerably more away-from-home than you have now." Kinsman had replied, "Yes, I know, but I'm sure we'd be able to overcome that."

Kinsman had ranked 8th in sales volume in 1978; currently he ranked 10th. Morton estimated that his 1979 earnings would be about $37,000. He was 34 years old and held a BS degree in biology from Suffolk University.

Daniel Mace

Daniel Mace was the sales representative in Miami. He had been with the company in this capacity for three and one half years. Prior to joining IDC, he had served for three years as vice president of sales for one small IDC competitor and for five years as a sales representative for another. In both of these companies, he had left because he was passed over for further promotion.

Mace was married and had two children. In 1977 and 1978, he was the top salesman in both growth and volume; currently, he was fourth. Morton estimated his 1979 earnings at around $46,000. Mace was 43 years old. He was a high school graduate—and had no college experience. Morton considered Mace to be unselfish in his dealings with people, but overzealous. On one occasion, Mr. Mace had said to Morton, "I'm the best sales representative that you have. I want the opportunity to be a manager in this company. I promise you this: should I fail, I will go back and sell in any territory you put me. I will knock myself out for this company, but I want the opportunity."

Morton commented: "Dan has won awards, he has done it all, and he was placed on the list because he deserved a chance to be on the list. He earned it."

George Slate

George Slate had been with the company for three years as the sales representative in Portland, Oregon. Before joining IDC, Mr. Slate had three years experienced as a technical sales representative for a competitor company and five years experience as a high school teacher. Since Arnold Nelson's appointment as western regional sales manager in 1978, Mr. Slate had served as his "unofficial assistant," handling administration and field training on the West Coast. Slate was married and had two children. In 1978, he ranked fifth in sales volume; currently he ranked third. Morton estimated that his 1979 earnings would be about $39,000. Slate was 34 years old and held an MBA degree from Southern Illinois University.

According to Morton, "George has turned in a consistent level of sales performance for the entire time he has been with the company. He has no motivation problem. He is highly respected. He doesn't have a great deal to say in a sales meeting, but when he says anything, everybody stops talking to hear him. He is very happy in Portland. An outdoors type of person, he came from Chicago to the northwest partly for that reason. In his previous company he had been offered a field management spot which required a move. He felt complimented, but he also felt pressured into a position he was not yet ready for. So he turned it down. Subsequently, he felt that the opportunity would not come again with that company, so he left."

Sheldon Farmer

Shelly Farmer had been with the company for two years as the sales representative in Detroit. He had worked for a competitor as a sales representative for two years and as a sales coordinator, an intermediate position between direct selling and direct field sales management, for a year. That company had moved him three times that year, and had kept promising him promotions which were not forthcoming. Mr. Farmer decided to leave his home in Texas and join IDC because he believed that IDC was about to develop a sales management structure and he wanted to be on the ground floor. Farmer was married and had two small children. In 1978, his first year with IDC, he ranked third in sales volume; currently he was first. Morton estimated that his 1979 earnings would be approximately $35,000. He was 29 years old and held a BBA from the University of Missouri.

According to Morton, "Shelly is an energetic, enthusiastic sales representative. He has more than proven himself in the two years he has been with us. He will be a genuine superstar if he doesn't burn himself out. We feel that he has paid his dues, and he deserves to be considered."

Case 6
Caduceus Corporation

The Caduceus Corporation was a large international medical supply company which manufactured and marketed a wide variety of medical care products for hospitals, clinics, and health care facilities. It employed approximately 120 district managers in the United States who supervised a direct sales force of over 700 men and women. This case comprises interviews conducted in the summer of 1980 with three of these district managers, selected for their districts' outstanding sales records. Senior executives of Caduceus were interested in examining the philosophies and practice of these managers to uncover common denominators that might help them to improve the performance of other first-line sales managers.

BARRY WINGATE

"I came on board in December 1970, after a stint with engineering OCS. After three months in training I became a salesman in the Little Rock territory. I worked there for five years; I guess I did a pretty good job. In late 1975, the district manager in Tennessee was promoted and I was asked to take that district. I didn't particularly want Tennessee, but it seemed like a good opportunity. Three months later, we split the divisions and my boss asked me if I would take the Georgia district. I've had this district since 1976.

THE DISTRICT MANAGER'S JOB

Hiring

"Certainly one of my most important jobs is hiring the right people. With the high turnover in this company, it's disastrous if we don't hire the right people—it's costly to me, to the company, and no good for the person hired.

Copyright © 1981 by The Colgate Darden Graduate Business School Sponsors, University of Virginia. Reproduced by permission. This case was prepared in collaboration with Timothy A. Hill.

"We don't get a whole lot of training on how to hire. When I became a DM they said, 'You're a DM, go out and hire two people.' I had never hired anybody in my life. Of course, you can only learn how from experience.

"I have some concrete rules that I use in hiring. One is that I won't interview anyone who isn't presently holding a job. Maybe once in a while I will miss out on a good candidate because he was fired or left on his own. But generally I feel that if a guy is really good, he's going to be working.

"Second, I will not interview anyone who has had three jobs in the last three years, under any circumstances. There are enough ups and downs in sales to caution me against looking at a guy who hasn't shown stability in a lesser company. If those companies would make a man leave, then the demands this company makes on its salespeople are going to make him leave that much sooner.

"Third, I want a guy who can show me a record of success and who is proud of that record. I believe that successful people want to be successful. They set goals, they reach their goals, and they brag about it.

"Fourth, I look for a guy who can get along with other people, one who talks well on his feet, who can walk into a hospital that's going down the tubes on our product and go to the administrator or chief of staff, handle all the flack, get the hospital settled down, and walk out of there with a contract.

"Finally, I want someone who is ambitious, who is promotion-oriented. I don't particularly want to hire life-long salespeople. Those people are more difficult to motivate. I would like to have half a dozen of my people, in the long term, be DMs in strategic places around the country. I get a lot of friends that way—makes my job easier.

"I generally don't interview until I anticipate an opening. I am constantly in touch with about 15 agencies in key cities in my district. They send me paperwork on individuals so that, even though I don't interview these people right away, I'll have some people in mind, or at least on hand, that I can talk to at any particular time.

"I like to interview a couple of months in advance of an opening. Then I interview until I find the right guy. The first time around I interview 20 people. If there are five that I like, I'll interview them a second time, and maybe one or two the third time. After the second interview, I'm pretty confident about who I want. So the third time I interview, I'm more concerned that he wants Caduceus.

"One of the mistakes you can make is to oversell the company. Two months or a year later the guy bails out. When you ask why, he says, 'This isn't what I want, I didn't know what I was getting into.' So I take great pains. I bring in the catalog and the products and show the guy exactly what he's going to be doing. Some people don't like to sell urinary drainage bags or catheters, especially if they sold bulldozers before.

"Then I usually follow up that evening or that weekend with dinner with him and his wife. I want to see how he handles himself socially, see what his wife is like, whether she supports him. Once I've made a choice, my regional manager and then a few people at headquarters talk to the guy. He's on board, unless they shoot him down.

Allocating Time in the Field

"I don't believe in taking the worst people and spending all kinds of time with them and trying to get them to do a little better. If I can move the worst two producers up 10 percent, I'm still not getting a lot out of them. If I have two superstars and I can motivate and direct them, move them up 10 percent, that 10 percent is 10 times more than the first 10 percent. So I spend most of my time with the top people.

"In the long run, I don't think you always end up with that type of situation. In the long run, you're going to be rid of those two people at the bottom if you're managing properly. Eventually you're going to be replacing those two bottom guys with two top performers. And you're going to motivate some of the mediocre guys up to the top, if the guys are half-way decent and you do a good job of managing.

Supervising in the Field

"I don't believe in a canned sales approach. Of course, without one, you'll always be going on calls with your people and hearing something you don't like, whether that person's been around six months or five years. Even so, I don't like to jump in and say too much, under the assumption that the sales rep is accurate in what he's saying. If he's talking about selling our surgeon's gloves and the question comes up, 'How are they sterilized?' and he says, 'With ethylene oxide,' which is a blatant error, than I will correct him, saying 'We now have a much improved process; we do it with gamma radiation.' That doesn't happen too often. If the guy is starting to drift off and maybe lose the sale, I will step in kindly, and in a nice manner, and try to direct it back where it should be.

"Other than those situations, I don't like to get involved. I would rather have him make a small error. Same thing in a closing situation. If I feel that situation is absolutely ripe for closing, and we can walk out of there with a 10-case order, but he's not doing that, and he can't do it the next time around because something is going to change—either next closing call we're not going to have that audience, or competition is going to come in and cut the price—then I might step in and say, 'Why can't we go with it?' Otherwise, I would not do that. This does happen occasionally, whether the guy has been around six months or six years.

"In selling our products, generally one sales call is not all that critical unless he's right up there before the key committee. I will try to let him go his route and then critique the sales call when we get back in the car or have a cup of coffee. I'll say, 'Look, that was fine, you made these gains, but then you drifted off. You brought in this objection, you could have closed at this particular point and didn't, and so on.

"Sometimes I get too excited. All sales managers think they're the greatest salespeople in the world. And they are pretty good, or they wouldn't be sales managers. Sometimes I wish that I could go out for a couple of days and just sell. So sometimes when you're in a particular situation on a call, you get excited. You think you're going to close, but he's not closing it, and you have a tendency to take over. The more I'm in this business, though, the less I do it.

Motivating Salespeople

"One of the toughest problems is motivating salespeople. A big factor is the money, of course. These guys get a company car, free lunch, $35,000 a year, and all kinds of commission plans. Generally, though, the most important motivation is not the money. It may be in the short run. He may have a new boat, a new car, so he's going to go out and really have a tremendous third quarter to make the money to pay it off. But in the long run, money is not the most important factor.

"Recognition is the main thing, gaining the manager's approval and the other guys' respect. If a manager displays the fact that he is unhappy with them, that has a big impact on them. When my regional manager comes out and works with my salespeople, and has a good day and writes them a nice, sincere note, 'Hey, you did a super job,' they brag about it. They think it's the greatest thing in the world.

"In this company we have a lot of camaraderie and high morale. In light of that, how well a guy performs and whether he's doing his share is very important to him. We let it be known if you don't do your share. We're a very tough company. When rankings come out you feel real bad if you don't look good.

"So one way to motivate people is to put big goals in front of them. They may not achieve your goals all the time, but if they achieve 70, 80, or 90 percent you'll still come out ahead. People become high achievers in this company, or they get out. In my 10 years here, we're still as dynamic and cocky as ever. I've seen people go in and out after 2 years. They just can't keep up with it.

"And you have to help them achieve confidence in themselves that they can reach these goals. Confident people can do a lot more than those who are not confident. Confidence comes from know-how, and know-how comes from confronting each individual situation. I am here to help that person get confidence.

"Let's say a hospital is using our surgeon's gloves, and we're ready to be kicked out. The salesman who has never faced that situation panics—says the wrong thing, does the wrong thing. It goes down the tubes. On the other hand, if he has gone through that situation five times before and has won four times, he knows what to say and do.

"The only way the individual is going to get to that point is by his manager leading him by the hand into those situations. When they're new, salespeople have a tendency to shy away from difficult situations. I did, myself. As a manager, I'll tell him ahead of time, 'This is a bad situation, let me do some of the talking.' You do it a couple of times and he sees how it works; he plays that role the next time. He tries it, it works, and he thinks the next time, 'It's not so bad.'

"And confidence is a two-way street. You need to listen to your salespeople, learn from them what's right and wrong in the district. Nobody knows more about production performance, competitive activity, customer's desires. So you can figure out what the problems are and can give your people some direction.

"Money, goals, confidence—these are the starting points, but they're not always enough to motivate some people, especially if they've been around a few years. The older a guy gets, the more comfortable he becomes in his territory. Anyone who's been out there more than five years must be motivated continually.

"If he's a top performer who's slipping, you give him some positive motivation. I'll say, 'You can make more money. You've got a shot at going to Bermuda this spring. Let's get going.'

"Or he may be getting tired. It's hard to be out there every day in head-on competition. It wears a man out. Maybe his wife demands more time, his children are growing up, he's got to spend more time with the Little League. I motivate the guy who's slipping back by making that niche he's in uncomfortable. I'm going to be writing letters, working with him, whatever. He's going to say, 'I've had enough of this. If Barry wants me to get these five conversions, it's better for me to put up with the garbage and get them than it is to put up with Barry.'

"Or he may be an average performer. For this guy you set short-term goals. I'd have a very frank discussion with him, make him a little uncomfortable. I'd say, 'This is what I want from you in the next three months: I want this conversion, bring your dollars up to this. I'm going to monitor your performance, I'm going to work with you to achieve these goals.' At the end of the three months, I'd critique the guy. If he can be motivated and he has skills, he'll have hit those goals, or come damn close. But if you've monitored him for a couple of quarters and he's not coming near, then I'd say you've got to terminate the guy. There is no place in my district for the guy who will never be a winner, who just does a job.

"Then there are specific problems that may come up. If a really good salesperson is starting to develop problems—poor paperwork or trouble working with the group—I'd sit down with the guy and explain to him the problem and how it's hurting him. If he's the right kind of guy, he's going to understand the situation and he's going to be mature enough and motivated enough to say, 'Yes, I've got to correct the situation.'

"If it's paperwork and he wants to get promoted, then explain that paperwork is an important facet of the DM's job and that he has to learn to handle it correctly. On the other hand, he may be a career salesman who says 'I'm not doing paperwork because I don't like to do paperwork.' It has to be done, so I'm going to show him how. If he does it quickly, streamlined, and with no bullshit, it will help him achieve his goal of not wanting to do a lot of paperwork because he's going to get it done real quick. If he plays around with it and screws it up, he's going to be more uncomfortable because I'm going to make him uncomfortable with that paperwork. I'm going to insist that he does it correctly.

"Of course, sometimes a person has problems right from the start. When I hire a guy, he goes to headquarters to learn and to be the best person in that training class. I let him know from the day he's hired that I want him to be the best in everything he does with the company. If he's up there doing all the wrong things, then I made a mistake. Probably I'm going to sit down with the sales trainer and figure out how serious a mistake. Maybe the guy has a serious problem and I totally misjudged him. If the sales trainer and I sit down with him and talk with him, and if we find out we made an error, we should probably let the guy go. But I've got to be damned sure that's the case. And I'm not going to fire him because of the sales trainer's story. I have to talk to the guy. Maybe he's up there having a good time and still learning. Maybe that's part of his personality.

"At times your relationship with a particular salesperson, for a short period of time, gets to the point where you say, 'Hell, I'm going to fire that son of a bitch. He screwed this up. He went overboard on that.' You learn to ride over times like these, to weigh them in the balance.

Managing Turnover

"I have very little turnover. I have four salespeople who have been with us for more than 5 years, two of them for 10 years, and three new people who have been around less than 3 years. If I did have turnover, I'd want to find out why they were leaving.

"If your people are leaving because another firm is paying twice as much money, then you've got a sales job to do. You've got to convince them that the opportunity for promotion, the open-end commission plan, and the potential with our company is better than at that other company. I believe that. I don't think there's anybody in this company who's been around very long who doesn't believe that. Our people make a ton of money if they know what they're doing. We don't lose many people to competition.

"You might lose people because they get all charged up and then they don't get the region or don't become national sales manager in three years. Sometimes there's nothing you can do. I had two situations like that. One was when I took over the Tennessee district. When I came in, this man said, 'I deserved this job and I'm going to leave.' I talked to him and said, 'It doesn't work that way. There is opportunity and promotion, let me work with you a while, I'll do everything I can.' He didn't buy that, so he left. I didn't try to keep him. In a situation like that sometimes you're spinning your wheels.

"On the other hand, there are situations where you can lead the guy down the road and promise him too much. That could be a mistake that we make at this company. If he feels that he's not getting promoted, you have to explain to him in black and white what the criteria are that we promote on, what he's doing well, what he's doing not so well, and who's he competing with. Quite frankly, I believe that if he is promotable, then he is a mature person and, if so, then he will understand everything you lay out and it will work well. If he is not mature, he obviously is not promotable, he's too excitable, and he will leave.

THE MANAGER IN THE MIDDLE

"What the home offices say I have to do and what the salespeople can produce may be two opposite things.

"A good example is what's going on right in the division now. One of our competitors has just entered our market with a product identical to the most important product in our division. We stand to lose a third of our business. They are cutting prices and Caduceus just had a price increase. I don't know who made that decision, but it was made, and I'm sitting here on top of a few million dollars worth of business with a 10 percent price difference between us and them. Customers have decided that pricing will be the determining factor, and the doctor's support won't persuade the buyers to stay with us. So I sit down with my supervisors and try to negotiate. 'Can we roll back?'

"You negotiate. Then you sell the decision to your people. 'I want you to pass that price increase on to your customers.' Not 'the damned company had a price increase; I think they're crazy, stupid, but we've go to do it, so let's try.' The first thing is to make the sales force understand that it's what *I* want. They don't really care about the regional manager or the vice president of sales. They don't work for the home office, they work for me.

"How do you sell that decision? I like to break it down in writing. If I have to hit a 35 percent increase in surgeon's gloves, I'll say, 'OK, I've got seven territories, which means I have to pick up four to five accounts per salesman.' All of a sudden the goals are not impossible, just hard to reach. Then I sit down with the salespeople and say, 'You've got to do your share of it. This is what has to be done.'

"I try to break down the goals even further. You just don't go out and pick up five accounts. You say, 'Maybe I can get two right away. A bid is coming up. If I renegotiate that correctly and get some help from those people, maybe I can pick up two more accounts.' All of a sudden the four or five accounts become one and two. I set up a plan and a date, I give each its priority, and I put our resources into the best one. When that one looks good, then I go to the next priority.

"Because managers are in the middle, we need to have outside diversions, hobbies. You'd go crazy if all you thought about all night long was 'What am I doing? The company wants this and that, I can't do it. My poor salesmen are crying,' etc. You put it all into perspective. The important thing is that you don't go home and say, 'This is killing me, having to do this, having to do that.' None of that will help. If you have a problem, take action. If you can't take action then forget it. It's not my problem, it's somebody else's problem.

MANAGERIAL PHILOSOPHY

"I think a lot of my own manager, and I want him to think that I'm one of his best people and that I'm helping him to achieve his goals. By the same token, I'd like to be recognized by my salespeople as a good sales manager. Your people ought to respect you and respond to what you want. I think good sales managers are liked. I don't buy the philosophy that good managers just set goals and beat people to reach them. I very definitely want to be liked. I think my salespeople do like me.

"Some of the wackiest, craziest people I know are salespeople in this company. That's the nature of selling. If we had a bunch of normal people out here, I don't know that we'd sell much product. I modeled myself after the district manager I had when I was selling. We had the craziest people you can imagine. Never did anything really wrong, but they had one hell of a good time. If they thought they could chase women and get away with it, they did it. My manager's philosophy was, as long as there's no damage done, as long as the guys are producing, let them have a good time.

"It takes that craziness to survive out here, with the rejections and the pressures. We ask our salespeople for the impossible all the time. Growing at 25 percent, we're down a little bit in our quarter, so we get a phone call from headquarters saying, 'We need an extra $500,000 in sales.' And we produce!"

JOAN BOSWELL

Joan Boswell was the district sales manager for Houston. She joined Caduceus in January 1977 as a sales representative in south Texas. After six months' field experience, she was promoted to field assistant, a position that the company used to groom potential district managers. She served as field assistant for 17 months, becoming the longest-tenured field assistant in the division's history. In February 1979 the division created a new district to reduce the manager-to-sales-rep ratio. Boswell was chosen to manage the new district in Houston and had held the position for one and one half years.

She attributed her swift rise in the company in part to her previous sales experience. "I brought seven years of experience in selling with three other firms. I've been in this business for 11 years, so just from exposure and experience I can empathize with what people go through. I frankly feel that that is partly why I've moved as fast as I have. I think that you earn the respect of the people you're dealing with, as opposed to just assuming their respect if you have maybe one or two years' experience. However, I don't believe my getting the management spot was easy to accept on the part of a

84

lot of field people who had had more time in the company. Fortunately, I was perceived as the best candidate, and I was lucky to get it.

THE DISTRICT MANAGER'S JOB

Setting Priorities

"When a sales rep becomes a manager, the most important change in thinking is the realization that she has to get together a team of people who are going to get the collective job done. That means recruiting the right people, hiring the right people, training them, motivating them, controlling them, directing them, giving them enough latitude so that they can grow in the job and develop themselves. That doesn't happen all the time. Say you're lucky enough to have five superstars. If you just let them run, you're going to get good performance, but is it the best? Is it cohesive?

"Getting the team to function smoothly means that the manager has to orchestrate her own efforts. Suppose that a manager has four people working under her. One is a star, one pretty good, one fair, and one poor. How does the manager allocate her time to each sales rep?

"It's not 25 percent across the board. Sometimes a manager feels she has to work with a new employee closer to get him up to speed. And as a result, she slights the number 1 and number 2 people. That is a real error. The top two people may not ask for or want direction because they are superstars, but they still need it. I think you can increase their productivity by giving them more attention.

"If the one at the bottom is there because of inexperience, then I would spend probably 30 percent of my time with him. If I feel that in X amount of time I can bring the bottom man up to speed, I'll spend the time. If not, I'd spend that time in looking for another person. As for the average performer, you have to estimate the payoff in time spent on him—could he become a star, given some help?

"You've got 180 or 190 working days in the year. That means only about 12 days that you can spend with each person, if you divide the time up evenly. That's not much time. And the whole thing is harder than it looks. You can't say I'll spend 25 percent here and 10 percent there, or eight days a year with this guy. It just doesn't work out that way. You have emergencies two or three times a week. It's difficult to work three or four days in a row with one guy. So it's a good idea to review at the end of the year how much time you really have spent on each person and figure out if you've really given them a fair shake. A good manager recognizes that she's slighted people and takes steps to allocate time to them.

"A good employee is going to ask for it, too. We had a management advisory council, where you bring in five or seven of the top people recognized over the years for consistent performance. Good-quality, veteran salespeople. The DMs aren't present at those meetings. The crème de la crème of the sales force said, 'My district manager is not spending time with me.' Everybody in this life needs some direction, coaching, channeling, and acknowledgment when the job is being done well.

"Managing one's time is more than just allocating time in the field to each sales rep. I have to juggle administration and recruitment and training as well. Administration can be a burden. It should be a one-day-a-week job. No DM can do it in just one day. If you establish the goal of being out in the street with your people the other four days, there is only one other place that work can come from. That's at night or weekends. Recruitment can take a lot of time, too. And if you have a particularly high turnover and have to recruit and train people all the time, then you can't take enough time to be in the field with your people. This can get to be a Catch-22. If you don't direct your seasoned people, they'll quit too, and you find yourself chasing your tail.

Dealing with Turnover

I handle turnover by proper hiring, honesty with my people, and making sure that I'm getting the most out of my people. When you hire the wrong people with the wrong expectations of the job, you'll find turnover. Where you don't work enough with the people and don't find out what they want in their jobs, economically and in their own development, then you'll get turnover. If you don't have equitable, uniform means of evaluating people as objectively as you can, you're going to get turnover. And I can't control all the causes of turnover. There could be distribution problems. If the products are back-ordered for nine months, and we have nothing to sell, it's going to be hard to hold those people.

"Of course, to some degree, turnover in sales is a good thing. You get new blood, an employee who is a stone pony, who will walk through walls. The new sales rep is going to do things that the guy who's been in the territory for five or six years wasn't doing. Chances are he's going to open up new avenues. He doesn't know it hurts yet. He doesn't know he's going to get hurt when he walks into an account that hasn't seen a Caduceus person for years and that harbors a resentment for something we did 10 years ago.

"Our division has done pretty good lately. We haven't lost too many people that we didn't want to lose. That's also a sign of the perseverance and the survivability of people, too—their ability to weather the bad times.

Recruiting and Hiring

"Probably one of the most important features of the job is to make a decision to hire someone who can affect you.

"What do I look for in candidates? I want the top 10 percent of the field. Of course, the top 10 percent of the field is often happy where they are. They're not going to move unless you catch them at the right time—maybe they're dissatisfied with the present manager, or the commission program.

"I wouldn't hire an average performer. You can assume that that person is going to give the same average performance when he's working for you—unless you can see him as a person you're going to groom, personally. But it makes your job a little easier if you can get someone who's a star at the start.

"So my emphasis is on track record—how he competed in his last arena. I also want to know what motivates him—money, a chance for personal development? Does he have a high energy level? I'll hold out, rather than take someone who's just looking for a home to make an average income. And I want someone who's able to get along with people, persuasive—and most of all, aggressive. We need good salespeople who are killers when they need to be and they're soft when they feel they need to be. There has to be a latent aggressive instinct to get the job done and get the sale at all costs.

"At the interview, I generally try to establish a comfort level and then occasionally will try to make them uncomfortable to see if they can react quickly, to see whether they have the aptitude to understand and deal with some of the difficult situations they are going to be in. And I ask them about their previous jobs, and check their references as deep as I can. We've all been stung with candidates who have sometimes not been truthful. If you can screen that out initially, you're going to save yourself a lot of time.

"As far as their personalities go, you don't want a mentally unstable person. You sometimes shy away from circumstances that might lead to bigger risks—like if someone's going through a traumatic divorce. But I have hired people who've been recently divorced. I think you can tell whether their heads are on straight.

Setting Performance Standards

"Everyone's quota is last year's performance. At the beginning of the year we get district budgets. I give each sales rep a figure that he should reach by year-end—a figure that I think he can achieve. You're not going to give your average performer an unreasonable number to shoot at, whereas to your top person you're going to give a good amount. The number is based on their ability to get the job done—plus enough of a challenge so that, if they reach it, they are rewarded.

"Sometimes we're handed goals that we know aren't going to be realized. That doesn't mean we don't try to achieve them. Maybe I'll establish subgoals. Sooner or later, whoever decreed those difficult goals figures out that they won't be realized. Sometimes if I'm given goals that are really unreasonable, I'll convey that to the manager and say, 'This is what we're told to do, and we're going to try, but here's a reasonable approach. This is what our minimum level of performance should be.'

"Basically, we evaluate people on their sales figures. Certainly administrative skills are not at the top of the heap. Our profession is one where you can, in general, look at those numbers on a daily, weekly, monthly, yearly basis, and know what your batting average is. That's the final result, given some interpretation of those numbers. Still, I think we sometimes lose track of evaluating people. We look at the numbers monthly, but do we really examine them? Do we acknowledge that employee as often as we should? Do we tell him, 'You're really doing a good job?'

Supervising in the Field

"One of the difficult parts of the DM's job is to lead by example. Yet you still have to allow them to make mistakes. I've always been one to allow them to make mistakes, in front of the customer, in back of the customer. Of course, if they get the facts wrong, you have to correct them. You don't have to say outright, 'You're wrong.' You might let it go by, and then correct it at the conclusion of the presentation. If there's a deliberate distortion of product, it stands to be corrected at the time.

Deciding to Terminate People

Boswell described a recent situation in which a new sales rep in the company's centralized training program had skipped sessions and spent his evenings bar-hopping. 'I went to confront him face to face. I explained the terms of his employment and how he's expected to perform in training before-hand. I gave him a second chance to see if he changed his behavior in the next few days. Fortunately, this guy shaped up. If he hadn't, I'd have terminated him. You can't tolerate that sort of behavior. Of course, if he hadn't shaped up, I'd have seen it as my failure. It's my job to ensure that we've hired candidates who are responsible, who are prepared for training and see it as an exercise that's going to benefit them.

"We have two candidates right now who did not meet certain perform-ance standards at the three-week training session. They are going to have to come back for one or two weeks of remedial training. We'll decide then whether they have the basic technical skills to get the job done. I may still terminate them, after putting the extra time and money into their training.

"If the rep is in the field and having problems, then you decide whether you can salvage him or whether he's on the way out. If you want to try to develop him, you give him goals that he can reasonably attain and sit down and discuss how you and he are going to get there.

"If you want to terminate him, then you develop an unattainable program so that you'll have documentation when you terminate him. A smart person will know that if he's put on a program, it may well be time for him to go. That makes the manager's job easier, if you don't have to outright fire him.

"Another problem is the long-run average performer. If he only lacks administrative skills, I'll tolerate that any time. But if it's his numbers, that's another question. You realize that not everyone is going to be a star. Some people might be inclined to keep him, if his performance was acceptable. I wouldn't.

"I wouldn't just put a gun to his head, either. I'd have to respect the amount of time that he's been working for us. Why hasn't he been a star? I'd try to make him a star, first.

"What motivates a supersalesperson? With some it's the public exposure—they like to be in the limelight. Some like the challenge of meeting goals. There's a real basic instinct in the supersalesman, something in that man's blood that makes him do whatever it takes to get the job done. Sometimes it's that self-confidence that says, 'I'm doing what it takes, and going one step beyond.' Getting up a half-hour earlier and staying an hour later. It's a self-competition, a desire to succeed and go beyond what your own body says you can do. I may not necessarily like the guy's behavior, but he gets the end result.

"But some people have a comfort level that's just too low for this job. They don't want more than $30,000 a year. Those guys just aren't hungry enough and they give you an average performance. We had a guy who was 39 years old, had been eight years with the company, and was just too comfortable. His energy level wasn't high enough. The job outgrew the person. You have to weigh in his customer following, of course. But if he's been in that territory for eight years, it's likely that a turnover was necessary three or four years ago. I had to fire this guy. It sounds mercenary. But the decision had to be made.

"This is a hard thing for new district managers. They aren't responsible for the reps being there, and they hope they can bring the poorer performers up to snuff. But you have to decide early on whether the raw material of that person is worth developing. If you've decided that you've spent time developing the person and he's not going to get better, you put him in a program so that he knows exactly where he's going. You do your homework and get your ducks in a line so that when the final day of reckoning occurs, both parties are prepared. And then you handle it in a straightforward, nonvindictive, businesslike, professional manner.

MANAGERIAL PHILOSOPHY

"You can't lose your cool, especially over the uncontrollable factors that come up. You just try to cope and learn something for the next time. A new district manager feels responsible for everything that happens. But you finally realize you can't worry about everything 24 hours a day, every day of the week.

"It also helps to realize that you can't make any really bad decisions if you get input from the people below you. If the situation's really difficult, discuss it with your superior and the people you work with. And usually, given three ways to go on any decision, the difference in end result between one and three isn't very great.

"In dealing with people every day, you need a straightforward no-nonsense approach. Mutual communication is the key. 'Here's where we need to be, when we have to be there, and what we have to do to get there.'

"I also believe that you have to be a bit distant from your sales reps. You may like or dislike them, but you can't let your feelings either way affect the way you work with them. I think you shouldn't socialize with them, either. Of course, you have to recognize their personal problems and acknowledge that side of their lives, because it's going to affect their performance.

"My own style is authoritative. But that's not the only way to manage. The main thing is to be honest. You're controlling their lives, to some extent. Being honest means not taking them for granted and jerking them around or manipulating them or using them for your own benefit. If I had a manager who was doing that to me, I'd find ways to get even. No one likes to be used.

"I think that being district manager is one of the toughest jobs in this division. We have to juggle different strategies for different products. And the pressure to get the job done, to develop, and to be perceived as successful to get the next job is pretty intense.

"The main thing is to get the right people to do the job. And then work hard. There's no substitute for it. No matter what uncontrollable factors come up, no one can ever say you're not doing the best damned job you can."

ED PERRY

Ed Perry had been the district sales manager in the St. Louis district for the past 10 years. He had been with the company for 17 years. When the former district manager was promoted to a position in Los Angeles, Ed took over the job and was given the title "assistant district manager" while the former manager was deciding whether or not to keep his new job. Six months after his boss had left, Ed became the new district manager.

THE DISTRICT MANAGER'S JOB

Recruiting

Ed clearly felt that recruiting and hiring were among the most important aspects of his job. "Let's illustrate it this way: you can have a stable full of horses, and train to your heart's content until you've done the best training you can do. But if they weren't thoroughbreds to begin with, it's for naught. I want people who are winners.

"One source is the employment agency. Since my time is limited, I make certain that I get good quality people from an agency, or I'll stop working with it. But I'll stick with a good agency. Even within the good ones, there are probably only one or two counselors who are worth much. Those people I'll work with closely, and we'll have a good conversation about those people after the interview. If they make a mistake, I'll let them know.

"What am I looking for? I want a person who is in the top 10–15 percent of the sales organization. I'm looking for the individual who didn't just inherit that position, but one who earned it. I'm looking at the written proof. What were their stacked rankings? What position did they wind up in after the past year or quarter? Of the trips or incentives that the company offers, how many did they win, compared to the other sales reps?

"I'm also looking for an individual who I feel will mold into a given territory and will fit closely with the kinds of people he'll be calling on. I try to avoid flaws, such as personality conflicts with other salespersons nd employees. A common question I'll ask is 'How did you get along with your boss? Have you ever had a problem with him? What were his strengths and weaknesses?'

Interviewing

"The first interview usually lasts about an hour. My style is to put people at ease. I'm not interested in routine questions or answers. I almost avoid those questions because I know what the answers will be. Is a guy going to say, 'I'm a bad salesman?' He's aware that what he says is going to influence his career and his ability to earn money over the next period of years, and he's going to be very much on guard. So I take my coat off, I'll have a pot of coffee sent to the room, ask him to feel free to take off his jacket, if he'd like. I want to get to the individual rather than the facade.

"The first thing I look for is sales background and ability to sell. I tell them, 'Since we're hiring for a sales position, and since your ability to earn money, or to be promoted, depends on your ability to sell, I want to know as much about you as a salesperson as I possibly can. Sometimes I'll ask, 'Why are you a good salesperson?' By assuming that he or she is good, I'm not attacking—but I want to know.

"The second thing I want to know is what brings them to sit down and talk to me. I want to know what's gone through their minds and what they hope to accomplish by commercially divorcing their previous company and joining this company.

"Third, I tell them that one objective of the interview is to give them whatever information they need to make a valid decision on whether to continue the interviewing process with this company. I usually ask that their questions about the company be held until the last few minutes of the interview.

"Getting back to that first point, their sales abilities, I need to find out what their weaknesses are. That's not easy. They're on the witness stand and are not going to condemn themselves. One way to get at their weak points is to ask, 'If your most recent boss were sitting here, how would he describe you? What would he tell me that would have to be worked on the most?' That way I'm not attacking in the same way as if I said, 'Tell me your weaknesses, dummy!'

"At the same time, I'm looking for believability, persuasiveness, and the ability to understand oneself. For example, many people will say, 'Well, I hate to do paperwork.' (That's almost always true.) When someone gives me a negative about himself, I always want to see if they've learned enough about selling to add, 'I've been able to conquer it. If you compare my paperwork to others' within my organization, you'll find it is superior to theirs. It was something I really had to work on.' I might ask his employer later about his paperwork: 'How did it compare to others?' If I get a different answer from the one the interviewee gave me, depending on how well I liked him, I'd sit down and talk with him and cover this area again.

"I usually have three or four interviews with someone I'm interested in. You can't be with a person too much. First of all, I don't want to give the impression that it's easy to get into the company. Something he doesn't have to fight hard for has less value. And, second, I want to know him. We're supposed to make an important decision in just a few sessions. It's a very heavy responsibility, to both the company and to the individual.

"After talking with the candidate maybe three times, I call his former employer. Sometimes that's futile. One employer would not tell me anything but name, rank, and serial number. Other people in that organization had said, 'He is good, damn good.' I didn't hire him. When I don't get information, the first thing in my mind is that the guy is worrying about a legal suit. He has something negative to say that he can't. On lack of evidence, I'm going to convict the guy.

"Once I've decided on someone who I feel confident is the one I'm going to run with, I put him out in the field for at least half a day, sometimes a full day, with one of my top people in the nearby territory. I want him or her to get a feel for what our people do, the problems they run into. Of course, a half-day or one day doesn't give them anything more than an eye-opening experience, but at least they get some basis for liking or disliking what we do.

"I've got another reason for doing this. It shows my confidence in my people, and I want to build them up. I ask the sales rep, 'What is your assessment of this individual? Will he or she be a success, and why? Hopefully, they will appreciate this confidence and will grow, becoming better prepared at some future time to take additional responsibility. My people are good. If I hear some negatives and they're realistic, often I'll go with my own people. The candidates will often let down their guard a little bit because they're not being interviewed and they think they're out there learning about us—but we're learning a lot about them.

"All in all, I rather enjoy interviewing. It's only unpleasant when other things have to be done. If we have excessive turnover, obviously a larger portion of my time is going to be spent interviewing, which means I can't develop my people the way I should, nor can I make as many calls on customers, nor can I anticipate problems quite as well. It just takes time, and that's the commodity we have so little of.

Allocating Time in the Field

"Ideally, I'd like to spend 60–70 percent of my time with the above-average people. The best people are already getting a major portion of the business, whether you're with them or not. The point is to get that business faster. And I need to learn, so that I can train the others. My knowledge is limited by what I've experienced, what I've been taught, and what I've read. For example, if I'm not selling a new product, I have no direct experience with that product. I definitely have to improve my knowledge. And who am I going to do it with? My winners. I go to them when it comes to new products and new concepts, or when I want to test something I've read about, or see something that's been reported in my own district as working. I want to understand what's making my best people successful in certain areas.

"Realistically, though, my time winds up being evenly distributed, with a little more emphasis on people at the top and the bottom. I'll raise my hand as one who spends too much time on the poor-to-unsatisfactory performers.

"Why spend time with the people at the bottom? You're actually spending time with the account so that it doesn't fall apart until a new person takes over the territory. We're assuming that I will be getting rid of that person as soon as I possibly can. In my experience, I've never been able to turn one around. Since that individual is going to be gone, I have to bridge the gap between old and new. And, of course, the other reason for spending time with these people is that my boss will be asking: 'Have you put him on a program? Have you done this? Have you done that?'

Dealing with Poor Performers

"We're not in Japan, we're not in Germany, we're not paternalistic. This company is results-oriented, and he's going to have to perform. If he's in the middle of the heap, we're going to talk about his 'middle-of-the-heapness,' and we're going to do what we can to make sure he's at the top of the heap. If he's not in the top 25 percent of the sales force at least every so often, then he's in the wrong job. That's a good way to waste a life. I would tell him so, just that way.

"I do need steady performers—don't misinterpret what I'm saying. But there's a difference between a steady performer and the guy whose high point is the middle of the pack. If he is the middle of the pack, he's with the wrong company and certainly in the wrong district. Steady performers are consistently in the top half, but not consistently middle.

"In the words of a former director of this company, 'Has he had five years' experience, or one year's experience five times? After five years, he should be hitting his stride. This company is not designed to keep and nurture the individual who is still a middle-of-the-pack performer after that amount of time.

"And of course, it's not just the company. *I* want the superstars. I can't be satisfied personally, or within this company, unless I am a winner. I like to take the accolades. I like the style I live in. I like to associate myself with winners. But I can't be a winner and my district can't be a winner unless I've got winners on my team. And if management is going to come to my district to look for potential promotions, or to come to me to be sure something gets done I've got to have winners on my team. Probably my job would be easier if I had more middle-of-the-roaders, because I would probably have less turnover. There would be fewer promotions, and fewer people would go to other companies because other companies would not want them either. I'd have a comfortable, smooth life, and would not have to work so hard. But I wouldn't be happy.

Supervising and Developing People

"I personally think that good DMs have everybody in programs at all times—programs geared to that person's needs and to the company's objectives. And I've almost decided that I'm not going to design programs for people any more. The salesperson has to adopt the program himself.

"What the manager needs to do, of course, is get at the motivations behind the person's substandard performance, help him understand his own motivations, and help him to design a program that will help him. Why is he not doing his work? Is he just discouraged? Is he afraid that he's soon going to be a turnover figure? He may be motivated by promotions, by extra earnings, by being named to the president's club.

"So when you help him design the program, you tie it to those motivations. 'I know you'd really like to be promoted, to be given additional responsibilities. I think you're capable. But there are a couple of areas I've been concerned about.' If he needs help, I'll help him. But he or she has to accept the problem and want to correct it.

"Being aware of their motivations is important when I'm supervising in the field, too. They want respect and recognition. For example, if someone makes a mistake in a sales presentation, I don't want to attack that person's credibility in front of a customer. Usually, I will not contradict him. I'll wait until afterward to discuss it, and he'll learn from the experience. If the problem can't be corrected later, and if it represents a large amount of money, then I'll interfere. I'll try to soften the blow, though, by simply saying, 'Gee, Bill, I thought I heard you tell other accounts that this is the situation.' Or, 'I'm sure you wanted to include, as you did elsewhere, this bit of information.'

"On the other hand, if he's deliberately screwing up, I'm not going to worry about his reputation. That guy is out, period. Deliberately changing facts and figures is lying. I can't tolerate that. That sort of behavior I usually put down to a bad attitude. Attitude is awfully difficult to work on, especially with a new person and there's no time to dally with it. So if he makes misrepresentations, or misses more than one training session—for any reason—it's time to let him go.

Evaluating People

"I evaluate my people in terms of personal development, educational development, additional responsibilities they've taken on, teamwork, administrative work. But I put most emphasis on the bottom line: whether or not they reached the company's quarterly sales quotas.

"I think that's why I like sales. It's so directly related to corporate objectives, and achievement is so clearly defined. It's easy to say, 'You've done your job,' or 'You haven't done your job.' When I was selling I liked the reinforcement and the ability to judge my progress on my own. I don't need anybody to tell me. I know.

THE MANAGER IN THE MIDDLE

"The toughest part of the job is being between top management and my own people. That position means a lot of different frustrations.

"First of all, being in the middle means having to support a principle or decision, made above me, that I feel is wrong. It's particularly difficult for me, because I don't disguise my emotions, I don't lie. And when I'm not part of the decision making, sometimes I feel like a clerk, passing along decisions like a robot. But my job is to carry out those decisions, as quickly and efficiently as possible. That's it, like it or not. You have to take the bad along with the good. I take my frustrations out on the tennis court and by jogging.

"One of the key policies I disagree with is the company's system of rewards. For one thing, this company does not do a very good job of portraying to its employees that it offers continuity in income. Instead, we spend too much time talking about people with exceptional salaries. And the money is big. But by emphasizing the exceptional, the company loses the exceptional people. The superstars don't feel that they're going to be able to perform that way over a prolonged period of time. They figure, more often than not, that they'll get their money and run.

"The other problem with compensation is that it doesn't always correlate with promotions. The top salesperson knows that any promotion will be worth less money in this organization. He knows that it would take a series of promotions—maybe three and four jobs up the line, maybe five or six years away—before he could make what he made as a salesperson. This happened to me personally. The only way to correct it is to make sure that we consistently reward outstanding performance outstandingly.

"The compensation is one of the key reasons for turnover among our good people. In fact, this company is programmed to have high turnover. That's frustrating to me personally, because I hate to develop personal relationships with people who I know are not going to be around for very long. Conversely, turnover works to my benefit, professionally. My name has been around for a long time. People pick up the phone and ask for me to help them out because they remember me from years ago.

"Being in the middle also means that you have to develop a tough skin about how your own people feel about you. I have to make unpopular decisions sometimes. The issue of being liked is particularly interesting when one is in transition from salesperson to sales manager. To be a good salesperson, you have to be liked by the customers you do business with. Given very similar sets of opportunities, customers do respond to people they like. So it's conceivable that the salesperson who has been a good one, who has been well liked, may have difficulty moving into the role where now he's got to make decisions that may or may not be popular with the people that report to him.

"To make these decisions work, you've got to have the respect of your people—whether or not they like you. My having been successful in sales has been very helpful. Managing is much easier when you have the credentials of having done it well. Hopefully, I am well liked, as well as respected. But if not—that's the way it goes.

"Being in the middle has also made me very aware of the need for teamwork. From time to time I'll get a prima donna. They are the good people who have succeeded in a short period of time. All of a sudden they'll say, 'The SOB down the road flubbed the job,' as if they never made mistakes. We lost an account because of a problem in the loading system. We just did not have the product to ship. I can't go out to the garage and make it. Maybe we had the problem because the chairman said, 'I'll accept this level of complaint and loss.' But no matter whose fault it was, we've got to remember we're all in this business together. In this case, one poor guy up there caught hell from everybody. Before the prima donna goes shooting at other people, he's got to be aware that we need every part of this corporation: distribution, manufacturing, procurement of raw materials, support, quality control, and on and on. Everyone of these people are just as important as the next person. I am just as dependent upon a young woman on a production line who packages properly, as I am on the salespeople.

"I spent a lot of time last week defending the company and trying to solve a quality control problem. I can't go out and get new business while I'm doing that. But it's part of my job. I hope I do it better than any manager ever has. I'll try.

MANAGERIAL PHILOSOPHY

"The good manager selects quality people. He trains them to meet their daily challenges and trains them to assume additional responsibilities as they come along. He's a good counselor. He takes into consideration the individual's whole being. And he'll do everything necessary to help that person perform at his peak. The manager has to be goal-oriented and has to elicit that kind of attitude from those who report to him. He has to be the kind of person that others can respect.

"I'm motivated by the same kinds of things that motivate other good people. I like to consider myself a good person, a good manager. I like to be considered by my peers and by my superiors as being an outstanding manager. I like to be considered by those who report to me as being an outstanding manager, a winner. Along with that, of course, come the financial re-wards. I like the recognition of those with whom I come in contact daily, which includes everyone within the company, the customers, the people in my community. I like to be the best of the best, consistently.

"I'm still learning. I would like to know how to recognize problems be-fore they become problems. How do you recognize when anyone is not telling the truth? A guy said to me a few weeks ago, 'You're sure you're not a lawyer?' This was a guy who wouldn't give in answers. I had to go about it 15 different ways. And I still wanted an answer.

"My overall philosophy is to encourage people and be honest with them. The two go together. I want to encourage those who report to me to become the very best that they can. Honesty is part of that. It's important for long-term relationships that people are able to trust me and I them. Of course, I'm not going to tell someone that he's ugly. I've learned in this business to accentuate the positive. But you understand what I'm saying: be honest, and treat others as you'd like them to treat you. Expect the absolute best from your people. Give your best. And expect the best of those above you.

"So the main thing is to be concerned with the individual—his needs, goals, drives. That's getting at the cause, rather than focusing on the symp-tom. Human-related issues are infinitely more important than the numbers. I respond to people who give a damn about me, and I suspect that every-body does. I care about the people I bring in. I'm jealous about getting the best people to begin with, I'm jealous of helping them reach their potenti-als, and I will do everything possible to help them do that. I usually get the same kind of loyalty in return."

Case 7
Medical Technology Products, Inc.

Mr. Houston W. Eastland, general sales manager of Medical Technology Products, Inc., was reviewing a consultant's report entitled, "Motivation and Organizational Climate: A Study of Outstanding and Average Sales Offices." The study had been based on the premise that a manager's style created an organizational climate that could encourage or discourage salesmen. Eastland was now evaluating the study's premises and its findings, so that he could determine what specific managerial changes might be made to turn average sales districts into outstanding ones.

COMPANY BACKGROUND

Medical Technology Products (MTP) manufactured, sold, and serviced electrical, electronic, and mechanical equipment used in hospital operating rooms and laboratories. MTP was a leader in this rapidly growing industry, and its products were known for excellent quality. MTP's sales were in excess of $100 million. Sales had been growing at an annual rate of nearly 20 percent, and the company was very profitable. MTP employed 4,000 people.

THE SALES ORGANIZATION

As general sales manager, Eastland supervised 3 regional sales managers and 30 district managers. The district managers in turn oversaw about 1,000 people in all, including over 200 salesmen, 450 service people, and 300 clerical workers. Districts ranged in personnel from 4 salesmen and 8 servicemen, to 15 salesmen and 45 servicemen.

The MTP salesman designed configurations of equipment to meet the needs of each hospital. Each salesman called on 30 to 40 hospitals. He or she

Copyright © 1968 by the President and Fellows of Harvard College. Reproduced by permission. This case was prepared by J. A. Timmons under the direction of Jay W. Lorsch and George Litwin.

worked closely with the doctors and technicians who would use the equipment, and also dealt with the purchasing agents in larger hospitals. The job required wide ranging skills: the salesman had to be something of a mechanic, an engineer, an electrician, a carpenter, an architect, and a draftsman. The salesman usually acquired this knowledge by spending several years as a service technician. He or she often had a degree in electrical engineering, or had had similar training through prior work experience. Doctors placed great confidence in the recommendations of a good salesman.

A normal sale was $50,000 to $75,000 although smaller items ranged from $5,000 to $20,000, and complete systems might cost $250,000. The salesman usually sold about $500,000 worth of supplies and equipment in a year. He or she received a base salary of $8,000 to $10,000, depending on length of service, plus a 2 percent commission on collected sales. Top salesmen earned $30,000 to $40,000 per year; average salesmen earned about $19,000. Income could vary considerably from year to year, because of the high price per unit sale.

Repeat sales depended largely on the quality of the service that MTP provided for installed equipment. MTP's service people were responsible for installing and maintaining the equipment. They often worked overtime, sometimes for an entire weekend, to meet installation deadlines or to make repairs. They were often called to out-of-town hospitals for emergency service work. Corporate senior executives had set nationwide wage rates for the servicemen. Depending on prior training and experience, a new serviceman started at $125 per week, receiving time and a half for overtime. On regular time, a serviceman could earn a maximum of $225 per week; the average serviceman earned $190 per week. None of the servicemen belonged to a union.

THE DISTRICT MANAGEMENT

While the district manager supervised the salesmen directly, he or she oversaw the servicemen and clerical staff indirectly. A service manager supervised equipment installation and maintenance, and a commercial supervisor managed bookkeeping and order processing.

The district office was practically autonomous. Eastland and regional sales managers reviewed district results each month, via uniform accounting and control reports. But the specific means of organizing and controlling the district were left to the discretion of the district manager, under the regional managers' supervision. One district manager, for example, stressed service as the key means of maximizing long-term sales. One method he used to carry out this objective was an elaborate system of recording each serviceman's training and expertise. A large master board hung on the wall in the district office, showing categories for progressive levels of knowledge and training. Symbols entered on the board for each serviceman indicated his or her general level across all categories, as well as a particular rating in each category. Another district manager stressed cost cutting as the number one priority, and he insisted on twice-daily call-ins to keep track of service and salesmen's activities. A third manager used no formal system, relying instead on informal contacts to monitor her sales and servicemen. A fourth manager gave few directives, emphasizing individual responsibility.

Methods of appraising customers' satisfaction and salesmen's performance also varied across the districts. In one district, an annual performance review was supplemented with spot-check calls on customers, reviews of each salesman's weekly report, and information on sales and expenses from the commercial supervisor. Another manager held no formal reviews, and had daily conversations with his people and worked with them in the field. Still another manager relied almost entirely on feedback he received from key customers.

THE CONSULTANT'S STUDY

MTP's corporate staff, with Eastland's approval, had contracted with a consulting firm to conduct a study of district sales management. Specifically, the study was designed to identify (1) *managerial styles* that distinguished superior from average sales districts and (2) *personal characteristics* that distinguished salesmen in superior districts from those in average districts. Eight districts were singled out for study: four ranked as outstanding and four as average. Rankings were based on sales growth, market share, profitability, sales quota achievement, and expense ratios.

To examine managers' styles and salesmen's characteristics, the consultant used three methods: questionnaires, interviews, and observations. One questionnaire was designed to assess the climate of the district organization, as perceived by salesmen and service supervisors. Another set of questionnaires measured salesmen's motivation as well as certain personal characteristics that the consulting firm had found to be correlated with success in sales. A third set of questionnaires assessed the salesmen's satisfaction with their jobs, their pay, and their managers. The consultant interviewed managers of each office to determine their managerial philosophies and styles. Salesmen and service managers were also interviewed to uncover their perceptions of how the offices were run. Finally, a researcher spent two days in each office, observing personal contacts, subjects covered in meetings, managers' activities, and the like. The researchers who made the interviews and observations had no prior knowledge of these offices' ratings. This precaution was taken to ensure that the researchers would not be biased.

Salesmen's Characteristics

Through its studies of other companies, the consulting firm had identified two types of salesmen: the entrepreneurial salesman and the integrative salesman. The entrepreneurial salesman tried to make a sale to each prospective customer on each call. The integrative salesman tried to make a sale by applying the company's resources to the prospective customer's problems. These previous studies enabled the consultants to draw up composite ratings for top entrepreneurial and integrative salesmen on the basis of three basic motives. The consultant then compared these scores with those obtained by salesmen from MTP's outstanding and average districts. Exhibit 1 charts these comparisons.

Exhibit 1
Characteristics of Salesmen

	Test Scores									
Basic Motives	*Low* 1	2	3	4	5	6	7	8	9	*High* 10
Need for achievement (success, measured against competitors and against one's personal standard of excellence)	★ ★ ★ ★ ★ ★ ★ ★ ★ ★ ★ ★ ★ ★ # # # # # # # # # # # # # # E E E E E E E E E E E E E E I I I I I I I I I I I I I I									
Need for affiliation (warm, friendly, compassionate relationships with others)	★ ★ ★ ★ ★ ★ ★ ★ ★ ★ ★ ★ ★ # # # # # # # # # # E E E E E E E E E I I I I I I I I I I I I I I I I									
Need for power (control or influence over others)	★ ★ ★ ★ ★ ★ ★ ★ ★ ★ ★ ★ ★ # # # # # # # # # # E E E E E E E E E E E E E I I I I I I I I I I I I I I I I									

★ Salesmen from top MTP districts.
Salesmen from average MTP districts.
E Top entrepreneurial salesmen from other firms.
I Top integrative salesmen from other firms.

Organizational Climate

The consultant compiled ratings of the district's climate, as perceived by salesmen and service managers. Six characteristics of the organization's climate were rated from 1 to 10.

Structure referred to the degree to which the manager used specified procedures to control the district. A score of 9–10 would indicate that the organization was "run by the book"; a score of 1–2 would indicate disorganization or chaos. The *delegation* score showed the degree to which people felt that they had individual responsibility. A very high score would indicate that the manager was perceived to abrogate all responsibility for the actions of his or her personnel; a very low score would indicate the perception that the manager seldom allowed anyone to do anything without his or her approval.

Freedom measured the degree to which employees felt that they were encouraged to take risks. A very high score would indicate an "anything goes" atmosphere; a very low score would indicate that they felt they must avoid mistakes at all costs. *Pressure* measured managers' encouragement as perceived by salesmen. A very high score would indicate that the managers' demands were perceived to be unreasonable; a very low score would indicate that there was no pressure to perform well.

Rewards and support measured the adequacy of rewards, support, and recognition for good work. A very high score would indicate flattery; a low score would indicate a hypercritical atmosphere. The *team spirit* score measured the degree to which each individual felt that he belonged to the group and took pride in it. A very high score would indicate a "country club" atmosphere; a very low score would indicate excessive tension and competition within the group.

Exhibit 2 presents the average scores of outstanding (★) and average (#) districts on the basis of these six characteristics.

Exhibit 2
Organizational Climate

	Questionnaire Ratings									
	Low									High
	1	2	3	4	5	6	7	8	9	10
Structure	★ ★ ★ ★ ★ ★ ★ ★ ★ ★ ★ ★ ★ ★ ★ ★									
	# # # # # #									
Delegation	★ ★ ★ ★ ★ ★ ★ ★ ★ ★ ★ ★ ★ ★ ★ ★ ★ ★ ★ ★									
	# # # # # # # # # # #									
Freedom	★ ★ ★ ★ ★ ★ ★ ★ ★ ★ ★ ★ ★ ★ ★									
	# # # # #									
Pressure	★ ★ ★ ★ ★ ★ ★ ★ ★ ★ ★ ★ ★									
	# # # #									
Rewards and support	★ ★ ★ ★ ★ ★ ★ ★ ★ ★ ★ ★ ★ ★									
	# # # # # #									
Team spirit	★ ★ ★ ★ ★ ★ ★ ★ ★ ★ ★ ★ ★ ★ ★ ★ ★									
	# # # #									

On the basis of the researchers' observations, the consultant also charted the amounts of interaction among managers, salesmen, and nonsales personnel in outstanding and average sales offices. Exhibit 3 documents these results.

Managerial Style

By combining information from observations and from interviews with salesmen and service managers, the consultant compared the managerial

Exhibit 3
Interaction among Managers, Salesmen, and Nonsales Personnel in Outstanding (★) and Average (#) MTP Sales Offices

	Experimenter's Ratings Based on Observation									
	Low									*High*
	1	2	3	4	5	6	7	8	9	10
All interactions	★ ★ ★ ★ ★ ★ ★ ★ ★ ★ ★ ★ ★ ★ ★ ★ ★ ★ ★ # # # # # # # # #									
Manager and salesmen	★ # # # # # # # # # # # # #									
Among salesmen	★ # # # # # # # # # # # #									
Manager and nonsales personnel	★ # # # # # # # # # #									
Salesmen and nonsales personnel	★ # # # # # # #									

Exhibit 4
Performance Characteristics of Managers in Outstanding (★) and Average (#) MTP Sales Offices

	Experimenter's Ratings Based on Observations and Interviews									
	Low									*High*
	1	2	3	4	5	6	7	8	9	10
Amount of coaching	★ # # # # # # # # # #									
Sets high standards	★ # # # # # # # # #									
Makes unilateral decisions	★ ★ ★ ★ ★ ★ # # # # # # # # # # # # # # # # # #									
Mutual (two-way discussions) or problems	★ # # # # # # # # # #									
Amount of criticism	★ ★ ★ ★ # # # # # # # # # # # #									
Amount of praise, recognition, and related nonmonetary reward	★ # # # # # #									

Exhibit 5
Salesmen's Perceptions of the Job and the Manager in Outstanding (★) and
Average (#) MTP Sales Offices

	Questionnaire Ratings									
	Low									High
	1	2	3	4	5	6	7	8	9	10
Interest in and satisfaction with the job	★ # # # # # # # # # # # # # # # # # # #									
Satisfaction with compensation plan	★ # # # # # # # # # # # # # #									
Satisfaction with total rewards and punishments	★ ★ ★ ★ ★ ★ ★ ★ ★ ★ ★ ★ ★ ★ ★ ★ ★ ★ ★ # # # # # # # # # # #									
Liking for manager as a person	★ #									
Respect for manager's ability and judgment	★ # # # # # # # # # # # # # # # # #									

techniques used in outstanding and average districts. Exhibit 4 presents these results.

To complement these data, Exhibit 5 summarizes the salesmen's perceptions of their jobs and their managers.

THE CONSULTANT'S RECOMMENDATIONS

On the basis of this study, the consultant made three general recommendations to district managers.

1. *Define the sales task broadly* to encompass sales, service, customer relations, and accounting and clerical support. The district manager would then recruit salesmen capable of handling this enlarged sales task. For example, a candidate whose only or strongest asset was high motivation of individual achievement might not contribute as much to the success of the overall operation as a candidate who could work well with other sales, service, and support personnel.

2. *Emphasize positive feedback*, giving praise and recognition for satisfactory performances and offering support and coaching rather than criticism and punishment for unsatisfactory performances. It is natural for managers to spend most of their time and energy in trouble shooting. But criticism and punishment not only stifle creativity and energy, they also cause distortions in communication from subordinates.

3. *Use a participative approach in managing the district*, communicating current issues and problems to all personnel and including them in decision

making. The manager should seek results through the team's work rather than through his own individual efforts. He or she can then concentrate on planning, stimulating, and integrating the effort of individuals within the group.

CONCLUSION

Mr. Eastland recognized that the consultant's findings and recommendations were potentially useful. But what specific actions could he take, what policies could he set up, to help his district managers develop better integrative selling teams? And what could he do to help his district managers cope with the increasing complexities of their own jobs, as MTP's sales multiplied and its technologies became more and more sophisticated?

Case 8
Kramer Pharmaceuticals, Inc. (A)

In August 1978, executives of Kramer Pharmaceuticals, Inc., received a number of letters from irate customers who complained about the firm's terminating the services of one of the Kramer detailers, Mr. Bob Marsh. Because customer reactions of this nature were extremely rare, and because Kramer's reputation in the industry for enlightened management practices appeared to be in question, the sales vice president decided to look into the Marsh case in detail, to determine whether Marsh's discharge was a "management failure" and, if so, what could be done about correcting the situation. Accordingly, the sales vice president collected all the data in company files that pertained to the Marsh case, including managers' comments that allegedly gave insight into Marsh's feelings toward company management personnel.

BACKGROUND INFORMATION

Kramer was a major manufacturer of prescription drugs for the medical and dental professions. All its products were carried by reputable drug wholesalers and drugstores for resale to the general public by prescription, or to hospitals and physicians. Kramer competed with such firms as Abbott, Lilly, Merck, Upjohn, and Schering. Kramer sales in 1977 exceeded $400 million.

Kramer fielded a sales force of over 500 detailers who called regularly on hospital personnel, doctors, and dentists to describe the Kramer line and to persuade these medical personnel to use and prescribe Kramer drugs. A typical Kramer detailer was responsible for about 200 physicians and hospital accounts within an assigned geographic territory, and he or she was expected to make between six and nine doctor or hospital calls per day.

Most Kramer detailers were pharmacy school graduates who had joined Kramer after a few years' experience as registered pharmacists in retail drugstores. Each new Kramer detailer received a month's training in product characteristics and selling (detailing) skills at the company's Denver headquarters. In addition, both new and experienced detailers received regular on-the-job training from the 35 district managers. A Kramer detailman could expect between 10 to 15 days of these field visits in a year, depending on his or her experience and performance. All Kramer representatives returned to headquarters regularly for continued training throughout their careers.

Kramer executives considered these detailers second to none in the business. About 60 percent of the detailers had 10 or more years with the company; 25 percent had fewer than 5 years. About half were aged 40 or older, and one fourth were under 30. Senior executives were also gratified that turnover in the sales force was much lower than the industry's average. Only about 8 percent were lost each year from quits, discharges, retirements, and deaths.

Kramer detailers were salaried and received an annual bonus based on corporate performance. In 1978, a detailer's total earnings ranged from $20,000 to $36,000. The corporate bonus typically amounted to about 15 percent of these totals. In addition, each detailer was provided with a company automobile, generous fringe benefits, and reimbursement for all normal business expenses.

Every Kramer detailer was evaluated in terms of both sales volume and improvement in his or her relationships with customers. Quotas were established yearly for each of the dozen or so major product categories to stimulate proper concentration of detailing efforts. Every Kramer detailer received a formal performance evaluation from his or her district manager once a year and informal evaluations whenever necessary.

Almost all of the 35 Kramer district managers had been chosen from among the sales force for leadership, administrative, and selling activities. Evaluated chiefly on ability to develop personnel, each was expected to spend three to four days per week on field visits with his detailers. The individual district managers reported to one of the six zone managers who reported in turn to the sales vice president.

BOB MARSH

In June 1966, Bob Marsh, the 32-year-old manager of a prescription department in a major drugstore in Toledo, Ohio, had submitted his application to Kramer for employment as a sales representative. Marsh presented a good academic record and a history of successful drugstore experience since his graduation from a top-flight pharmacy school in 1960. He was also an experienced U.S. naval pilot with a fine officer-service record.

Marsh had grown up in a Toledo suburb and married a woman from the same town 12 years before. The couple now owned their own home in this suburb, where they were active in community and church affairs. They had two children.

Marsh had explained that he had been considering joining Kramer for over a year. He knew several career ethical drug detailers and had talked with them about the job. Since the earliest days of his training in pharmacy, Marsh had considered Kramer one of the finest firms in the industry. After a few rewarding but unexciting years in retail pharmacy, he had decided to become a sales representative. His first territorial preference was his home state, although neither he nor his wife felt that moving to another part of the country would deter his joining Kramer. Marsh also had expressed interest in being considered for an international assignment in the future, as he and his wife had lived in or visited almost every major European country during his years in the navy.

A Kramer detailer who knew Marsh quite well had arranged for him to meet John Meredith, the district manager in Toledo. Meredith had been impressed with Marsh and had rated him highly in sincerity, aggressiveness, attitude, enthusiasm, learning ability, judgment, character, affability, and appearance. His personal references were outstanding. In a note to his zone manager, Meredith had said, "I am quite hopeful that we will be able to obtain the services of Bob Marsh. I have every reason to believe that he will develop into an excellent salesman."

WORKING WITH JOHN MEREDITH

About a month after the interview with Meredith, Marsh joined the Kramer sales force and was assigned a territory in Toledo, which greatly pleased the Marsh family. Although his new salary level of $14,000 a year was below his current salary at the drugstore, he believed that his earnings potential with Kramer would be considerably greater in the long run. Marsh had an advantage in that he knew personally many of the physicians and hospital personnel whom he would be calling on.

Marsh's initial field training went smoothly, and Meredith was certain that he had made an excellent decision in hiring Marsh. Marsh quickly grasped all facets of the job, including product characteristics and basic selling skills. He was exceptionally well received by physicians, office receptionists, and hospital personnel. His district associates also welcomed him cordially. The only characteristics that caused Meredith even momentary concern were Marsh's seeming lack of attention to organization, planning, and follow-up, and his tendency to question the logic of some of the company's major promotion programs. But since these attitudes were not unusual with beginning salespeople, Meredith wrote them off to inexperience.

After four months on the job, Marsh joined a group of other recently employed representatives at Kramer headquarters for a month-long sales training program. The new detailers studied customer preferences, product characteristics, and sales promotion practices, as well as the pharmaceutical industry and Kramer's competition. Top Kramer executives lectured on corporate history, policy, goals, and philosophy. In addition, the salespeople had ample opportunity to share their problems and experiences with other novice detailers during social get-togethers. The training department's report on Marsh was excellent.

Shortly after Marsh's return to the territory, Meredith spent a couple of days in the field with him. Although it was apparent to Meredith that Marsh had benefited greatly from the home-office training program, Meredith was disappointed with Marsh's seeming indifference to organization. Marsh gave little advance thought to the physicians he hoped to see—and worse yet, he had no definite plan or approach once in the physician's office. On each call, his attitude was "catch-as-catch-can." His approach to hospitals was much the same. He also displayed more interest in developing his own promotion programs than in following the plans outlined at district meetings. And he tended to second-guess the scheduled promotion program by deciding himself what products to promote.

Meredith also thought that by this time Marsh should have better records of physicians and should have known more about their backgrounds, practices, hospital affiliations, and product preferences. Marsh also tended to prejudge his customers' interests. His sample bag was cluttered and poorly organized, and he often did not have the appropriate promotion literature to accompany the product being discussed. Materials stored in his automobile and at home were in no better shape.

Meredith reminded Marsh that serendipity was not the pattern of a successful salesman, and he pointed out that Marsh ought to change these bad work habits early in his career. Meredith also suggested that Marsh should do less "visiting" during his hospital calls and use this valuable time for more sales presentations. Nevertheless, a good number of Marsh's physicians had increased their Kramer prescriptions in recent months, indicating Marsh's ability to influence physicians favorably. There was also an increase in the number of physicians buying Kramer products for office use. Marsh's hospital sales were also showing gains.

In January 1967, Marsh's salary was increased to $15,000, a level even with that on his previous job. Marsh seemed to be becoming increasingly more comfortable with his physician and hospital accounts, and sales throughout his territory were growing steadily. Meredith continued to stress the need for better planning, follow-through, and responsiveness to direction. He reiterated that Marsh could do much better with his good customer rapport if he were better organized and if he pressed harder for commitments to adopt Kramer products.

Near the end of his first year, following another two days with Meredith, Marsh received his first formal performance review. As on all previous occasions, Meredith instructed Marsh about ways to improve his performance. Meredith did most of the talking, and there was little discussion. From the interview Meredith gained a clear impression that Marsh had found his suggestions helpful and would try to do better.

Meredith also drew up a written appraisal to be reviewed by the zone manager and the sales vice president. On the favorable side of the report, Meredith had this to say:

A hard worker—loyal and dedicated.
Well received by physicians and hospital personnel.
Anxious to do well.
Appreciates and follows instructions and suggestions.
Cooperative and helpful with fellow associates.

These notations were made on the adverse side:

Should overcome the tendency to prejudge customers and promotion programs.
Should be more responsive to management directives.
Should give more attention to planning and organization.

Marsh's overall work performance was recorded as *below standard.*

In January 1968, Marsh's salary was increased to $16,000. In July 1968, his second year-end performance review resembled the first: Work performance, *below standard;* Attitude, *standard.*

At this time the zone manager and the sales vice president took note of these performance reports and asked Meredith for his assessment of Marsh's potential. Meredith replied that Marsh was making substantial progress and that he expected him to overcome his deficiencies in the near future.

In January 1969, Marsh's salary was raised to $17,000 and in July, as Meredith had predicted, Marsh's progress review indicated substantial improvement. His overall performance was now *standard.* The only areas still needing improvement were planning and organization.

The July 1970 performance appraisal report was even better. Marsh's effort to improve his call planning and overall organization had impressed Meredith to the point that he now rated this aspect of the job as *completely satisfactory.* Meredith also indicated that Marsh's attitude could not be better and that he had made great strides in overcoming his tendency to prejudge management, customers, and promotion programs. Marsh's judgment and responsiveness to supervision were now *excellent,* and his overall rating was *above average.* In January 1971, Marsh's salary was raised from $18,000 to $20,000.

WORKING WITH BILL COUCH

In March 1971, Meredith was transferred to another district. He was replaced by a new district manager, Bill Couch, an experienced and highly regarded supervisor. Couch's initial field visits with Marsh went well. Couch was impressed with Marsh's customer rapport and acceptance throughout his territory. Couch frequently heard doctors refer to Marsh as one of the best detailers in the area. A prescription audit of several of the larger drugstores in Marsh's territory confirmed an impressive share of prescriptions for all major Kramer products. Kramer products were being used in every hospital pharmacy. In July, Marsh's first performance review under Couch recorded *satisfactory* ratings across the board, with the exception of planning and record keeping.

Later in July, on the occasion of Marsh's fifth anniversary with Kramer, the firm's president sent Marsh a personal letter congratulating him on this important anniversary and expressing "sincere gratitude for your fine contributions during your first five years with Kramer."

Over the next three years with Bill Couch, Marsh's performance ratings remained *satisfactory*, and he was given steady salary increases. In 1973 he was given the added responsibility of overseeing a distributor. Couch suspected, however, that while Marsh considered this activity interesting, he found the attendant work with drugstores a bit time-consuming.

Marsh's salary progress in 10 years was impressive: his salary reached $24,000 in 1974. His final progress review with Couch in July 1974, a few months before Couch too was transferred to another district, was the best yet. Couch recorded

> Outstanding reception in physicians' offices and drugstores is a great asset.
> Most gratifying improvement in drugstore sales.
> Good acceptance by fellow associates.
> Contributions at district meetings greatly appreciated.
> Excellent attitude and company loyalty.

Marsh's overall work performance was recorded as *well above average*. His attitude was graded as *well above average*.

WORKING WITH JIM RATHBUN

In September, Marsh began reporting to Jim Rathbun, who was gaining a reputation in the company as a bright, young, energetic manager with a lot of new ideas about how to increase sales. Marsh appeared to find Rathbun's emphasis on teamwork stimulating.

At first, Rathbun was complimentary about Marsh. Like previous district managers, Rathbun was quick to observe Marsh's excellent rapport with virtually everyone in his territory. According to Rathbun, however, Marsh was not using this selling asset to its fullest advantage. Rathbun pointed out more opportunities for increased sales than previous supervisors had ever mentioned.

First, Rathbun expressed dissatisfaction with Marsh's record in establishing new products with physicians. Second, he criticized Marsh's poor penetration with dentists—a facet of Marsh's job that previous supervisors had not noted. Rathbun asserted that an improved attitude, and better organization, planning, and follow-up would remedy Marsh's performance. Rathbun also outlined some preliminary sales goals for Marsh to reach within the next six months.

During the next four months, Rathbun made several specific suggestions to Marsh. Rathbun advocated pinpoint detailing, that is, presenting one or two items of particular interest to each physician depending on his or her type of practice, rather than "rambling on," as Rathbun put it, about five or six products. Rathbun also talked about "getting the doctor involved" during the detail call.

Rathbun also announced that the disorder in Marsh's detail bag and automobile was deplorable. Rathbun could not understand how any detailer could operate effectively with working tools in this kind of disarray. Marsh's lack of an organized record and filing system was also beyond Rathbun's comprehension.

During this four-month period, Rathbun spent five different days with Marsh in various parts of his territory. During one of these field visits Rathbun expressed interest in seeing a specific physician. Marsh informed him that the doctor was never in on that day. On his return to the zone office, Rathbun discovered that Marsh's doctor call record showed that he had seen the physician in question regularly during the past two years on various days of the week—including the day in question.

During his next visit, Rathbun called Marsh's attention to this discrepancy. Rathbun referred to the gravity of falsifying reports and reminded Marsh that company policy provided for dismissal in such situations.

Marsh explained that although this physician did not have office hours on that particular day, she did occasionally see salespeople in the morning while catching up on her paperwork. Marsh had sometimes taken advantage of this opportunity and had then "saved" the call report slip for days when he had not been able to meet his doctor call quota. Marsh stated that he would never do so again and that his future record keeping would be flawless. Rathbun confirmed that nothing less would be acceptable. "Rules are rules, and that's the way it's going to be," he added.

In January 1975, Rathbun and Marsh had a lengthy discussion. After notifying Marsh that he would get no salary increase for 1975, Rathbun cited several specific incidents in which Marsh's poor attitude, careless organization, and inattention to planning and follow-up had been directly responsible for missed sales opportunities. Many of the sales goals that Rathbun had set four months ago had not been met. Marsh's new-product placement was seriously deficient, and his sales from special promotions to retailers and hospitals ranked in the lower half in the district. Rathbun closed the discussion by challenging Marsh's attitude toward management directives and company sales objectives.

Most of this lengthy discussion was carefully committed to paper. An apparently stunned Bob Marsh signed a statement confirming that he was now on *probation* and that failure to improve within 90 days would lead to dismissal.

At the end of the probationary period, after spending several days with Marsh in the field, Rathbun informed Marsh that his intense efforts to measure up to Rathbun's expectations during the past three months had paid off. The most dramatic changes were his newly organized detail bag and automobile, and his spruced-up records. His reporting accuracy was unquestioned. Rathbun also complimented Marsh's change in his detailing approach from rambling discussions to pinpoint presentations. Marsh was also now sticking to the promotion schedule as outlined by the home office and ratified at district meetings. His increased effectiveness in drugstore selling was confirmed by recent special orders. Several new-product goals had been reached in selected hospitals. His attitude toward the detailer's responsibilities met Rathbun's criteria. Accordingly, Marsh was removed from *probation*. His performance was now recorded as *satisfactory* on all counts.

In January 1976, Marsh was given a salary increase to $25,000 and in July his performance, according to Rathbun, was still *satisfactory* on all counts. In August, shortly after Marsh was sent another letter by the president of Kramer congratulating him on his 10 years of "fine, loyal service," there was another change in district managers.

WORKING WITH VINCE REED

The new district manager was a much newer and younger man than Rathbun. Toledo was Vince Reed's first supervisory assignment. He had only been with the company half as long as Marsh, but had established himself as a competent detailer and promising management candidate.

According to Reed, his first few visits with Marsh were pleasant and uneventful. Reed had access to Marsh's complete file and felt thoroughly familiar with his background and the obstacles to his development. The two men frequently talked about Marsh's ups and downs with previous district managers, and it seemed to Reed that Marsh appreciated these opportunities to discuss the problems of the previous years.

Reed found Marsh's performance generally satisfactory, especially in view of his earlier problems. Reed was impressed with Marsh's customer rapport, as previous supervisors had been. Reed talked with Marsh about the progress he had made in planning, organization, following direction, and effective use of time granted him by physicians. Reed also commended Marsh's attainment of sales goals.

However, Reed still questioned the slow acceptance of new products among Marsh's customers, and he indicated that physician sales in general were not what they should be. He felt that Marsh could follow district and home-office directives more promptly. And he felt that Marsh's organization was still deficient—his records of hospital and wholesaler personnel were inadequate, and the samples and promotional literature in his bag and car were disordered.

Reed recommended a salary increase of $1,000 for Marsh in January 1977. But later that spring Reed made some substantial additions to Marsh's file. In a carefully detailed letter to his zone manager, Reed outlined several of the points that he and Marsh had talked about on many previous occasions. Specific instances of Marsh's failure to comply with Reed's suggestions were itemized.

By July, Marsh's overall performance had slipped, and he was notified during his annual review that his rating had gone from *satisfactory* to *com-*

pletely unsatisfactory. Reed closed with an admonition that Marsh's performance would now have to reach an acceptable level within 90 days. Once again, Marsh was on *probation.*

Marsh was instructed to submit to Reed's office a written plan outlining his intended approach to extricating himself from this current status. Although Reed provided the basic outline for this master plan, Marsh had only to fill in the details—which he found easy to do, since he merely needed to agree with Reed's ideas on how the job should be done.

WORKING WITH TOM WILKENS

Vince Reed's being transferred to another district in September 1977 prevented his following through with Marsh. The new district manager, Tom Wilkens, whose background was comparable to Reed's, was only able to spend two days in the field with Marsh before he too was reassigned to another district in March 1978. In view of his brief exposure to Marsh, Wilkens made no change in the record, although he confirmed some of the observations made by Marsh's four previous supervisors. Although he did not discuss Marsh's probationary status in detail, Wilkens implied that the time limit set by Reed was no longer valid. While Marsh received no salary increase in January 1978, at least the probationary status had "evaporated."

WORKING WITH TED FRANKLIN

In the spring of 1978, Marsh's 12th year with Kramer, his 6th field supervisor, Ted Franklin, arrived on the scene. Franklin was also younger than Marsh, but he had been a supervisor a year or so longer than had the previous two district managers. Although Marsh had not had a salary increase during the last two years, his present base salary, plus annual bonus and other allowances and benefits, placed him in an income bracket enjoyed by few of his pharmacy school contemporaries who were still working in retail stores.

Before his first meeting with Marsh, Franklin went over Marsh's sizable personal history folder in detail. Franklin also assured the zone manager that with proper guidance Marsh could be remodeled into an above-average performer. In view of the complex history of the Marsh case, Franklin took considerable time writing a detailed narrative report to use as a discussion guide in his interview with Marsh.

Franklin began by summarizing all of Marsh's deficiencies as seen by earlier supervisors. He pointed out that the record was not good and that the time was fast approaching when substandard performance could no longer be tolerated. Franklin then turned to a long list of "survival" procedures that would save Marsh's career and his job. Marsh would have to improve his sincerity, company loyalty, job interest, enthusiasm, cooperation, deference to supervision and his work habits. Nothing but complete success could prevent dismissal.

Franklin set no time limit for the necessary turnabout. Instead, he instructed Marsh to call him at an appointed time each week to discuss his adherence to the outline and to review his daily progress. Franklin's program also included a weekly reading assignment of technical and promotion literature, designed to help Marsh establish new products. Marsh was to submit written summaries of the reading assignments each week. Marsh was also required to fill out questionnaires on each of his major hospitals. These forms were designed to give Marsh the market intelligence he needed for improving his hospital sales.

Marsh agreed to every point in the step-by-step program. Franklin required that he sign each page of the master plan to indicate his complete understanding of what had to be done as well as of the consequences of failure. The interview had lasted four hours.

By now the zone manager had also been transferred. The new manager, Pete Mallick, was a seasoned field executive with an excellent reputation in the company. He and Franklin carefully reviewed the blueprint for Marsh's rehabilitation. Mallick approved of the program and asked that Franklin submit to the zone office periodic reports on Marsh's progress.

Subsequent weeks did not go well for Marsh. He got off to a bad start with late phone calls and written reports. He began to fall behind schedule in reading assignments and in collecting the required market data for his files. Sales volume within his territory was unchanged.

In Franklin's judgment, Marsh appeared moody, unfriendly, indifferent, and lethargic. He had less and less to say, and offered fewer and fewer explanations about his failures on each subsequent weekly report.

Franklin's field visits fell far short in eliciting the kind of response that Franklin had hoped for. Even reminders that time was running out for the dismissal decision no longer appeared to have any stimulating effect on Marsh. The only attitude that seemed constant was his professed fondness for his company and job and his desire to do better.

By July of 1978, after several interim conferences, Mallick and Franklin agreed that time had run out. Marsh should be separated from the company. Franklin arranged a hotel meeting with Marsh. The discussion was short and centered on the well-documented facts that Marsh had been given ample opportunity to succeed and that in view of his long history of failure he had no alternative but to resign.

According to Franklin, Marsh accepted the ultimatum with surprisingly little resistance or comment. He told Franklin that he understood why the job was no longer for him. Franklin felt that Marsh was relieved that it was all over. He expressed gratitude for all the help he had received through the years, and he said that he would always have a warm spot in his heart for Kramer Pharmaceuticals and his colleagues. At age 44, he now planned to return to the same drugstore from which his sales career had been launched 12 years before.

Franklin reported to Mallick that the dismissal session had gone exceptionally well and that Marsh completely understood and agreed with the decision and was leaving the company with no ill will. The only touchy spot in the entire session was Marsh's request to talk over the decision with his family. Franklin pointed out that the conditions of his employment were no longer negotiable and that no point would be served in his discussing the situation with anyone. Marsh also understood that his entire case had been reviewed many times with the zone manager and corporate headquarters. The decision was irreversible.

THE AFTERMATH

A week later Bob Marsh called the Kramer zone office for an appointment with Mallick. He said that he had been treated unfairly and that he would like to talk over several other circumstances regarding Franklin's handling of his case, as well as his overall management of the district. Mallick replied that he was thoroughly familiar with every detail of Bob's history and that he was in complete agreement with Franklin's action. He saw no reason to meet with Marsh.

During the following week, the president of Kramer Pharmaceuticals received a lengthy and thoughtful letter from a prominent physician in Marsh's territory. The doctor expressed disappointment and chagrin over Marsh's dismissal. He was "stunned" that a representative of Bob's reputation and stature with so many of his medical colleagues could be dismissed so abruptly and for such arbitrary and flimsy reasons. He also cited "irregularities" in some of the current management and promotion practices in the area. He wondered what was happening to the long-standing ethical policies that had given Kramer such a fine reputation among physicians, pharmacists, and hospitals.

The president promptly replied that he was requesting an immediate investigation and that the zone manager, Mr. Mallick, would contact the physician. A meeting between the doctor and Mallick was quickly arranged.

Mallick attempted to explain to the doctor the long history of Marsh's unsatisfactory performance, poor attitude, and reluctance to improve. He also related the abundant patience and help that had been given Marsh by each of his district managers. He reiterated the long and thoughtful managerial consideration that preceded Bob's dismissal. He also reminded the doctor that Marsh had completely agreed with the decision.

The doctor was not satisfied, since this explanation failed to agree with his and other physicians' impression of Bob as an outstanding detailer. The doctor asserted that many other physicians and pharmacists in the area were talking about Bob's dismissal, expressing similar surprise and concern. Since Mallick's explanation was not satisfactory, the doctor again wrote to the president to tell him so.

In the meantime the district and zone offices received several similar letters and calls from other physicians and pharmacists. The sales vice president also heard from several doctors and druggists throughout Marsh's territory. The main theme was the same—surprise, disbelief, and perplexity over the abrupt and unexplained dismissal of one of the finest and most helpful career detailers in the area. The central question seemed to be— "How could this possibly happen to a man like Bob Marsh in a company like Kramer?"

Case 9
Kramer Pharmaceuticals, Inc. (B)

In January 1979, Mr. Edward Vallery, Southern zone manager for Kramer Pharmaceuticals, Inc., was debating a problem concerning a detailer, Mr. Alexander Brooks, whose performance had slipped when he had been assigned to a new sales territory. The new assignment was part of an overall territorial realignment prescribed by the company's Salesman Redeployment Program (SRP). In line with the company's policy to avoid unnecessary dislocations and disruptions to personnel, Kramer executives were trying to enact the program as rapidly as possible, without causing undue personal hardships for the reassigned detailers.

Primary responsibility for Alexander Brooks' performance lay with his immediate supervisor, Mr. Charles Jarrell, who was the Alabama district manager. But Vallery had recently found Jarrell's work to be unsatisfactory as well. Vallery was now trying to decide whether to reassign Brooks, to leave him where he was, or to induce him to take early retirement.

KRAMER PHARMACEUTICALS

Kramer was a major company in the ethical drug industry, manufacturing a wide line of prescription drugs for the medical and dental professions. Its products were sold to hospitals and to reputable drug wholesalers and drugstores for resale by prescription. Kramer competed with such firms as Abbott, Lilly, Merck, Upjohn, and Schering. Sales in 1977 exceeded $400 million.

Kramer fielded a sales force of over 500 detailers, who called regularly on hospital personnel, doctors and dentists to inform them of the merits of the particular items in the Kramer line and to persuade them to use and prescribe Kramer drugs when treating specific ailments. A typical Kramer detailer was responsible for about 200 physicians and hospital accounts within an assigned geographical territory. The detailer was expected to make between six and nine doctor or hospital calls a day.

Copyright © 1980 by The Colgate Darden Graduate Business School Sponsors, University of Virginia. Reproduced by permission. This case was prepared by Armen J. Malikian under the supervision of Prof. Neil H. Borden, Jr.

Most Kramer detailers were pharmacy school graduates who had joined Kramer after a few years' experience as registered pharmacists in retail drugstores. Each new Kramer detailer received a month's training in product knowledge and selling (detailing) skills at the company's headquarters in Denver. In addition, both new and experienced detailers received regular on-the-job training from the 35 district managers. A Kramer detailer could expect between 10 to 15 days of field visits in a year, depending on his or her experience and performance. All Kramer representatives returned to headquarters regularly for continued training and development throughout their careers.

Kramer executives considered turnover among the sales force to be much lower than the industry average. Only about 8 percent of the detailers were lost in a given year from personal choices, discharges, deaths, and retirements. By the same token, Kramer executives considered the detailers second to none in professional competence. Approximately 60 percent of them had 10 or more years of company service; only 25 percent had fewer than 5 years of service. About 50 percent were 40 years of age or over and 25 percent were under 30.

Kramer detailers were salaried and received annual bonuses based on corporate performance. In 1978, the individual detailer's total earnings ranged from a low of $20,000 to a high of $36,000. The corporate bonus typically amounted to about 15 percent of these totals. In addition, each detailer was provided with a company automobile, generous fringe benefits, and reimbursement for all normal business expenses.

Every Kramer detailer was evaluated in terms of the sales volume produced in his or her territory and the degree of personal improvement shown in relationships with accounts. Quotas were established yearly for each of the dozen or so major product categories to stimulate proper concentration of detailing efforts. Every Kramer detailer received a formal performance evaluation from his district manager once a year and informal evaluations whenever necessary.

Most of the 35 Kramer district managers had been chosen from among the sales force for their leadership, administrative, and sales abilities. Evaluated chiefly on ability to develop personnel, each was expected to spend three to four days per week on field visits with detailers. The individual district managers reported to one of the six zone managers, who reported in turn to the sales vice president.

THE SALES REDEPLOYMENT PROGRAM

The primary purpose of SRP was to realign sales territories to reflect certain changes in the medical profession and in the pharmaceutical industry. Prior to the early 1970s, Kramer sales territories reflected the earlier patterns of a predominantly rural population and a medical profession composed primarily of general practitioners. Thus, the Kramer sales organization contained many rural territories, and the selling job was not specifically oriented toward medical specialization.

During the 60s and 70s, as the general population became more urban and suburban, the medical population tended to locate more in large population centers. Also, the proportion of general practitioners among all medical doctors declined from 75 percent to 25 percent. Physicians, including general practitioners, began to locate closer to hospitals and medical centers which had emerged as the primary sources for medical treatment.

In the profession of pharmacy the druggists' role in mixing or compounding prescriptions had decreased significantly. Trade names took on even greater importance as doctors tended to prescribe more drugs by brand rather than by generic name. In addition, pharmaceutical manufacturers introduced more and more products that, because of their short storage lives or complex techniques of administration, had to be given to patients under the specialized supervision of hospitals or medical centers.

These changing conditions prompted Kramer executives to announce SRP in 1975, although the program did not get under way to any great degree until the fall and winter of 1976–77, because company executives had decided to realign territories and to make personnel changes only when normal attrition permitted. The Alabama district was one of the first in the company to come under the program.

The SRP program was administered by a director and staff at the home office. These executives used a sales potential measure, called doctor quotient (DQ), to determine the most appropriate territory and district alignment. The SRP director and staff at headquarters assigned to each territory a DQ based not only on the number of physicians but also on the degree of medical specialization in the area, the types of specialties practiced, the number and size of hospitals and medical centers, and the size of each physician's practice. For example, a rural general practitioner might contribute a fraction of a point to a territory's DQ, while a metropolitan anesthesiologist with a large practice might contribute as much as 1.8 points. Kramer executives believed that the aggregate DQ assigned to a territory more closely reflected the area's potential prescription levels than did the sheer number of physicians.

Determining the DQs for the current territories within the six zones was only the first step in the realignment program. The SRP staff then used a linear program to determine the computerized optimal territorial alignments by weighing DQs with travel distances, call frequencies, and territorial headquarters' locations. The computer program could be adjusted to accommodate special circumstances, but such changes would produce territorial alignments that were less than theoretically optimal.

In addition to realigning territories to correspond with theoretical prescription levels, the SRP's second objective was to structure the selling effort. For example, SRP staff assigned priorities to physician accounts according to the physician's specialty and practice size. Rather than call on all physicians in rotation, detailers were required to call once a month on A-level physicians, every two months on B-level physicians, and every three to four months on C-level physicians. Also, doctors and hospitals were now given priority over pharmacies. Whereas the ideal call frequency had been five doctors and five drugstores per day, detailers were now to call on six to nine doctors and hospitals, but only two pharmacies per day. Another means of structuring the selling effort was to assign accounts to detailers according to their specializations. For example, metropolitan hospitals were now treated as complexes requiring specialized detailers for various departments.

The SRP director advised each zone manager on the computer's recommendations for the most appropriate territorial alignments. Some territories were not combined if their doctor quotients did not warrant a full-time detailer. (For example, some rural territories had comprised fewer than 100 physicians, while some city territories had comprised over 400.) The program increased the number of doctors and institutions that most detailers were responsible for. Final territorial alignments were determined jointly by the SRP director, the zone manager, and the district manager. Specific personnel assignments were made by zone managers, in consultation with their district managers.

Kramer sales executives believed that SRP would make the sales organization more responsive to its markets. But one executive outlined a few of the problems with the new system.

> All of a sudden new markets and relationships have appeared that will require new sales expertise. The young, relatively new salespeople take it well well and willingly. Some of the senior salespeople, however, do not want to change and resent it. They are upset because the company is now telling them where and how to spend their time—they're not accustomed to selling in hospitals, for instance. But if we had not instituted the program, we would need double the number of detailers to get the same job done. We've been telling them since 1975 why we need the program; now we're moving on it.

THE ALABAMA SALES DISTRICT

According to SRP studies made at headquarters, the average DQ of the 16 Alabama territories was too low. To raise the average DQ per territory, the SRP staff had recommended a reduction of one territory. Late in 1977 two detailers retired, giving the opportunity to implement this recommendation. These retirements took place in the Gadsden territory and in one of the Birmingham territories. The studies indicated that the Cullman territory with a DQ of 149 should be discontinued and reapportioned to increase the DQs of adjoining territories (see Exhibit 1). In November 1977, Vallery[1]

---

[1]Edward Vallery joined Kramer in 1966 at the age of 26. After five years as a detailer in Virginia, he was promoted to district manager in North Carolina. He became southeastern zone manager in 1976. He held a BS in Pharmacy, an MBA, and was a captain in the army reserve. As zone manager, he supervised the activities of six district managers, and reported directly to the vice president of sales.

Exhibit 1
Proposed Realignment of Alabama District by Doctor Quotient

Territory	Present DQ	Proposed DQ
Auburn	140	140
Tuscaloosa	141	141
Selma	142	142
Anniston	134	171
Florence	156	156
Huntsville	164	168
Gadsden	144	166
Cullman	149	0
Montgomery A	161	161
Montgomery B	167	167
Montgomery Hospital	248	248
Birmingham A	140	165
Birmingham B	145	165
Birmingham C	138	165
Birmingham Special	153	165
Birmingham Hospital	246	246
Total	2,568	2,568

Details of Realignment by Territory

Birmingham
      576 DQs (excluding Hospital)
   + 86 from Cullman
   ─────
      662 ÷ 4 = *average*

Gadsden
      144 DQs
   + 59 from Cullman
   ─────
      203
   ─ 37 to Anniston
   ─────
      166

Cullman
      149 DQs
   ─ 59 to Gadsden
   ─────
      90
   ─   4 to Huntsville
   ─────
      86
   ─ 86 to Birmingham (mostly to Birmingham C)
   ─────
       0

Huntsville
      164 DQs
   +   4 from Cullman
   ─────
      168

Source: Company records.

announced the discontinuance of the Cullman territory, effective January 1, 1978, and gave Alexander Brooks, the Cullman detailer, the choice of the two territories opened by the retirements. Brooks chose the more rural Gadsden over the urban district in Birmingham.

The Alabama district now comprised 15 territories as follows: three detailers called on physicians in Birmingham, one detailer called on Birmingham hospital personnel, and one detailer called on pediatricians and surgeons in Birmingham; two detailers called on physicians in Montgomery, and one detailer called on hospitals in Montgomery; and seven detailers were assigned to each of the seven rural territories. These latter were relatively large in area, and required long travel distances between calls. Each contained a minor population center such as Gadsden, with a population of

53,000. Exhibit 2 gives a map of the Alabama sales district. (Southern Alabama, not shown on this map, was part of the Mississippi district.

Vallery's current dilemma over Alexander Brooks seemed to have begun with this territorial realignment. But performance in the district as a whole had been slipping for some time and was now well below the company average. DQ measures and overall economic potential indicated that Alabama should have ranked among the top half of all districts in the company. Instead, the district was in the bottom third. The average age of Alabama detailers was 48, considerably higher than the company average, and Vallery wondered if that was not part of the problem in Alabama. But he also suspected that a larger part of the problem lay with the Alabama district manager, Mr. Charles Jarrell.

Jarrell had taken over the district in 1975 upon the retirement of James Soper, who had managed the district since 1956. Jarrell was born in 1932 and had joined Kramer in 1957, after serving in the Korean War and then

Exhibit 2
Area and Mileage Covered by Alabama District

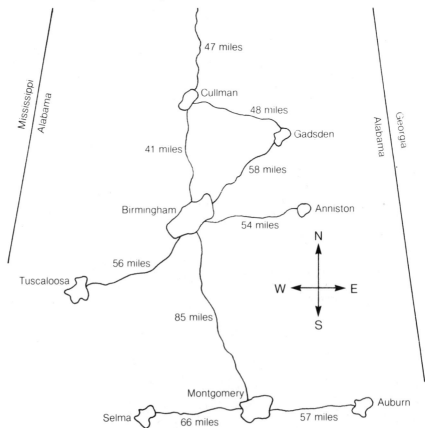

finishing pharmacy school. In addition to a BS in pharmacy, he had earned a master of commercial science degree at the evening division of the University of Alabama. Upon joining Kramer, he had served first in quality control and then had spent eight years as a detailer in the Georgia district. In 1968 he had been promoted to district manager in Mississippi, where he remained for seven years before moving to Birmingham to take over the Alabama district.

Although Kramer executives had considered Jarrell an average-to-good district manager in Mississippi, Vallery had become critical of Jarrell's performance in the Alabama district. Vallery had visited Birmingham on October 24, 1978, for a two-day review of Alabama sales and of Jarrell's own work. Vallery's follow-up letter to Jarrell included the following remarks:

Dear Charles,

After our discussions in Birmingham October 24 and 25, it seems desirable to record and confirm the conclusions reached.

First of all, the performance of the Alabama District is inadequate. Sales per detailer are lowest in the region in 9 out of 12 important product categories. Growth of the district, as measured by percent of increase in dollar purchases, is below national average. While some progress is evident in some areas, the new effect is still not satisfactory.

In short, the time for "shock therapy" is *now!* Your reference to a basic company philosophy, to wit, "Our products are our people," is apt. The facts are that one of the best ways to develop people is to demand that they always deliver their very best performance.

No one wants to be unreasonable and it is important that we avoid pettiness or meanness by insisting on a top-level performance from all personnel. Those who do not meet satisfactory levels of performance must be relieved of their responsibilities to make way for more productive personnel. This may be accomplished either through their taking advantage of acquired personnel benefits, or by our making it possible for them to direct their efforts in some other endeavor outside our company for which their talents and capabilities more effectively suit them.

It has been the acceptance of poor performance by some of the personnel in the Alabama District which accounts for the deterioration in the district's total accomplishment. As we agreed, this situation can no longer be tolerated. To this end, it was further agreed that you would spend four to five or more consecutive days with detailers whose performance is substandard. At the conclusion of this time in the field, you will conduct a realistic progress review outlining minimum acceptable objectives and establish a time when these objectives must be met. Further, you should clearly state the course of action you will take if the goals or objectives are not met in the prescribed periods of time.

Charles, you have an excellent background of experience and education. You had a good record as a District Manager in Mississippi. You have a keen mind and it does seem a shame to minimize the value of these attributes by accepting inferior performance from the men whom you manage.

MR. ALEXANDER BROOKS

One of the detailers whose performance Vallery had termed inadequate was Alexander Brooks. Jarrell had concurred with this evaluation but had suggested that Brooks be given more time to work things out.

Alec Brooks had begun his career with Kramer in 1949 as a detailer in the Alabama district, and he had been given military leave during the Korean War. Brooks held a BS in pharmacy and had completed a Dale Carnegie course in 1971. He was active in his local Elks Club and American Legion, and was a member of the Alabama Pharmacists Association. He had four children.

When offered a territory in Birmingham, he had refused and had convinced his manager that he should live in Cullman. Brooks had explained that after undergoing some harrowing experiences in the Army's Chemical Corps, he had developed a fear of gaseous pollutants and was concerned that living in Birmingham would endanger his family's health. Birmingham was heavily polluted at this time.

Cullman, population 13,000, was centrally located in the territory as it existed at that time. Cullman was not very far from the northern suburbs of Birmingham, where many of Brooks' accounts were located. Brooks subsequently resisted several more efforts made by Mr. Soper, his district manager from 1956 to 1975, to persuade him to move closer to the most active part of the market in his territory.

On several occasions, Brooks had taken it upon himself to write the company's top executives. For instance, in 1968, he wrote the president of Kramer applauding the sales vice president for having increased base salaries in a new compensation plan. Again in 1974, in response to the president's letter congratulating him on his 25 years with the company, Brooks wrote,

> Time passes all too quickly. Therefore, the most important decision a man must make is how he wants to spend his working years. Never have I felt I should have chosen to do other work, nor ever once did it occur to me to feel anything but pride in my association with Kramer. This of course has been fostered by the ethics and integrity of the men that dictate the standards and policies of the company.

Throughout his years with Soper, Brooks' performance had ranged from satisfactory to above average. In his 1974 performance appraisal, Soper commented to Brooks:

> You do an above average job in detail work, a fine job at the retail level, and you have utmost respect from physicians and druggists alike. You have not done the type of job you can do on the Prednophine.[2] This I am sure you will correct. You have come from below average to above average on all Cortoflex products and have a better increase than anyone in our district. You have a

[2] Disguised trade names.

> very creative mind, contribute most effectively to our sales meetings, and it is
> a pleasure to watch your forward progress.

These comments were typical of the appraisals that Soper had given Brooks over their 19 years' association. Brooks also held Soper in high regard. He once responded on one of his own evaluation forms:

> Although I have heard physicians and druggists tell how a district manager pressured or embarrassed a representative in their presence, no one has ever seen such tactics on the part of Mr. Soper. He is always helpful, a gentleman, and the welcome mat is always out for him. I feel pride in his supervision.

After Soper retired, Mr. Jarrell, in his first appraisal in July 1975, gave Brooks a rating of above average, complimenting him on his abilities. In July 1976, however, Brooks' rating was dropped to satisfactory without any explanation noted in the records. No further performance appraisals were filed on Brooks by Jarrell until July, 1978.

In the meantime, the SRP recommendations were being enacted. In November 1977, Brooks agreed to move from Cullman to take over the Gadsden territory, effective January 1, 1978. He received his official notice of transfer in December with a letter from Jarrell, which pointed out the company's desire to reimburse his moving and extra travel expenses coincidental to the transfer, and which set out the procedure by which Brooks was to keep a record of these expenses. Corporate staff real estate personnel estimated the value of Brooks' home at $50,000, which became the price at which the corporate real estate subsidiary would buy the home, making funds available for a new home in the new territory. This option was to be open to Brooks for 90 days from the effective date of his transfer.

At the beginning of the new year, Brooks began working the Gadsden territory. On January 15, 1978, Brooks wrote Mr. Robert Barnes, manager of corporate real estate, relating some of his problems in relocating.

> Because of a very tight housing situation in Gadsden, I'll be staying out or commuting until something becomes available. I do not intend to sell my home or start the wheels moving in any direction until I find a home to buy. Maybe with warmer weather and spring more listings will be available . . . .
>
> Also of importance is that we have a 21-year-old daughter with encephalitis. She was paralyzed two years ago and has had to be under intensive care since. We want to be very sure of a place to move into before proceeding with the disposal of our present property. I will be 56 this summer and do not want to take a mortgage at this stage of the game. I'm sure you now understand why this can't be a hasty move. We are in hopes something of our liking will turn up soon. Thus, I beg your patience and indulgence, plus luck, in finding a suitable home.

Vallery was not certain whether the plight of Alec's daughter had been previously mentioned to headquarters; there was certainly no previous written record of it. Due to the circumstances, Vallery authorized an extension of the real estate option to June 1, and Brooks was so notified by Barnes late in February. Vallery could not determine how much effort Brooks had put into finding a new home in Gadsden. But this issue seemed immaterial, for Vallery received the following note from Jarrell in late April:

> For your information you should know that Brooks' daughter has been re-admitted to a hospital in Birmingham for extensive tests. The medical people have told Alec that the prognosis is not very good.

At this point, Vallery wrote Brooks to extend his sympathies, expressing hope for the best results in the tests. In May, Barnes sent a letter to Brooks noting the problems in his family and suggesting that he take up the matter of a further extension of the real estate option with Vallery. A copy of this letter went to Vallery. Jarrell also wrote to Vallery supporting an extension of the real estate option and reporting a further deterioration in the daughter's condition. Although an extension meant that the company would continue to cover Brooks' commuting expenses to Gadsden, Vallery agreed to extend the option to August 1. Upon receipt of the second extension in early June, Brooks wrote Vallery:

> We appreciate the extensions accorded us in finding a suitable home in Gadsden. The same homes we looked at in February and March are for the greater part still for sale, but by different brokers. With the shortage of homes, prices are being kept high, and the taxes are the highest in Alabama. Trailer towns of mobile homes are sprouting up, but we have found nothing adequate for a family of six. We know that before too long our needs will be less and the square footage will not be necessary.
>
> Our second request for an extension was specifically because of the deterioration of my daughter's condition, which the doctors are now calling "grave."
>
> I am sure it must appear that we are fighting this move, but this is not true; it's the awkwardness and strain of the problem which is apparent on my family. I'm willing to stand outside expenses of travel myself, but we want to avoid buying something inadequate which will mean a move to something better after we are located in Gadsden. We have also been looking for a rental that will temporarily solve the situation.
>
> I know this has been a period of frustration for you and Mr. Jarrell as well as ourselves. But I want you to know that we're trying desperately to locate in Gadsden. Kramer has been my life and has been good to me. It has been my dedication and I want very badly to keep it this way.

Early in July 1978, in lieu of a formal performance appraisal, Brooks received from Jarrell the following note:

> Although you have not been living in your headquarters town, you have, in the past six months, made good progress in developing new business and have shown sales growth in important products. Obviously, when you live in Gadsden, your sales growth will be even greater and will be up to and over the district average.

The final extension, however, was to no avail. Brooks failed to move to Gadsden, although he continued to commute and make his daily calls. On August 5, 1978, Jarrell informed Brooks in writing, as a record of their telephone conversation, that the extension had expired, and that the company would no longer reimburse the mileage from Cullman to Gadsden or the motel and meal expenses in Gadsden. Jarrell suggested that Brooks should make inquiries into building an adequate home. A few days later, Brooks wrote Barnes to inform him that he would not be able to take up the option and would himself incur the commuting expenses. "To commute 50 miles isn't the worst thing in the world—especially since conditions are such as they are," Brooks wrote.

By the time that Vallery made his October field visit to Alabama, Brooks' sales had begun to deteriorate, and coverage of his territory appeared to Vallery to be inadequate. Jarrell suggested that Brooks should be given more time. Vallery decided to try to induce Brooks into early retirement, so that a more active detailer could take over the Gadsden territory. Vallery mentioned this idea to the sales vice president in a report that he made in early November.

> I would not want to take action at this time because of the tremendous emotional stress the Brooks family is currently subjected to. However, if the prognosis of his daughter's disease is acute, it may be terminal at any moment. As soon as feasible after this, of course, it would seem to be desirable to be in a position to offer Mr. Brooks some financial inducement to accept early retirement. He has more than enough service to qualify for early retirement. And if his income could be supplemented over a period of five years, it would bring him very close to the age where he could obtain additional benefits under the provisions of the social security laws.
>
> In spite of Mr. Brooks' announcements of wanting to work until he is 65, I do believe that there is a chance he might accept such an inducement as I mentioned above. Mr. Brooks has a number of friends in the Cullman area and several physicians and pharmacists wrote to protest his transfer to Gadsden last January.
>
> Any arrangement under which Mr. Brooks terminates his status as an active employee should be one with which he has evidenced acceptance and complete personal agreement. With Mr. Brooks' current performance, there is no doubt that a new, effective detailer would be able to produce so much more additional sales volume that it would be a worthwhile investment to induce Mr. Brooks to accept early retirement.

Any such plans, however, were set aside when Vallery was informed of the death of Brooks' daughter on November 28, 1978. The following January, Brooks addressed a letter to Kramer's president and to the sales vice president, in which he recounted in detail the sad events relating to his daughter's death, as well as the difficulties he had in finding a home in Gadsden. Brooks also questioned the closing of the Cullman territory and his transfer to Gadsden. Excerpts from his letter to the sales vice president follow:

> Enclosed is a clipping relative to the loss of our daughter this past November. Two days before Christmas three years ago she was severely stricken with

encephalitis. The doctors gave her about 18 months to live; not more than 2 years at the very most. She made it to within a few weeks of three years . . . .

I had correspondence and telephone conversations with Dr. Swenson of our research division regarding a new agent being tried on animals. I appreciated the concern of our laboratories in trying to help, but we were aware of what we were up against.

You can imagine how stunned we were a year ago Christmas to be told I would have to move to Gadsden, Alabama. This is a time when everyone in the family depends on friends for a morale boost.

I looked at many, many homes in Gadsden, but the real estate situation was and is critical because of rapid expansion of local plants. I had a choice of so-called shacks or homes too expensive, in a tax bracket $500 to $800 more per year than my present home. In other words I was faced with a cut in salary on this basis, as this is just a lateral change with no increase in compensation.

A man from Birmingham was to travel into the country to take my territory. I would be taking over a strange territory in Gadsden, but a new man hired at that time was allowed to stay in Birmingham because he didn't want to change his location.

After 28 years of loyal and enjoyable years with Kramer and at the age of 56, of the three territories involved I was the one told to move—told, not asked how this would affect the family, especially my daughter. The indifference to my problem was unbelievable.

I stopped a flood of letters to management from our customers who couldn't understand my having to move at this time. I requested them not to write as I was sure this would be resolved. My professional relationship with customers has always been excellent . . . .

The pressure was unrelenting. To find a home I had to find one especially suitable to our daughter, who naturally preferred at times to isolate herself, or a home such as ours with a gentle staircase that has two landings, making it easier for her to manipulate her way around the house. Attached is a letter telling me that as of August I had to assume a large portion of my travel expenses. This is not the empathy that one would expect after so many years of service.

My sales have always found me in the top bracket in the district. I have been on virtually every sales program, either individually or as part of a panel for many years. I have been asked many times to MC anniversary or retirement parties. I have given many talks to schools and professional groups. I am not ashamed of my record. I am sure I have only added prestige to the name Kramer.

I had thought of going to the age of 62, but now 60 seems more attractive. A move for three years doesn't seem to accomplish a great deal. It's like pushing friends and everything worthwhile one has into a hole.

With over 500 men in the sales force, I know it is a virtual impossibility to keep tabs on all individuals, but I feel that I know you well enough, and that with your time in the field you would know my feelings. It still seems to me that a simple realignment of territories can be accomplished without anyone's having to move and without loss of coverage to the areas involved.

In response to this letter, the sales vice president asked for and received from Vallery a report reviewing briefly Brooks' history with the company and details leading up to his letter. The following paragraphs concluded Vallery's report, dated January 23, 1979.

> We discontinued paying "expenses incidental to moving" on August 1, since it was apparent that he would not be moving any time soon. No further efforts were expended to get him to move or to get him to do anything other than meet his family obligations after August 1. His daughter died on November 28. Mr. Jarrell and several others attended the funeral and flowers were sent from the company. There have been no further efforts on our part to effect his move, to enable Mr. and Mrs. Brooks to overcome their grief. At this point, Mr. Brooks' "expenses incidental to moving and relocation allowance" payments totaled $4,662.70. In December, we were asked by our financial component to notify Mr. Brooks that this amount was to be added to his 1978 income and grossed up for taxes. We decided that we would prefer not to bother him with these kinds of details during the very stressful situation in which Mr. Brooks found himself, and we elected to hold this until he had overcome his grief.
>
> We have tentatively planned to approach him in February about this matter and give him any additional help that we can in relocating his family. As it now stands, he must drive in excess of 130 miles each day to work his territory.

Upon receiving the inquiry from the sales vice president, Vallery realized that the situation would have to be resolved soon. On the one hand, Vallery was tempted to turn the problem over to the sales vice president, because Brooks, as a long-service employee, would probably appeal "upstairs" any decision that he believed unfair. On the other hand, Vallery knew that the SRP had given zone managers the final say in relocations, so perhaps this decision was his own. Vallery recalled the company's official SRP policy—to move as rapidly as possible while avoiding undue personal hardships—and was uncertain how to apply it in this situation. He believed that his alternatives were (1) to force Brooks into early retirement; (2) to allow Brooks to continue to work Gadsden out of his home in Cullman and either (*a*) reimburse him for travel expenses or (*b*) require him to pay his own travel expenses; or (3) to realign the territories as they had been before January 1978, or by some scheme using the present number of detailers. Another option, of course, was to ask Jarrell to make the decision.

Part Three
The Sales Executive

The sales executive's major responsibilities are: (1) to determine the precise role that the sales force is to play in the firm's marketing strategy and (2) to design and implement a sales management system that encourages the salesman to enact that role.

DETERMINING DESIRED BEHAVIOR

Anyone who has spent time observing salesmen from different companies as they make their sales calls will appreciate that defining these activities as *selling* is a vast oversimplification. Selling is much more than merely asking for the order. The activities can range from "hand holding" to pressuring the customer to buy; from long involved negotiations with numerous customer "influentials" to door-to-door canvassing; from making highly technical presentations to sophisticated customers to haggling over price on bulk items that are purchased repeatedly. Within the same industry, salesmen selling practically identical products to similar classes of customers will exhibit different behavior. This variety of activity is, or ought to be, a function of the role assigned to the sales force within the firm's marketing strategy, not a function of how salesmen think they ought to behave. If each salesman believes that he is in business for himself, the firm will have as many marketing strategies as it has salesmen. Experienced sales executives, therefore, begin with a clear understanding of the specific desired behavior and do not sidestep this necessary analytical task by describing sales force activities in generalizations such as "they are paid to sell." Overgeneralization may cause executives to ignore sales force activities that are vital to the marketing strategy.

The first step in determining desired behavior is understanding the firm's marketing strategy. This first step is more difficult than it sounds. Sometimes the sales executive's ignorance of marketing strategy arises from his or her failure to participate with marketing executives in formulating marketing strategy. The sales executive's nonparticipation can lead to a lack of

131

understanding of how the firm has chosen to compete, lack of commitment to marketing objectives, and improper direction of field sales activities.

Sometimes the sales executives' lack of participation is caused by the formal organization itself. Reporting relationships often do not require communication between sales and marketing. Furthermore, sales and marketing personnel often have different backgrounds and personalities. Marketing executives tend to be analytical, tend to have formal educations in business administration, and tend to talk in a language of their own, using terms such as *positioning, segmentation, gross rating points,* and so on. Many sales executives, on the other hand, are people who have made their mark as salesmen, have less formal business training, and are more at ease taking a customer to lunch than analyzing quantitative data. Most firms' methods of evaluating performance reinforce these differences: marketing executives are frequently evaluated in terms of profitability and return on investment; sales executives are more frequently evaluated in terms of sales volume.

Sales executives who make the more useful contributions to strategy formulation are the ones who are familiar with marketing concepts and terminology. Some companies help sales executives to achieve this familiarity through management development programs, other firms use a career path that gives promising salesmen positions in marketing early in their careers. By the same token, some companies insist on sales experience before giving marketing executives positions of greater responsibility. It is as important for the marketing strategist to understand the realities of the marketplace as seen through the eyes of a salesman as it is for the sales executive to understand how the firm has chosen to compete.

The sales executive must also keep up with subtle shifts in marketing strategy that may affect desired sales force behavior. Nearly all companies modify their marketing strategy from year to year. Prices are changed, new dealers are added or dropped, new products are featured, new advertising campaigns are begun, and so on. Every time a company modifies its strategy, it inexorably modifies the desired behavior of the sales force. Even though these modifications are minor, over time they add up. Most marketing and sales executives, if they were to examine their marketing plans of five years ago, would be surprised at the difference between those plans and their plans for this year. Similarly, if these executives were to examine in detail what specific activities were required of the sales force five years ago, they would be surprised at the differences in today's activities.

For example, one company that made some subtle changes in its product line several years ago ended up reducing its volume with smaller customers and increasing its volume with more profitable, larger customers. As marketing's efforts toward the larger customers intensified, sales executives found themselves with obsolete call standards, badly aligned sales territories, and a sales force largely ill-equipped to explain new-product benefits to more sophisticated purchasers. Furthermore, many field sales managers were uncertain about the company's new sales emphasis and were continuing to coach and direct salesmen to call on the older, smaller accounts instead of training them to be more effective with purchasing agents. Before any policies can be instituted to encourage desired behavior, before any supervision can help the sales force perform desired behavior, the sales executive must know what that desired behavior is. If that behavior does not have a foundation in marketing strategy the company will not get to second base.

DESIGNING THE SALES MANAGEMENT SYSTEM

The sales management system is that collection of policies, procedures, and practices that encourages salesmen to carry out their role in the firm's marketing strategy. Experienced sales executives are cautious about accepting advice from outsiders on how to design a system, or how to change one. What competitors do, what prestigious firms do, what articles in learned journals suggest may not be relevant. What may be good practice for one sales force may be wrong for another. Thus, thoughtful sales executives continually ask themselves such questions as these: Are the salesmen deployed correctly? Are selection and training procedures effective? Are controls sufficient? Are salesmen being paid too little or too much? Are they adequately supervised? In short, are management policies and practices still appropriate to the selling task as we define it *today*?

Of course, a company's management policies and practices will not constitute all the influences on sales force behavior. Common sense suggests that *how well* a firm's executives implement their policies has a greater impact on personnel performance than *what* policies these executives choose to implement. And the effects of a firm's practices are often influenced by outside factors, such as industry norms or particular competitive situations.

Nevertheless, sales executives are responsible for deciding the most appropriate form of organization for their sales force, the most appropriate selection criteria, compensation plan, span of control, and so forth. The major obstacle to thinking clearly about these decisions is mythology. Webster defines *myth* as "an ill-founded belief held uncritically, especially by an interested group." A major set of sales management myths hold that certain sales management practices are associated with high performance and others with low turnover. Although the myths are legion, here are some common ones:

Salesmen work harder for straight commission.

College graduates are not interested in selling.

Salesmen are born, not made.

Any one of these conclusions may have validity in the context of the particular situation within which it originated. But the theorems do not necessarily remain valid when they are applied to other, quite different situations. The point is that "best practice" needs to be highly particularized, and particularized right down to the individual company. Mythology is no substitute for a good, hard, close look at reality.

Given a clear understanding of the firm's marketing strategy and expectations regarding the behavior of its sales force, sales executives can influence performance favorably by employing a judicious *combination* of policies and practices. To choose these policies, the executive must consider the following factors:

1. The organizational approach that best encourages the kind of sales force behavior that the marketing strategy calls for.
2. The territory assignments that provide the best strategic support—that is, the most efficient and effective market coverage.
3. The kind of salesman best suited to the company's selling task.
4. The amount and kind of initial and subsequent training that best prepares the sales force to fulfill its role in the marketing strategy.
5. The level and method of compensation that best rewards the sales force for performing its required tasks well.
6. The measures and controls that best serve to direct and monitor the desired sales force behavior.
7. The system for evaluating sales force performance that best encourages the desired performance.

It is the *combination* of policies that is important. To rely too heavily on one element of the sales management system is to depend on mythology. For example, experienced sales executives avoid placing a disproportionate emphasis on compensation plans. In effect, these sales executives have overcome the notion that "I can rely on my pay plan to get better performance." Most experienced sales executives agree that there are no magic wands. Compensation will influence sales force behavior. But compensation decisions will also have an impact on selection and training decisions. Sales executives who accept the fact that all of these decisions are highly interrelated recognize that the proper combination of policies and practices, each designed to encourage the desired behavior, produces a total effect greater than the sum of the parts.

THE ELEMENTS OF THE SALES MANAGEMENT SYSTEM

Organization and Deployment

Effective sales force administration calls for sales executives to decide what type of organization approach suits their products and markets. Should the organization be structured from the standpoint of the customer, the product line, or the geography of the market?

Sales forces are most often organized by customer groups when specialized knowledge of various businesses is an essential sales force skill. For instance, many computer manufacturers assign one group of salesmen to call on retailers, another to call on banks, another to call on utilities, and so on. Each of these customer groups has different computer requirements. The training required to understand these businesses well enough to sell computer hardware and software to them is sufficiently different to warrant separate sales groups. Similarly, sales forces are more often organized by product line when the lines are sufficiently different or complex to warrant product specialists. For instance, many manufacturers of medical equipment assign one group of salesmen to sell kidney dialysis equipment, another to sell X-ray equipment, another to sell surgical equipment, and so on. Organization by geographic boundaries most often occurs when customers are fairly homogeneous in their need for the product, when the product line is homogeneous or nontechnical, or when customers are so scattered that travel between accounts precludes efficient use of a customer or product line specialist's time.

Deployment, or territory assignment, can require a complicated set of decisions. Most sales executives strive for sales territory assignments that require a full week's workload—no more, no less. Before delineating territories that meet this goal, however, the sales executive must make judgments about the minimum account size for profitability, the optimal call frequency, and the optimal number of salesmen the firm can deploy. Often, sales executives then use computer programs to draw territory sizes, taking into account desired hours spent on each account, hours available, and geographic contiguity.

Given territories with equal workloads, however, sales executives may or may not want to make territories equal in potential. Some executives try to create territories with equal potential in order to (1) give salesmen equal earning opportunities (assuming equal competitive activity among territories) and (2) permit comparisons in performance. Other executives make some territories better than others in order to place the best salesmen with the best customers, to take advantage of sales personalities (such as "country" and "city" selling types), or to allow for promotions within grades and to create training territories for new salesmen.

The assignment of territories is one aspect of the mechanical side of sales management. Even when territories are assigned to perfection, there is no guarantee that salesmen will perform to the limit of their capability. On the other hand, if the territories are badly aligned, sales will always suffer, as some territories will be overmanned and some undermanned. Poor alignment can also cause sales force morale problems.

Selection and Training

Sales executives must decide what kind of person is best suited to the company's selling task. This decision involves determining the best sources of applicants for sales positions, the economics of poor performers and sales force turnover, the desirability of psychological testing, and the role of personal judgment in selecting salesmen. Sales executives must also decide how much and what kind of initial and continuation training their salesmen need. They must decide on the location of these training activities and the qualifications of training personnel.

Mythology can hamper the process of making good selection and training decisions. Experienced sales executives try to understand the particular requirements of the sales job, rather than seeking the "ideal sales type." The analysis behind the selection and training activities of a company can be outlined as follows.

Determine the realities of the selling task. What activities need to be performed—(trade, missionary, technical, entrepreneurial selling)? How much supervision is available? What is the risk to the company if the salesman fails to perform well? What are the travel requirements? How much liaison is required between salesmen and other company personnel? Answers to these and similar questions help sales executives appraise realistically the details of the sales job and thereby avoid the usual generalities, which provide few useful hiring guidelines.

Determine minimal prerequisites. Such things as experience, education, and other prerequisites, developed from an analysis of the realities of the job, can usually be inspected from an application form.

Determine required skills. Skills and aptitudes are often fairly easy to observe or measure. A good interviewer can evaluate a candidate's articulateness and to, a lesser degree, selling ability. Analytical skills can either be observed or measured through a variety of easy-to-administer tests.

Determine the personal qualities needed. Beyond minimum acceptable levels, personal qualities are usually hard to observe or measure. A good interviewer can evaluate a candidate's appearance and poise. Beyond these, however, identifying the degree of such qualities as judgment, maturity, motivation, leadership, character, and so forth, seem to defy both skilled interviewers and written tests (short of psychiatric diagnostic devices such as the Rorschach and Thematic Apperception Tests).

Determine whether to use more complex tests. The truly critical attributes—what you would *really* like to know about the applicants—are unmeasurable. How will customers react to them? Will they work hard? Are they dependable, honest? Will they show initiative? Two circumstances will suggest the utility of psychological testing. First, such testing is useful if a clear need exists to limit management discretion. If line managers are exercising poor judgment in their selections, the use of tests to screen out the worst of the applicants has merit. An alternative course is to have selection decisions made by a staff specialist. The obvious disadvantages in both using tests and having selection decisions made by others are that line managers lose the opportunity to develop their judgment and be accountable for their actions. (Hiring a few mistakes has the effect of making the manager much wiser much faster!) Second, testing is warranted if critical requirements are measurable. If the selling job requires a quality that can be evaluated with psychological tests, not to test for it would be foolish. Unfortunately, even these kinds of tests are usually better at predicting failure on the job than they are at predicting success.

Mythology can obscure decisions about training, by causing executives to perpetuate entrenched and outmoded programs or to subject the sales force to canned programs that bear little relationship to desired behavior. Instead, thoughtful sales executives determine what specific behavior is required and then analyze how well the salesmen—new and experienced— are equipped to exhibit that behavior. Training systems can then be designed to narrow the gap between the salesmen's capabilities and the job's demands.

Compensation

Most thoughtful sales executives agree that the objective of a good sales force compensation plan is to *reward* performance, rather than to *stimulate* it. This difference is subtle, but important. The former view suggests that *compensation is but one element* in a system of policies and management activities designed to encourage salesmen to perform well. The effectiveness of training programs, the quality of field supervision, the presence of nonfinancial forms of recognition, and many other factors that create a climate encouraging high performance all combine with the compensation plan to encourage desired behavior. On the other hand, the view that compensation plans stimulate performance can lead to overreliance on compensation, to the substitution of compensation for management. This view also overlooks the fact that people desire security, recognition, advancement, challenge, and camaraderie in their work, as well as money.

The choice of the kinds of behavior that financial compensation is to reward can be a puzzling one. On the one hand, if the firm stresses short-run goals—such as opening new accounts, pushing products with higher margins, unloading products about to be phased out, or attempting to meet time-period volume objectives—its compensation scheme is likely to include highly specific and objective criteria. On the other hand, if the firm stresses longer-term market development, has selling cycles (from initial contact to signed order) that are longer than normal accounting or performance appraisal periods, or requires tasks wherein the selling effort only indirectly produces a sale, as in some types of trade and missionary selling, the firm will probably have compensation schemes based on very general and subjective criteria.

How much to pay salesmen is another puzzling choice. A balance must usually be struck between an amount that will attract and retain good people

138

and an amount that makes economic sense to the company. Paying too little generally promotes excessive turnover; paying too much neither improves performance nor lowers turnover.[1] Within the dilemma of how much to pay are questions of the size of the pay differential among the salesmen and of whether the differential should be based on performance, merit (if it differs from performance), or seniority. Some executives approach these issues by asking the following questions: What am I willing to pay for the lowest acceptable performance, for average performance, and for outstanding performance? A graph can be constructed similar to the one below.

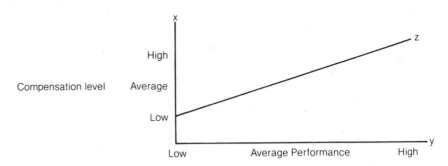

The x axis and the points high, average, and low are usually determined by the marketplace—industry norms, competitive factors, and the supply of and demand for labor. The y axis and the points low, average, and high are usually determined from an economic analysis of what the cost of selling is to the firm. The slope and shape of the line z is a function of the importance of personal selling in the marketing activity of the firm. Indeed, if the salesmen's efforts are directly related to sales volume produced, it may be possible to reward them in a linear fashion, as the solid line above indicates.

When an individual salesman's performance can be directly related to his or her sales volume, a high proportion of variable pay is warranted. This condition is most apt to be present when the selling cycle is short, when salesmen are the dominant element in the firm's marketing activity (the customer is created and maintained through the activities of the individual salesman), and when the sales force shares little responsibility with other groups within the firm for ensuring customer awareness of product benefits and satisfaction with product usage. Examples of direct relationships between sales performance and sales volume produced can be found in many areas of entrepreneurial selling, such as door-to-door selling of vacuum cleaners.

In some firms, it is difficult to relate performance to sales volume produced. Many sales require long periods of time to consummate, are the result of teamwork with other departments in the firm, and involve a variety

[1] See monograph by Derek A. Newton, "Sales Force Performance and Turnover" (Cambridge, Mass.: Marketing Science Institute, 1973).

of activities that, when performed well, eventually produce both sales and long-term relationships with customers. To evaluate salesmen's contributions to this kind of sales effort, some executives redefine performance as *merit*, a term that comprises a number of activities that *indirectly* produce sales volume. These executives attempt to evaluate salesmen according to their performance of these activities and compensate them accordingly, recognizing the dangers of subjectivity inherent in these evaluations. The nature of this kind of indirect selling, and the subjective element in appraising its performance, suggests that variable pay will be a smaller proportion of the salesman's compensation. When neither sales volume nor merit is easy to assess, some executives rely on seniority to make distinctions among pay levels. Here the pay plans contain little if any variable element.

The format of the compensation plan can be important to both the salesmen and the firm. Even a carefully designed compensation plan can overpay for unintended results, as in the case of windfall sales; can underpay, as in the case of insufficient goods because of factory shutdowns; or can reward the wrong kind of behavior, as in the case of plans that reward the short-term sale at the expense of longer-term service requirements. The best compensation plans are those that are easy for the firm to administer, readily understandable, perceived as fair by the sales force, flexible enough to withstand windfalls and catastrophes, and related to an individual's performance, whether that be sales volume or merit. In other words, the rewards should be seen as going to the deserving.

Measurement and Control

Sales executives need to measure and control both direct and indirect sales activities. Good decisions about the kinds of information to collect and disseminate are keys to success in correcting and directing sales activity and in providing feedback for the overall marketing effort of the company. Quotas and reporting systems are two important elements in measuring and controlling sales force activity.

A key question in setting quotas is whether to base the quota on historical performance or territory potential. If the quota will be used to set production schedules, historical performance is obviously the better guide. If the quotas are to be used to compare salesmen's performance, territory potential may be the better basis for the quota. If the quotas will be used to motivate salesmen, the choice between historical performance and territory potential becomes more difficult.

Quotas. An example of a two-man sales force illustrates this problem. Let us assume that the company's two sales territories are equal in potential, as determined by objective measurement, and that the two salesmen are unequal in ability, as determined by last year's sales results.

If sales quotas are based on past performances (last year's results), Mr. Strong will get a quota representing 60 percent of the company's sales objec-

Salesman	Last Year's Sales as a Percent of Total Sales	Territory Potential
Mr. Strong	60%	50%
Mr. Weak	40	50
Total	100%	100%

tive for the year. This is a tough challenge for Mr. Strong. Assuming that market share and competitive activity are equal in the two territories, Mr. Strong must operate above the potential of his territory to make his quota. By the same token, this quota is an easier task for Mr. Weak, who will be operating below the potential of his territory.

If, however, sales quotas are based on territory potential, each salesman will have the same quota. Thus, Mr. Strong will have the easier job since he can make quota by operating at a level below his ability. Mr. Weak will have the tough challenge, since to make his quota he must operate above his ability.

If a quota's objective is to stimulate performance, the choice between historical performance and territory potential as the quota's basis will depend on the individual the executive wants to stimulate. A quota biased toward experience gives the stronger individual higher goals and the weaker one lower goals. Conversely, an emphasis upon territory potential lowers the figure for the best salesmen while raising it for the weakest. If the sales executive wants to give every salesman the highest reasonable quota, then he or she must vary the formula, emphasizing experience for the best salesmen and potential for the worst. But the variations make any comparison of salesmen questionable.

In summary, quotas can have different purposes and different bases. Every quota is the result of particular management assumptions and compromises, and every quota offers a range of possible effects. It can become, therefore, a useful sales management tool when used intelligently. In setting quotas, the greatest dangers are in giving an impression of precision where none exists and in appearing arbitrary. This latter danger can be a serious threat to morale if the salesman's compensation is tied to making quota and that quota figure seems unfair.

Reporting Systems. Sales executives need to know who their salesmen are calling on and not calling on, who their customers are, who their prospects are, what products are being purchased, and what customers are doing about paying their bills. These data help executives analyze manpower needs, redesign territories, uncover training needs, set goals, control product mix, control call frequency, improve individual performance, and reduce accounts receivable and bad debts.

The use of call reports and other kinds of reporting forms allows sales executives to generate data that they may then analyze in a variety of useful ways. The following matrix illustrates some of the comparisons that may be made.

Information	By Salesman	By Company	By Sales	By Hours Spent
Customer name				
Customer class				
Equipment inventory				
Products purchased				
Date of call				
Time spent				
Purpose of call				
Demonstrations per sale				
Trials per sale				
Calls per sale				
Percent travel time				
Customer–prospect ratio				
Percent office time				
Complaints				

The accuracy of the data that sales executives can gather—particularly of the data on time spent—depends on the trust between salesmen and managers. The degree of trust depends in large measure on four factors:

1. The firm's management philosophy. Is the philosophy to help salesmen sell or to force them to sell?
2. The firm's management problems. Is it more important to monitor *company* performance or *individual* performance?
3. The firm's management policies. Do policies complement communications flow or inhibit it?
4. The firm's management style. Do executives engender cooperation or do they inhibit it?

The rewards from a good sales information system can be great, if executives' behavior can gain the cooperation of the sales force. Since the salesman's time is the critical variable, any information system should try to measure this variable. The sales manager can then help the salesman to make the best use of each working minute.

Performance Evaluation

Sales executives must be concerned about, and have a system for, evaluating their own performance and that of the individuals reporting to them. Evaluation criteria can range from pure sales volume gains to return-on-investment calculations. Evaluation systems range from the highly subjective to the totally quantitative. Sales executives must make judgments in this area, fully aware that their decisions about how people are evaluated have enormous impact on how they behave.

For many managers, conducting an annual performance appraisal with subordinates is the single most unpleasant, difficult, and generally unproductive task among their many job responsibilities. Yet many theorists claim that performance appraisal can be the single most important tool in improving subordinates' performances. Executives in many companies have come to recognize that the performance appraisal *system* itself can create enormous difficulty for the average field sales manager. For instance, consider these typical burdens placed on the manager by some performance appraisal systems:

The need to appraise performance along dimensions irrelevant to the actual requirements of the job. ("Who cares if he uses crude language occasionally? He's the best salesman I've got.")

The need to appraise personal attributes, an activity that trained psychologists have difficulty doing well. ("How do I know how 'loyal' she is to the company?")

The need to communicate these appraisals of personal traits to a potentially hostile listener. ("How do I explain my reasons for giving her a '7' on 'Exercises Good Judgment'?")

The need to conduct and communicate a comprehensive recounting of the subordinates' accomplishments in the past year and—euphemistically—his "areas for improvement." ("Do I really need to remind him how upset I was last August when he failed to get that facilities report in on time?")

Not only have these traditional appraisal systems complicated the appraisal task for the individual manager, but such formal systems have increasingly failed to meet EEOC (Equal Employment Opportunity Commission) and other fair employment guidelines, which require the use of objective performance criteria in decisions affecting promotion, transfer, training, or retention.

Thus, many companies have shifted their performance appraisal systems and philosophies in the following directions:

From a focus on personality traits to a focus on job-related behaviors and results.

From an emphasis on recounting past peccadillos to an emphasis on developing future action plans.

From viewing performance appraisal as an annual ritual to viewing appraisal as an ongoing process.

From a focus on static job descriptions to a focus on specific task requirements identified by systematic job analysis.

From a focus on evaluation to a focus on development.

From unilateral appraisals to bilateral discussions.

Case 10
Fortress Rubber Company

In June 1977, Mr. Ralph Harris, sales manager of the Fortress Rubber Company of Boston, Massachusetts, was attempting to select one candidate among three to fill an opening in his sales force. Fortress executives had for some time retained the services of a psychologist, Dr. Robert Gold, to assist them in selecting new employees. Dr. Gold's reports on these three candidates were available to Mr. Harris.

COMPANY BACKGROUND

Fortress's 1976 sales were in excess of $30 million. The company manufactured and marketed rubber and plastic electrical tapes. These tape products were sold by the present sales force of five industry specialists to utilities, industrial plants, and electricians through a network of approximately 3,000 independent distributors. These latter were serviced by 27 manufacturers' representative organizations (reps). Exhibit 1 shows a partial organization chart of the sales operation.

The industry specialist's job was to acquaint end users with the specific technical advantages of Fortress electrical tape. The specialist also had to learn each customer's splicing requirements and other technical problems to be able to develop new applications for Fortress tape. The specialist actually spent only one fourth of his or her time working directly with present or potential end users, however. Most of the specialist's time was spent working with the reps, arranging and conducting frequent regional sales meetings to pass on new information. The industry specialist also attended similar regional meetings held by the rep groups for their distributors. Typically, the specialist spent one half of his time away from the main plant in Boston.

The industry specialists were typically in their 30s and earned about $30,000 a year, on the average. All had had previous sales experience. Ac-

Exhibit 1
Sales Organization

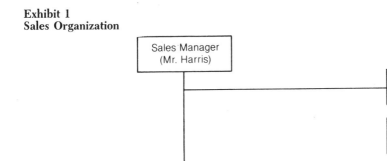

cording to company executives, the most desirable background for an industry specialist would include a college degree and selling experience. Fortress executives also looked for candidates familiar with the Fortress product line or with a group of Fortress customers. The executives preferred to hire people in their 20s or early 30s, because the work was fast-paced and required a good deal of traveling.

During the past few years, a sharp increase in business—especially in small orders—from the public utility and railroad industries led Mr. Harris to believe that his company could support a full-time specialist serving the public utilities and railroad market. This new position would free the paper industry specialist, who currently served the public utility and railroads markets, to develop the considerable potential in the paper industry.

Mr. Harris planned to have the new specialist report directly to him, as did the other industry specialists. The specialist would be based in Boston and would travel at least three fourths of the time. He would initially assist the reps by making missionary and follow-up sales calls on large-volume prospects. After two years, Mr. Harris believed, this missionary selling activity could be relaxed. The new industry specialist could then reduce the travel time and give more effort to maintaining a few key customers and guiding the reps.

This job could lead to the position of assistant sales manager to Mr. Harris, or to the position of regional sales manager, a post that Fortress sales executives planned to create within a few years to provide independent representatives and distributors with better supervision and assistance. A candidate's promotability, then, was important to Mr. Harris in determining which applicant to select.

THE SELECTION PROCEDURE

Mr. Harris and other Fortress executives were dissatisfied with interviews, resumes, and references as means of evaluating candidates. Mr. Harris felt that hiring judgments based on interviews were often subjective. While resumes provided concrete data, such information was often difficult to interpret. And Mr. Harris had never seen a negative reference. Moreover, most candidates requested that their present employers not be contacted, so Mr. Harris felt that the most pertinent information about their job histories was not available to him.

To make better hiring decisions, Fortress executives employed a psychologist, Dr. Robert Gold, to gather and assess more information about prospective employees. Dr. Gold's qualifications included a BS and an MA in psychology and sociology from Tufts University and a doctor of education degree in psychology from Boston University. He had an established practice in Brookline, Massachusetts, was on the faculty of a local college, and had done consulting work for various businesses and public school systems. Dr. Gold was a member dealing with psychological variables in normal and abnormal human functioning. Dr. Gold charged Fortress $600 per candidate. In return for this fee, Fortress executives received an interpretation of the applicant's personal history and a discussion of the applicant's qualities for the position.

Among the tests used by Dr. Gold were the following standard individually or self-administered psychological tests: Wechsler Adult Intelligence Test; Cooperative Reading Comprehension Test; FACT Arithmetic Test; FACT (verbal) Expression Test; FACT Judgment and Comprehension Test; Sales Comprehension Test; Strong Vocational Interest Test; and various projective personality tests. Dr. Gold also used special performance situations and his clinical judgment to assess other personal qualities, such as emotional stability, mental organization, resourcefulness, flexibility, tact, creativity, and motivation.

During the past several months, Mr. Harris had interviewed more than a dozen people for the position of industry specialist in the public utility and railroad industry. He had chosen three candidates to receive psychological testing. His impressions and those of other Fortress personnel are presented below, together with excerpts from the reports submitted by Dr. Gold on each of the three candidates.

MR. JOSEPH WARING

Mr. Joseph Waring had been referred to Mr. Harris by the company's largest distributor, who was enthusiastic about Mr. Waring's selling and managerial abilities. Although Mr. Waring was not actively seeking a job, he was interested enough in the opportunity at Fortress to arrange an interview.

Mr. Harris believed that Mr. Waring made a good appearance and would probably be an excellent salesman, although he tended to be "a little cocky." Mr. Waring knew Fortress's customers very well and had had experience calling on these customers, especially the larger distributors. He also responded very well to several questions on the rubber industry. Mr. Harris recalled meeting Mr. Waring at a trade show earlier in the year. They had a mutual interest in sailing, and Mr. Harris believed that he would enjoy working with Mr. Waring. The office secretarial staff was also favorably impressed with Mr. Waring.

During a luncheon with Fortress top management, Mr. Waring impressed these executives with his selling ability, but they wondered whether he had the capacity to assume a management position at a later date. This doubt was generated largely by Mr. Waring's comments about the problems of dealing with excessive paperwork.

Dr. Gold interviewed the candidate and reported the following information about Mr. Waring's background and personal history.

Mr. Waring is the youngest of four children; he has one older brother who is an engineer; his two older sisters are married. His father put himself through engineering college and owned a small company. Mr. Waring characterized his childhood as excellent, but says that he has not struggled as hard as his father did. He has been married for eight years. His wife is one year younger than he. They have a good marriage, according to him. They have three children, all boys, and there are no problems. His hobbies include boating, other water sports, hunting, fishing; his wife loves boating. He enjoys an occasional drink. He was in the army reserves for a little more than 10 years before resigning.

Mr. Waring has a long history of not applying himself, and his academic background and work history underscore this pattern. He was a fair-to-poor student in elementary and high school because, as he states, he did not "get kicked hard enough." He attended a local university for one year in the school of business administration, where he did fair work and again did not apply himself. He then moved to another local university "because of the school-work program." However, because the work program required very long hours (7 P.M. to 7 A.M., six days per week), he decided to leave school and work full time at this job (a governmental project). He remained in this position for four years. His work was largely technical, but he also did some work for the purchasing director. He felt that he was getting good experience, but the job offered little chance for advancement. He then worked for two years with a builder-real estate agent. Mr. Waring ran a branch office and supervised construction as well as property sales. He left because he preferred "more technical sales and getting around more." He then sold diesel motors for a large distributor for a year, but "the money wasn't there." His most recent job has been with a small company where he began as a product manager, then became an assistant sales manager, and then assistant to the vice president. He was let go along with many other administrative personnel during a company shake-up. He has been without work since last April. He does not need to make a hasty decision about future employment, because he runs a tow-boat business with his brother. He stated that he is interested in Fortress Rubber Company, but is considering another job as well.

After reviewing the test results, Dr. Gold submitted his assessment of Mr. Waring's abilities and potential.

> Mr. Waring's reaction to the assessment procedures was only fair. He complained about the tests to my assistant and also told her that he does not like to take tests. He has a tendency to talk a lot, but he expresses himself well and has a good sense of humor. He was well groomed. He had previously taken an extensive battery of tests for a position with a company in the South. However, only one of the present tests was a repetition.
>
> Mr. Waring has excellent practical reasoning ability. He approaches problems well and thinks before he acts, and his thinking is organized, flexible, and resourceful. He is above average in judgment and comprehension. His vocational preferences and work history show strength in business and sales. He performed at an average level in reading comprehension, arithmetic ability, and sales comprehension. He shows fairly good tact and fair creativity.
>
> In general, Mr. Waring has good basic intelligence. However, he apparently has not done too much with it. He lacks self-discipline and the ability to apply himself consistently to the tasks at hand. This lackadaisical quality naturally prevents him from fully using his talents. He also has difficulty making decisions; he procrastinates and avoids responsibility. Thus he needs outside direction, but he has good interpersonal relationships with authority figures, so he is able to take direction well. He is emotionally immature but basically stable. He shows real warmth in his relationship with other people.

MR. ROBERT MANN

Mr. Mann was referred to Mr. Harris by a well-known personnel placement agency in downtown Boston. The agency was especially enthusiastic about Mr. Mann and convinced Mr. Harris to come to their offices to interview him. After a very successful interview, Mr. Harris invited Mr. Mann to Fortress to visit the plant and meet other company executives. Mr. Harris enjoyed Mr. Mann's sense of humor and believed that the candidate would work out well at Fortress Rubber. Mr. Harris especially liked Mr. Mann's initiative in working his way through college and his general desire to move ahead. Mr. Harris also believed that Mr. Mann knew as much about Fortress's customers and products as some of the present salespeople—his answers to questions on technical aspects of electrical tape were flawless. His previous experience seemed to be ideal preparation for the job.

During a luncheon with Fortress top management Mr. Mann made a favorable impression and managed to keep the conversation relaxed with several humorous stories. The only reservations that the executives later expressed stemmed from some dissatisfaction with Mr. Mann's appearance and from some perplexity over his lack of progress in his career.

Dr. Gold's interview with Mr. Mann produced the following information about his personal history and background.

> He grew up in greater Boston and attended public schools. He stated that his marks in high school were below average: he had good marks in English and social sciences, but passed by "the skin of my teeth" in other subjects. He

also stated that he did very well in grammar school. After high school he worked for a year as a clerk with a supermarket chain; he felt that he was good with the customers. He then had a one-year enlistment in the navy, where he went to electronics school and college preparatory school, and achieved the rank of seaman second class. He hated the navy because "they wouldn't let you think." He then spent one year at a junior college where he did very well; following that he spent three years at a local university and finished with a low B average. While at college, he worked a full night shift to pay for his college career; he lost a great deal of weight because of overwork.

Following college he worked for the telephone company for three years as a communications consultant; he left for more money. He then spent seven years with a local company. He trained inside for a year, then moved to outside sales; he left for more money. He then spent seven weeks with a small company, and left because it was an "impossible situation and the wrong place"; apparently, the job had been misrepresented to him, for it turned out to require 100 percent travel. He then worked for a large company in selling for two years; he was asked to resign, and he is not sure why. He is presently selling computer instrumentation; he is leaving because "every order I have sold has been fouled up. The quality is adequate, but I am used to selling the best." He also says, "There is no place to go." He is currently interested in more responsibility. He feels that he is a proven salesman; he is now looking to make his last move. He feels that Fortress is a dynamic company, and says "I have a real solid feeling" toward Fortress.

Mr. Mann is the second of four boys; he characterizes his childhood as happy. As a child he had a temper, and he correlates his red hair with his fighting to defend himself. Both of his parents are living; his father has been a jobber and real estate salesman; his brothers are in sales and marketing. Mr. Mann has been married 12 years. His wife graduated from high school and secretarial school. They have three children: the oldest is a girl who is a good student, the next is a boy who is bright but has no motivation for school, and the youngest is a girl who is not yet school age. He states that he has an excellent marriage and that his physical and emotional health are excellent. However, he also mentions that he had an ulcer at age 30, due to tension. He states that his mother is an intense person. He feels that he has done a good job as a father in that he represents security to his children; that is, he does not vary in his discipline. His hobbies are fixing up around the house, reading, coaching a Little League team, and fishing; he and his wife do not go out very much. He is a beer drinker—three or four in the evening, and apparently each evening. He has an occasional highball with customers, but says that he does not like to drink at noon.

After reviewing Mr. Mann's test results, Dr. Gold submitted the following report.

Mr. Mann reacted well to the assessment procedures. He was alert, fresh, and motivated both at the beginning and at the close of the evaluation sessions. He stated that he had taken such tests on two previous occasions. He makes a good impression, speaks well, but he has a tendency to wander from the subject under discussion. He appeared to be tense, and he exhibited a constant small-amplitude hand tremor; the tremor did not vary even under stress. He has a ruddy complexion, and he chain-smokes cigarettes. He tended to try to impress me about the way he handles himself in selling situations.

Mr. Mann's vocational preferences suit him for work in sales, personnel, and public administration. Mr. Mann's mental performance was very high in nearly all the skill and ability tests: basic intelligence, reading, verbal expression, business judgment, and sales comprehension. Only in mathematical ability is he merely a little above average. He is very good in practical and abstract reasoning. He catches on quickly, thinks clearly, and approaches problems well in that he figures things out before responding. He does not become rattled under pressure. He also performed well in the tests for mental organization, resourcefulness, flexibility, tact, and creativity.

Emotionally, he is expansive, optimistic, motivated, and generally mature. He also has a good sense of humor. However, all of the personality tests showed that he is defensive—he held back in his responses, making them difficult to analyze. His defensiveness suggests that he may be hiding some emotional problem. He is tense, has constant hand tremors, and had an ulcer at age 30. Clinically, I wonder if he may be an alcoholic. An essential feature of his overall performance was his excellent stamina. We can infer that this stamina would carry over to the work situation. On the other hand, if he does in fact have some basic emotional disturbance and/or is an alcoholic, he would not be able to cover up his problems indefinitely.

MR. JOHN TURNER

The third candidate, Mr. John Turner, was referred to Mr. Harris by a small suburban sales placement agency. Mr. Harris went to the agency for a morning of interviews, and Mr. Turner was by far the best of the candidates. He was currently working for an ashtray manufacturer, and during the interview he showed his selling process by picking up the table ashtray and selling it to Mr. Harris. He cleverly described product differences among various ashtrays and convincingly demonstrated superior features of a particular style of ashtray. His relaxed and positive manner during this sales presentation convinced Mr. Harris of his natural sales ability. Mr. Turner also mentioned that he had traveled to Europe some years ago, working his way across the Continent. He had also worked his way through college. This initiative also impressed Mr. Harris, and he invited Mr. Turner to Fortress Rubber for a plant tour.

Mr. Turner arrived early, in a Mercedes-Benz, and accidentally met Mr. Harris in the parking lot. They walked into the Fortress building together. Mr. Turner made a noticeable impression on the Fortress Rubber Company receptionist and displayed a very winning manner to Mr. Harris's office staff. As a result, the entire office staff believed that Mr. Turner would make a valuable and personable contribution to the sales force.

Although Mr. Turner knew very little about Fortress Rubber's products or customers, he assured Mr. Harris that he would have little difficulty in this respect. Mr. Turner said that it had taken him less than two months to learn the specifics in his present position.

At a luncheon with company top executives, he impressed the group so favorably that they later decided that he didn't have to be assessed psychologically. However, Mr. Harris had already scheduled the evaluation procedure and could not cancel it.

Dr. Gold reported the following information about Mr. Turner's personal history.

Mr. Turner has one younger brother who sells calculators. He described his family as close, saying that "we have a great deal of fun together." He characterized his father as strong-willed, but said that he and his brother "survived" and now have a good relationship with him. Mr. Turner has been seeing a woman for two and one half years and he plans to marry her. She has a staff position at a university. He has not been engaged previously. His hobbies are skiing, scuba diving, and tennis. He describes himself as having been a "hard drinker" while in the service, but he has cut down a great deal since then; he now rarely drinks during the week.

He lived in many parts of the country while he was growing up, because his father was a salesman. He describes himself as an erratic student in the various public schools that he attended. He went to prep school for three years, where his performance was also erratic; at one point he won a prize for raising his average more than any other student in the space of one year. He then went to college for one year with the hopes of studying to be an industrial salesman, but found engineering courses uninteresting. He left college to join the Marine Corps, where he remained for two years, elevating himself to private first class. He then attended a business college here in Massachusetts. He said that the courses made sense to him and he did well the first year, although his grades went down the second year. Following his junior year, he left to tour Europe for six months. He states that he always worked during his schooling, primarily cutting trees on a contract basis. He stresses his need for money and his desire for the "finer things in life," and the fact is that he did make good money. When he returned to school, he achieved average grades.

After graduation he worked for a brokerage firm in New York for 20 months. Because he still wanted to do institutional sales he left the brokerage firm and went to work for his father as a manufacturer's representative. He left this job after three and one half years because the "rep business folded" (apparently only for him, not for his father). He then did not like the work because, as he says, "you had to be less than honest in getting in to see a person" and "you had to wrench the customer's money away from other things he wanted to spend it on." Thus, he says, "I could only go so far and not quite far enough to close the sale." He left the job after six months.

He has been looking for a new position for more than a month now, but says that he is not looking too actively because he wants to make sure that he is going into the right thing. He went to a prominent national personnel counseling firm for evaluation. He was told that he should aim for management through sales and marketing. He has found that he should stick to selling, and to tangible products. He states that he has had a couple of "interesting offers," but that he is favorably disposed toward Fortress. He feels that he is too "fidgety" to take an office job at this time. He also states that his value is a little higher than most companies are willing to pay for.

After testing Mr. Turner, Dr. Gold submitted the following assessment of the candidate's strengths and weaknesses.

Mr. Turner's reaction to the assessment procedures was fairly good at the outset. Initially, he seemed quite alert, peppy, interested. He showed a good command of the English language and generally spoke well, except that he tended to ramble and his explanations were not always to the point. He displayed a fairly good sense of humor and was at times quite definitely flip. However, about two thirds of the way through the tests and interviews he began to wilt. He was visibly tired and was comparatively unkempt in appearance and demeanor. It appeared that he had put up a front at the beginning of the assessment, but had lost it by the end. He stated that he had not previously taken so extensive a battery of tests.

In general, the test results showed that Mr. Turner has quite good basic intelligence and other abilities. His test scores were very high in intelligence, in verbal expression and reading ability, and in judgment and comprehension, although his sales comprehension per se was well below average. His vocational preference is for work requiring verbal expression.

Analysis of his intellectual behavior shows that he has excellent practical and abstract reasoning abilities. He thinks well on his feet and was not visibly bothered by pressure; he did not become rattled when he was obviously having difficulty with a task. He was methodical in his approach to problems, yet his thinking was resourceful, flexible, and creative. However, his performance was sometimes erratic, probably due to periodic lapses of interest. His performance was relatively weaker on tasks calling for immediate effort.

Emotionally, Mr. Turner is immature: egotistical, selfish, and spoiled. He seems to have little emotional interaction with others, although he presents himself well in interpersonal encounters. He projects a need for nurturance from father-figures. He avoids responsibility and decision making, although he can evaluate situations quite well up to the point of making decisions. He is a talker rather than a doer. His behavior is generally erratic, and there seems to be no stable pattern to his life.

CONCLUSION

Mr. Harris wanted to add the needed sales support as soon as possible, and he did not believe that further searching would glean any better candidate than these. Thus, he now had to decide which of the three men would be the best addition to his sales force.

Case 11
Morrison Publishing Company

Peter Wimsey, sales manager for *Nurse's Journal*, was reviewing the resume of Dorothy Sayer (Exhibit 1) and wondering if he should hire Dottie as an advertising sales representative. John Scott, *Nurse's* western sales rep, had known Dottie for several years, and he had urged her to look into taking over his job, as he was leaving.

Nurse's Journal was one of several medical journals published by Morrison Publishing Company. Company headquarters were in New Jersey, but the company maintained a sales office in Chicago for the western sales representatives of its various publications. *Nurse's* western sales territory consisted of 26 states and brought in a million dollars a year in advertising. The job required extensive travel; each sales representative was expected to visit each major account four to five times a year. The accounts that carried advertising in *Nurse's* varied from drug companies to hospitals. Usually men were hired who had previous selling experience because Morrison did not have a sales-training program. Morrison executives had never hired a woman to take over an established territory.

Peter had interviewed Dottie intensively and she had been very open in her answers. As a result he had a detailed picture of Dottie's life and her previous experience. Some of her responses are given below.

"I lived in Minneapolis, Minnesota, with my mother while I grew up. I had three father-figures: my next door neighbor, my godfather, and my uncle. My brother was 12 years older than I and had gone to college and then joined the marines. After leaving the service he had gone into sales and has been very successful.

"My father had been interested in agribusiness. During the 1920s he established a chain of food stores and had become affiliated with Swift as a buyer. My mother was 15 or 16 years younger than my father when they were married. I was five when he died, but he left us comfortably off.

"My mother has been successful. She went to work when I was in seventh or eighth grade. I had been her whole world until then. My mother worked

154

Exhibit 1
Resume of Dorothy M. Sayer

SAYER, Dorothy M., 600 North McClug Street, Chicago, Illinois 60611.
EMPLOYMENT HISTORY:
1975 to present: Advertising Manager, M/C Division, Sulver-Mond, Inc.,
Deerplain, Ill.
Responsible for budget, planning and execution of advertising, sales promotion of
maternal products in accordance with market plan. Direct advertising agency in
producting materials.

1973 to 1975: Assistant Advertising Manager, Haffor, Inc.,
Hospital Products Division, Chicago, Illinois.
Responsible for budget, planning and execution of advertising and sales promotion for three major product centers. Copy writing, creative concept, media planning as well as direction of graphics and print suppliers to complete projects.

1970 to 1973: Production Manager, BV Publishing Division, Continental
Communications Company, St. Paul, Minnesota.
Responsible for scheduling production of 15 publications (monthlies) from initial
typeset to printing, binding, and mailing. Also responsible for ad scheduling
within each issue. Interface with editorial, ad sales, production, and printing
departments. Total accountability for physical production of each issue.

1968 to 1970: Advertising Production Manager, Medical Publications, Empire
Publishing Company, St. Paul, Minnesota.
Responsible for layout and paste-up of four medical journals produced monthly.
Interface with medical associations and with editorial departments and production
and printing departments within company.

EDUCATIONAL HISTORY:
1964 to 1968: B.A., Political Science/Journalism, University of Minnesota,
Minneapolis, Minnesota.

part-time for a couple of years, until she was offered a full-time job buying
books for the University of Minnesota.

"I was never told that there were things I could not do because I was
female. When I played store as a child I was always the merchant, and my
childhood dream was to run a gas station when I grew up. I never heard the
excuse that "you can't do that because you're a girl," and I was encouraged
by my family to become an attorney.

"I attended parochial schools and found a lot of love and support there.
My confidence comes from my experience in school. I was in the top 10
percent of my class of 200, and I was the person everyone tried to beat at
grades.

"My high school was a private day-school for girls. I was placed into a
college preparatory program. I had good teachers and all the basic studies,
but my math had fallen behind because the new math techniques had just
begun to be taught when I entered high school and no one had been
equipped to teach them. I took math for three years and biology and chemistry for two years. Chemistry was a disaster for me, but I liked English. One

of my teachers, Sister Saint Mary, pushed her students very hard in English and I was pleased with my ability in the field. A complete understanding of English is important because it is the basis of communication.

"I always had a weight problem, but because the women I knew in high school had gone out as a group I never noticed being overweight. I was a good student because there had not been much else to do. When I went to the university, however, I found that I could be good friends with men. It was then I realized I was not all that bad and began to lose weight.

"I never thought about what kind of job I wanted after college, but I had always planned on college. I went to the University of Minnesota. From eighth grade on I wanted to be an attorney. Minnesota, which had a strong political science department, offered two programs leading to a law degree. One program was a prelaw and law degree combination which allowed completion of law school in two years. The other program was a normal four years of liberal arts undergraduate work and three years of law school. I opted for the second program.

"I wanted and needed a secular education but I was not sure I was ready for the change. The year I enrolled at the university another 9,000 people had done the same thing. My freshman year was difficult because I had to get acclimated to the large classes. I had an edge over the other students because of my strong educational background. I enrolled in psychology, sociology, and political science courses. Unfortunately, I contracted mono during the spring quarter and was forced to drop out, but I made up the credits later and graduated with my class.

"The next few years went quickly for me. When I was a sophomore, I still thought law school was possible. I particularly enjoyed my junior and senior years. My favorite courses were constitutional law and civil liberties. I liked reading the cases assigned in civil liberties and enjoyed doing the briefs. As an outlet for my interest in English, I minored in journalism. I enjoyed serving as a member of the board of governors of the student union. A good friend of mine was editor of the school paper.

"My senior year I found that I was not interested in attending law school for three years, and I was glad I had taken the liberal arts program: it had provided a good background. I graduated with a 3.1 grade point average. I thought that the world was just waiting for college graduates. I thought that I and all my fellow students were going to be able to go out and find excellent jobs because we were all members of the blessed generation and all of us knew we were management material. It took me two months to find my first job.

"The job I found was at an old-fashioned letterpress publishing company, Empire Publishing. Everyone was well over 50. I found, after four years of college, that I had not been trained in anything. My starting salary was $4,800 per year and I was glad to have it. I loved my title of advertising production manager. My job was to keep track of orders and papers, and I dealt with the agencies' and accounts' advertising problems. It was a golden opportunity for me to learn publishing and learn to get along with people.

Empire had had a union shop and I learned very early on how to work with the men. Mother had always believed that 'you could get more with honey than with vinegar,' and I found out she was right.

"I worked with a woman named Maria Morano who had been a journalism graduate. Maria had started out as a cub reporter for the *Omaha Times* and she had been a very good reporter. Maria was a neat, attractive, confident lady. Most men were intimidated by Maria, but I thought she was terrific.

"It was sad that Empire ran down because of a lack of care from top management. By the time I left I had become known as the 'gal in the medical field' because I had been putting all the medical books together. I did not want to leave, but I wanted more experience and money.

"Maria had moved to Continental Communications; she had been made associate editor of *Snowmobile*. *Snowmobile* began just at the boom in snowmobiles, it had been the right thing at the right time—a publisher's and salesman's dream, at least for a few years. Maria had helped open the door for me at Continental.

"Continental needed people to work on *Snowmobile*. It was a modern, clean, and highly successful publisher and an offset printer. Most everyone in the office was under 40; in short, it was the opposite of Empire. Continental was publicly owned, but everyone knew everyone else who worked there.

"Since I was only 24, Continental had not wanted to give me the title of production manager. I hated to lose the title. I was given the job of putting ads for *Snowmobile* together. The magazine had a 50 percent editorial to advertising mix; normally, the mix for most publications is 60 percent editorial to 40 percent advertising. I organized the ads by press time so that there was the most effective matching of color, layout, etc. I did most of the work alone; my boss had a drinking problem and I wound up covering for him. He was in his middle 40s. A year after I joined he was retired.

"When I started I was not given an office. I ended up with a desk between two secretaries. As I was in a new position, no one knew where to put me. The secretaries were my age, and I started out at the same rate of pay, $500 per month. Continental had two payrolls that had come out at different times, administrative and nonadministrative payroll. I reported to the man above my boss. I was pleased about that because I felt the higher up I reported the better.

"My situation in the office had begun to improve shortly after I went to work. At the end of my six-month review I brought up my seating location, but it took longer than that to change. I was given, however, more responsibility and put on the administrative payroll, much to the chagrin of the secretaries. Later, I was given an office built especially for me and the job I was doing. I had done some of the design work for the office, so my office had a central location relative to all the other *Snowmobile* offices and I enjoyed working in it.

"There were 14 or 15 books of *Snowmobile* to be put out each 12 months.

All of the staff traveled to snowmobile races and shows. They had all received *Snowmobile* outfits and I informally did their public relations work from their hospitality suite when everyone else had been out getting stories. The secretaries had been upset that I was traveling and that they didn't. The politics in the office had been such eventually that they traveled, too. Although I did not get along with the secretaries, I felt that I could depend on the printing foremen and they had worked hard for me. I shared my jokes with them. They told me I should have been in show business.

"I left Continental when I broke my engagement, because my ex-fiancé made it impossible for me to stay in Minneapolis. He was constantly harassing me. He followed me when I was out with friends, called constantly at work, and simply sat outside my house at all hours of the day and night. I looked for a job in Atlanta, but the pay scales were too low. I stopped in Chicago to visit some cousins and they suggested that I call a friend who had an employment search firm. I called, and it turned out that there was a position available at Haffor, Inc.

"Haffor hired me as an assistant advertising manager at $12,000 a year. I had done editorial writing before, but had never done copy work, so I felt that the job was a huge step forward. My boss, Fred Arbuthnot, was not very personable; he was a 'wet fish.' He was not moving any higher in the organization, but I thought that the job was an opportunity for me to broaden myself. My job was the only management slot with a woman in it; the only other woman executive was in government contracts and customer services.

"I was lonely in Chicago and found it hard to adjust to so many new things at once. I had been out of work for six months. When I first took the job, I felt I was not able to communicate with anyone. I went to the personnel department and talked with the man who had interviewed me. I enjoyed the interview and felt that the man gave me some helpful advice. He said my feelings were a reaction to my uncle's death that summer. But it seemed to me that because the woman I had replaced had been a 'people eater,' people expected me to be one, too. Once I got that perception straightened out, I became more effective at my job and was much happier.

"Haffor was in the process of being bought out by Linner, Inc., and there was a good deal of anxiety around the office. Linner was known to be pretty ruthless in cutting out deadwood. After the purchase Linner decided to move the office to Boston; only 50 people were asked to make the move and I was one of them. My boss, Fred, was asked to move, but he decided against going. I felt that if he did not move I could take over his job. I already controlled the budget and the marketing plan. I wanted to plan the journals that Haffor was going to use and to schedule the media buying.

"I was furious to discover that I was the last person to find out Fred had changed his mind and decided to go to Boston. I told Fred that he should have informed me first. I felt, however, that I should have been able to anticipate that he would change his mind, because I have never known him to be able to make a decision. But I had felt he would not want to take the pressure that Linner put on its divisions. I felt that unless I was able to get a promotion out of the move, there was not much point in going. I had just gotten settled in Chicago, and since I was not able to get Fred's job there was not much glamour to moving.

"Haffor was the one place I worked where I had a problem getting along with a co-worker, Scott Walters, a Harvard MBA. He was an assistant product manager, bright, attractive, and articulate, but he belonged in academia. He tried, but he could not apply all his theories to the practical world. He thought that I was the token, and he was very condescending. He and I were the same age, but he acted as though he knew everything there was to know about marketing. He and I were working on a product promotion project and he fell very far behind. He then began to sabotage my work to save his ass. I became so angry I wanted everyone to know just how incompetent Scott was.

"At a meeting to decide responsibilities, Fred took me off the project. At a sales meeting after I had been taken off the project, management had found out that no one had wanted *me* off the project, and what a bad job Scott had been doing. As a result of his work, Scott was fired.

"Shortly after the Linner purchase was announced, Sulver-Mond called me. After a series of interviews, I was hired to take over the advertising manager's position in the maternal products division. The position had been held by a man who had been a good industry-friend of mine and who had recommended me for the job. I was made responsible for the development and completion of sales detail work, promotions, and advertising. My advertising budget was about half a million dollars and my starting salary was $18,500. I worked with an ad agency in southern New Jersey and I felt I had become more of a manager than ever before. I had a good relationship with the agency, but I felt the contract had been given through friendship rather than merit. I had done a lot of traveling on the job. Sulver launched a new product and I found the product introduction fun, in spite of the fact that promotional activities were kept to a minimum.

"The company was very bottom-line-oriented; the goal had been to keep up the 20 percent growth rate, and I did not always agree with the way they did it. To me it seemed that people got carried away with their educations; I had been one of a very few people in management who did not have an MBA. Sulver had developed a much more sophisticated marketing approach than Haffor, but I felt that each of their approaches accomplished basically the same thing.

"I feel that it has been a long 10 months at Sulver. Everyone is concerned with their own asses. My boss, Phillip Storey, has no people sense and he does not know how to delegate work. I have never had a pay review, although company policy dictates a pay review every six months. Whenever I have made an appointment to get a review, Phillip has inevitably broken it."

Case 12
Gateway Corporation

Early in 1977, Mr. Brian St. Clair, president of the Gateway Corporation of Joplin, Missouri, was reviewing alternate proposals for the company's sales training program. Recently, the corporation had grown rapidly and its sales force had been expanded. Mr. St. Clair believed that expansion had been at the expense of adequate training and supervision, the lack of which had led to considerable sales force turnover. Because the company was currently making substantial changes in its formal organization, St. Clair believed that now was the proper time to increase the amount and quality of initial training, for both salespeople and sales managers.

COMPANY BACKGROUND

The Gateway Corporation designed, developed, and marketed more than 7,000 high-quality products used to maintain and repair machines, vehicles, and buildings. The products were manufactured to Gateway's specifications by more than 400 different manufacturers and were sold under the Gateway brand name. The company's suppliers, in conjunction with Gateway engineers, performed applied research to develop new or improved products or to help solve particular problems of Gateway's customers. Gateway's replacement products were often of higher quality than those found in the original equipment. In 1976 company sales were in excess of $50 million, and net earnings were in excess of $3 million. The average margin after sales commissions on Gateway products was 28 percent.

Gateway was organized into three operating divisions. *The Metal Division* supplied industrial fasteners, including cap, set, and sheet metal screws; hex, lock, and speed nuts; flat, lock, and finishing washers; carriage, machine, and stove bolts; cotter pins; rivets; brass fittings; and many other kinds of fasteners for standard or special applications. *The Welding Division* marketed industrial welding alloys, including special alloy electrodes and

Copyright © 1980 by the President and Fellows of Harvard College. Reproduced by permission. This case was prepared by George W. Scott, Jr., under the supervision of Derek A. Newton.

rods, fluxes, solders, and welding adhesives. *The Electrical Division* distributed products for maintenance of electrical systems, including electrical terminals, connectors, wire terminals, wire, and insulating and sealing tapes.

MARKET AND COMPETITION

According to a recent survey by a trade magazine, annual maintenance expenditures of industrial plants were $40 billion and of nonmanufacturing enterprises, $20 billion. Gateway's competition in the maintenance supply business was highly fragmented and varied greatly in intensity from area to area. Hundreds of firms manufactured commodity-grade products and distributed them regionally, either directly or to hardware or mill supply houses. Although a few firms competed directly with Gateway nationwide, most of these firms considered their maintenance products as adjuncts to other major product lines. These firms competed primarily on price. Gateway officials said that few companies competing directly with Gateway had as broad a product line or used as direct a selling strategy.

THE SALES FORCE

Gateway employed 350 independent sales agents, each of whom specialized in selling the products of a single division. (An organization chart of Gateway's sales force is shown in Exhibit 1.) As of December 1976, the

Exhibit 1
Sales Management Organization

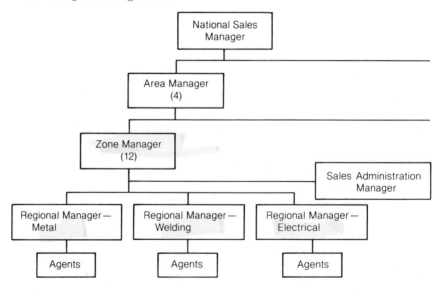

Metals Division had 194 agents; Electrical, 70; and Welding, 102. Each salesman's efforts were oriented to a specialist likely to use and order maintenance products—electricians, auto mechanics, welders, and custodians, for example. The agents were expected to help their clients solve specific maintenance problems as well as help them manage inventories.

Each agent was assigned to an exclusive territory for his or her product line. The Boston zone, for example, included 63 such territories in New England and upstate New York. These territories were distributed among the divisions as follows: Metal, 23; Welding, 19; and Electrical, 21. To make all territories equal in potential, territories were delineated on the basis of industrial purchasing activity. Because of the company's rapid expansion, boundaries were constantly fluctuating, and the number of territories had increased 30 percent per year for the past few years. In the Boston zone, for example, about seven new agents were hired per month, and an average of 20 territories were vacant. Agent turnover varied among the product lines, however. The Welding Division, requiring the most technical competence from the agent, had the lowest turnover rate; the Metal Division had the highest.

As agents, Gateway salespeople were not considered employees, but independent businessmen. Agents were paid a straight commission that averaged 23 percent of gross sales. The average size of a customer order was about $150; most ranged from $100 to $400. To earn $20,000 a year, an agent needed average monthly sales of $7,500. Agents received no fringe benefits, except for group rates on hospitalization insurance, nor were they reimbursed for expenses, such as transportation, phone calls, and souvenirs given to customers as part of the sales presentation. Frequent sales contests, usually timed for seasonal slack periods and for the fiscal year-end, had an impressive impact on sales.

About 20 percent of the agents grossed more than $40,000 a year. According to some executives, many agents who reached $20,000 to $30,000 annually pegged their output at this level by working only their best accounts and by shortening their workweeks to three or four days.

SALES SUPERVISION

Each agent was expected to contact his or her regional manager by phone at least once a week. Once every month or two, the regional manager accompanied each agent on calls. Each day the agent mailed orders to the nearest Gateway warehouse and called reports to the zone office.

Each agent was given monthly and yearly goals for his or her territory. Regional managers based these goals on the territory's past and projected sales, and on the manager's assessment of the agent's ability. Many senior executives believed that the agents should be given greater incentive to meet these sales goals, but the agents' independent status prevented managers from using quotas in a bona fide control system. Senior executives had experimented with salaries and drawing accounts, but these alternatives had been no more successful than straight commission compensation.

Regional managers comprised the first level of sales supervision. Of the 36 regional managers (RMs), 14 were company-employed, and the remainder were agents with supervisory responsibilities. The company-employed RMs, all with college degrees, helped to train new agents and were expected to move into positions of greater responsibility with Gateway. They earned salaries plus bonuses based on their agents' commissions. Company-employed RMs earned $25,000 to $30,000 per year. Agent RMs spent only half their time supervising other agents; they spent the rest of their time working their own territories. For supervisory work, agent RMs received a per diem based on their average commissions; for sales, they were paid straight commission.

Sales administration managers (SAMs) were salaried staff, each reporting to one of 12 zone managers. SAMs handled routine administrative problems for their zone managers, but spent about 80 percent of their time screening and hiring new sales agents. SAMs were evaluated largely on their abilities to staff open territories with good agents. SAMs, like company-employed RMs, were college-educated and were considered to be in training for more responsible managerial positions in sales or marketing. The newly hired employee with managerial potential usually began as a SAM or company-employed RM.

The *zone manager* was in charge of all agents in his or her geographic

Exhibit 2
Planned New Sales Management Organization

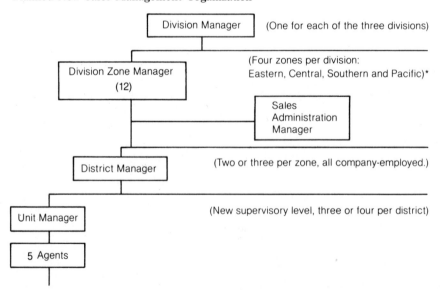

*Zone offices would remain in the same 12 cities. Each division would therefore have its zone office facilities separate from the zone offices of the other two divisions.

area, as well as sales volume, goal setting, and implementation of the sales programs received from company headquarters. Most zone managers spent a great deal of time on the road working with their regional managers. Zone managers received salaries plus bonuses based on Gateway's profits and on the performance within their individual zones. Zone managers earned between $30,000 and $40,000 a year.

Each of the 12 zone managers reported to one of four area managers who were responsible for sales performance in their respective areas. These area managers set sales goals, hired new managers, and supervised and evaluated all sales personnel in their respective areas.

By the end of 1978, Gateway executives planned to increase the ratio of field supervisors to agents from the current 1:10 to 1:5. The company had recently begun selecting and training a new level of supervisors, to be called *unit managers*. (Exhibit 2 shows the proposed 1978 organization chart.)

PERSONAL SELLING ACTIVITY

Predominant in Gateway's merchandising was the "structured presentation." All new agents and many experienced ones relied heavily on this presentation when working with new prospects. The approach structured the sale into four phases. The first, or *qualification*, phase involved telephoning the prospective account, determining the proper person to see, and arranging an appointment. Quite often this phase of the sale was the most difficult one for the new agent. The proper person to see was hard to determine in advance and hard to pin down for an appointment. After a brief interview, the first contact frequently passed the buck, forcing the new agent to locate someone else within the organization with authority to buy. The qualification phase was time-consuming also because most of Gateway's prospects were small firms located in the heavily industrialized part of the city; consequently many were hidden away in small alleys or otherwise nearly inaccessible places. Prospects not culled from past or current account records or from the Yellow Pages were often approached directly without previous appointment from the agent's noticing shop or store signs.

The second, or *souvenir*, phase was designed to break the customer's initial resistance during the first sales interview and give the agent a favorable climate for the presentation itself. Souvenirs such as pen knives or ballpoint pens were commonly used in industrial selling, regardless of the company's size or reputation. Gateway executives felt that the souvenir was a valuable device for opening the sales conversation, and experienced agents testified that Gateway's souvenirs were as good or better than those distributed by competitors.

During the third, or *presentation*, phase, the agent used the two large books he carried with him as sales aids. The first was the display book, which the agent opened in front of the prospect. Using a pencil as a pointer, the agent read each word aloud to the prospect. This part of the presentation took about ten minutes. It provided information about Gateway, called attention to the prospect's need for high quality in whatever product line the agent represented, and described the features of that particular Gateway product line. If the customer interrupted the presentation to ask a question about the product, the agent turned to the technical release section in the second of his two books, the price book, and read a more expansive treatment of the product. The agent then returned to the display book and completed his verbatim presentation.

To supplement the printed sales material, most agents used demonstrations. For instance, a small cap screw could be a crucial part of a customer's equipment. A screw with a broken head or stripped threads could cause severe damage or downtime to, say, a tumbling cylinder in a laundry, a sand and gravel truck, or a lathe in a machine shop. Using material available in the prospect's shop, a Metal Division agent could demonstrate the superiority of Gateway cap screws by placing one in a vise along with a standard cap screw, using a wrench to twist off the head of the standard cap screw, and then asking the customer to twist off the head of the Gateway cap screw. Most customers were impressed with these demonstrations.

In the final phase, the *close*, the agent turned to the prospect and asked for his participation. A Metal Division agent, for instance, would say, "What kinds and sizes do you use the most?" This question usually prompted some resistance on the part of the customer, such as the question "How much do these things cost?" The agent would respond by turning back into the display book and rereading the section on "Insignificance of Cost."

Once the Metal Division agent had elicited from the prospect three or four frequently used sizes of an item, he asked, "How about sending you a box of each?" He wrote the order up, and dealt with any further customer resistance by referring to the appropriate text in either the display book or the price book.

According to company executives, once a customer used Gateway products, selling further orders was no problem, as long as the account was serviced properly. On subsequent calls, the structured presentation was used only to introduce new items in the line and to explain packaged assortments. During follow-up calls, agents tried to expand the customer's use of Gateway products.

Once a customer had had experience with a Gateway product and became used to seeing the Gateway agent, the agent attempted to persuade the customer to buy a variety of items by offering to give the customer a storage bin with compartments labeled according to the customer's instructions. The customer could then be encouraged to buy an assortment of needed products from Gateway. Gateway personnel had carefully studied product use in relation to various types of businesses and could predict with a high degree of accuracy the amount of each item that a customer would need in a month. The customer was protected from being overstocked in any one item by a policy allowing customers to return items for credit on subsequent orders. Initial assortments for fasteners, for example, were usually priced from $200 to $400. Once the bins were in place, the agent visited the customer monthly, checked the stock levels in the various compartments of the bin, wrote up the order, and asked for the customer's signature.

AGENT SELECTION

Selecting and training new agents consumed a considerable amount of time and effort on the part of field sales managers. Selection began with placement of a "blind" advertisement in a local newspaper within the territory to be filled. Gateway was not identified in the ad because company executives did not wish the Gateway name to appear too frequently in the *Help Wanted* section. Copy for a typical ad is shown in Exhibit 3. When a potential agent telephoned to indicate his or her interest, the interviewer, usually the SAM, immediately conducted a structured three-minute interview. The SAM described the company and the sales job, and then determined the applicant's previous selling experience and his or her interest in commission selling. If these responses were favorable, the SAM set up a personal interview.

When the applicant arrived for the interview, he or she was given an application form and a package of literature. Once the application was completed, the SAM made a 20-minute structured presentation (*Career Opportunities with Gateway*), demonstrated the display book used in the structured sales presentation, and secured the applicant's reactions. Next, the SAM asked questions about the applicant's responses to the application form, to encourage the applicant to talk about his or her previous experience. When the interview was concluded, the SAM decided whether or not to hire the applicant.

Exhibit 3

SALES

Exceptional Opportunity

Multidivision industrial maintenance manufacturer has an opening in the _____ area for a career salesman, who is determined to make 1977 the beginning of a rewarding lifetime career.

Our salesmen sell the highest quality lines to the vast industrial maintenance market. They enjoy fully protected territories, frequent repeat business, and a liberal draw plus the highest commission rate in the industry.

Our men are trained thoroughly by successful salesmen, and are provided with back-up in the field to ensure immediate earnings. No overnight travel required. There are tremendous opportunities for advancement within the company.

Can you qualify? If you have had industrial selling experience or a related selling background, call COLLECT:

To help evaluate the candidate's suitability, the SAM used a set of criteria concerning the candidate's background, education, experience, and character (see Exhibit 4 for a complete list of these criteria). Adherence to these job specifications was not always strict, partly because of the lack of any known correlation between background and success, and partly because of the pressure to fill territories. Usually, no aptitude tests were given, nor was the applicant interviewed by other supervisory or management personnel prior to hiring. As company executives recognized, a great deal depended upon the personal judgment of the SAM.

Exhibit 4
Independent Agent—Metal Division, Ideal Job Specifications

Factor	Specification
Age	27–42
Marital status	Married with two or more dependents
Residence	Homeowner; lived two or more years in sales territory
Car	Late model car; collision and comprehensive insurance
Telephone	Have telephone
Education	At least high school graduate
Business experience	Has following of our type of accounts; and experience with fleet, contractor, or industrial field; commission experience
Product knowledge	Familiar with parts and hardware—their application to trucks, trailers, heavy equipment, industrial machinery, and other industrial applications
Job stability	Not more than three jobs in last five years
Employment record	Now employed; not out of steady work more than a few weeks in the last three years
Financial	Bondable, able to carry on first few months of training when earnings may be low
Physical	Good health and physical condition; no apparent physical defects; neat appearance
Travel	Willing to travel as necessary
Personality	Speaks well; capable to making friends easily; warm personality
Ambition	Success-minded; strong motivation for high income; interested in lifetime career in repeat-type sales
Reading ability	Should be able to read aloud effectively

The costs of the selection process were those incurred for newspaper advertising, about $1,600 per month per zone, and for interviewing. Since each prospective agent was usually interviewed in his or her home city, the cost of interviewing included the travel expenses of the SAM or company-employed RM. On the average, each zone had personnel taking 15 such trips each month. The out-of-pocket cost of a trip was estimated at $100, excluding salaries. The cost to put a new agent into the Gateway record system was about $60. Approximately 60 pounds of sales equipment was air-mailed to each new agent's home at an average cost of $60.

AGENT TRAINING

The formal training program for new agents comprised four days' instruction from a company-employed RM at the zone office. Each day's instruction lasted from 8 A.M. to 8 P.M. The RM delivered lectures prepared by headquarters staff and also conducted frequent role-playing sessions. The lectures were designed to familiarize the agent with the company, the structured presentation, and the mechanical aspects of ordering and expediting. The role-playing sessions were intended to convince the agent of the value of the structured presentation and to give the agent confidence in his or her ability to use this tool effectively. Other lectures were given separately for each product line, as necessary.

The costs of the training program included the agent's travel and living expenses (about $150), the RM's expenses (about $12 per day), and the RM's salary during the four-day period. The agent received no compensation other than expenses.

Following the formal instruction, the agent returned to his or her territory, spending the first two days in the field with the supervisor. After this period, the supervisor "revisited" the new agent for two days every other week, until the manager was either confident of the new agent's ability, or aware that failure would be inevitable.

Company executives believed that the agent's first 12 weeks were critical. The structured presentation was designed to provide all the product knowledge and selling skills required for survival of this period. While the agent was developing his selling skills, he or she was encouraged to call upon the small to medium inactive accounts in his territory. According to company executives, the chances of a new agent's mishandling an account were greater in the early stages, and large accounts generally required skill and persistance to gain interviews with the influential decision makers. Active accounts also generally required greater familiarity with the Gateway system and more skill and self-confidence than was usually possessed by a new agent.

During the early days in the new territory, the new agent's compensation from commissions could be quite low, both because of the type of account he or she was calling upon and because of the time lag in the company's accounting procedures. To counter this problem, the new agent was paid a weekly advance. After six weeks, the agent was placed on straight commission and paid semimonthly. During the time of low income, the agent was furnished with souvenirs. After six weeks, he or she paid into an escrow account a deposit on souvenirs and on sales aids, at a rate of no greater than 10 percent of his earned commissions. The cost to the agent of a typical souvenir was 30 cents. Sales aids for Metal Division products, for example, cost the agent $900 per year.

Executives maintained that a good agent needed four to six months in the territory to develop a base of steady customers. A recent company study of the average monthly sales of agents who had been with Gateway less than 12 weeks indicated that the average business written by a new agent was $1,600 a month. To make $20,000 per year, the agent would have to increase his orders by about $6,000 per month.

ALTERNATIVE TRAINING PROGRAMS

Termination losses were presently estimated at about $1,800 per month per zone. These losses included the costs of sales aids lost or redeemed, and souvenirs not paid for by departing agents. Although Gateway executives realized that changing the training program could not solve the turnover problem, some believed that a centralized program run by highly trained, permanent staff could do much to alleviate turnover. Other executives believed that intensifying the present training at zone offices would sufficiently improve the agents' skills. Both groups agreed, however, that the new program should include three phases: an agent basic school, field revisits, and an agent advance school.

The agent basic school would teach the four basic steps of the sale and outline the basic skills required for working a territory. The program would also describe career opportunities at Gateway. If the present localized training system were retained, these agent basic schools would be taught by certified field managers, those whose past records at agent training indicated that they were the best teachers in the zone. These teachers would use lectures and participatory devices, such as quizzes, verbal drills, role-playing sessions, and competitions. Each zone headquarters would have training facilities. The frequency of the schools would depend on the flow of new agents into the zone.

The field revisit phase would be essentially the same as the current schedule of field visits. However, executives believed that the visits would become more helpful to agents as their managers learned new methods of field coaching and counseling at the new field manager training programs, which would begin in 1978.

The agent advanced training would be done in a series of three or four schools, each covering advanced techniques in several of the following areas:

1. The four basic steps of the sale, especially the qualification and close.
2. Second, third, and ensuing calls.
3. Customer objections.
4. Customer inventory management.
5. Selling to purchasing agents and personnel other than maintenance supervisors.
6. Paperwork: sales orders, daily call sheets.

These schools would also increase agents' familiarity with Gateway products and their applications, as well as develop their enthusiasm for careers with

Exhibit 5
Economics of Centralized Training

Current zone training cost per man
    Agent expenses... $150
    Trainer expenses (RM)—4 days 48
    Trainer salary (RM)—4 days................................. 320

      Total .... $518 per man

Centralized training cost per man
    Assume: Additional $400 per agent in expenses
               3 full-time instructors @ $24,000 a year
               10 men hired per month per zone = 1,440 trainees
               3 division schools per month
    Assume: Agent expenses (1,440 × $550) = $792,000
    Assume: Trainer expenses (3 × $24,000) = $ 72,000
                                      $864,000 ÷ 1,440
                           = $600 per man

Gateway. Instruction methods would be similar to those used in basic schools, although more time would be spent in group discussions, to allow agents to share their selling experience. The schools would be held about six weeks apart, to allow agents to practice new skills and to allow time for field visits. If an agent needed more help in a particular area, he or she could repeat one or more schools.

Some executives believed that the three-phase program should be centralized rather than duplicated in each zone. They felt that formal training was a specialized job that could best be done by experts. Such instructors could use specialized training aids, such as films, programmed texts, and cases, which zone managers would rarely have the facilities or expertise to use. A centralized program would also give agents the opportunity to tour Gateway facilities and learn the company's climate. The zone office, some executives believed, did not offer the proper atmosphere to impress new employees with the organization's quality and resources.

To justify centralization in economic terms, one executive attempted to show that the cost of transporting the new agent to Joplin, the logical spot for centralized training, plus the fixed cost of a permanent staff and increased investment in training aids, would be close to the total cost of using RMs in the zone offices. Exhibit 5 gives his calculation of the economics of centralized training.

CONCLUSION

As Mr. St. Clair looked over the alternate proposals, he wondered whether his executives had raised all the proper questions. He felt that the structured presentation was basic to the issue of how the training was to be accomplished. He was particularly concerned with the future of this selling method, a method that had brought so much success to the company in the past. He also recognized that the new sales force organization, to be implemented by the end of 1978, would increase the ratio of field supervisors to agents. This change would affect his decision on the form, content, and location of agent training.

Case 13
Mid-American Supply Company

Mr. Spencer Hartley, general manager of Mid-American Supply Company (Masco) of Kenosha, Wisconsin, was reviewing the details of three sales force compensation plans. Plan 1, the current plan, paid a bonus annually to those sales personnel whose individual sales exceeded a quota based on the previous year's sales. Plan 2, a proposal submitted by a division manager, would pay commission and bonus if monthly sales targets were met. Plan 3, a proposal submitted by the director of marketing, would pay commission and bonus if product line targets were met. These plans, described in more detail below, were of great interest to Mr. Hartley in his search for a way to encourage his outside sales force to perform more effectively under current conditions of limited supervision.

COMPANY BACKGROUND

Masco, a large regional distributor of industrial machine tools, represented the product lines of several major manufacturers. The company's sales volume last year exceeded $17 million. The company's product line comprised approximately 30,000 items which, for accounting purposes, were divided into four groups: cutting tools, which included drills, reamers, milling tools and saw blades (about 30 percent of company sales); fasteners, which included all sorts of nuts, bolts, screws, and washers (40 percent); portable electric tools for industrial use, such as power drills and power saws (15 percent); and light metalworking machinery, such as small lathes (15 percent).

With the exception of fasteners—relatively undifferentiated products sold on a price basis—Masco carried only high-quality lines which carried a high margin to Masco. The amount and type of selling effort varied among the other three groups: cutting tools required a great deal of effort to justify the higher cost in terms of longer life; portable electric tools, made by a single manufacturer, were heavily advertised and Masco was the exclusive *industrial* distributor within its trading areas; metalworking machinery, well-known lines but not heavily promoted, often required extensive and highly competitive selling against other distributors carrying the same or similar lines. Typical prices ranged from $1 a gross on certain kinds of fasteners to 25 cents for a twist drill, $99.50 for an electric power drill and $2,000 for a small lathe. An average individual customer order was approximately $150.

Unlike most of its competitors, Masco did *not* sell to both jobbers and end-users, but chose to concentrate on larger end-users exclusively. Smaller customers who desired to purchase products carried by Masco on an exclusive basis were serviced either by the customer walking into a Masco showroom or by a Masco salesman making a prearranged call.

The company was organized into four geographical divisions, each representing a major Masco trading area: Kenosha, Milwaukee, Chicago, and St. Louis.

Each division had a showroom and a warehouse and was headed by a division manager who supervised all company personnel—warehouse, clerical, and sales—assigned to his division. The St. Louis division was typical. It served about 800 accounts in the 400-square-mile St. Louis area. Only about half of these accounts were considered to be "active"; that is, had purchased something from Masco during the last six months. Approximately one half the active accounts accounted for approximately three fourths of the division's sales volume. The division manager had reporting to him 7 outside salesmen, 2 counter salesmen, and 20 warehouse and clerical workers. Of the seven outside salesmen, two had been with the company over 10 years, two had been there over 5 years, and three were relatively new. Less than 20 percent of the division manager's time was spent in direct supervision of his outside salesmen. Each outside salesman was responsible for specific accounts within a geographic territory. The two counter salesmen served the walk-in traffic in the showroom and were considered as trainees for an outside territory when the occasion should arise.[1]

THE OUTSIDE SALES FORCE

Masco executives viewed the job of the outside salesman as involving much more than just selling. His basic responsibility was to maintain and increase sales to current high-volume industrial end-user customers and to prospect for new ones. His specific responsibilities included achieving personal sales goals, promoting and selling all company sales programs to his customers, maintaining a high degree of product knowledge and the ability to demonstrate all products, controlling travel and personal expenses, and

---

[1] Each of the four divisions currently employed two counter salesmen. In addition to the 7 outside salesmen in St. Louis, Masco employed 6 in Kenosha, 8 in Milwaukee, and 10 in Chicago.

organizing call activity so as to maintain the highest rate of selling efficiency at the lowest cost to the company. Masco salesmen were required to adhere strictly to company price lists; the only concessions allowed customers were volume discounts and credit extended over the normal 2 percent 10/net 30 terms.

The typical outside salesman averaged five sales calls per day and spent about 20 percent of his time prospecting for new business. A typical sales territory had approximately 25 major accounts which produced 75 percent of the territory's sales volume; another 75 or so accounts produced the remainder. The outside salesman was expected to see every active account at least once every five or six weeks. Territories were designed to comprise approximately 100 geographically contiguous accounts. An effort was made to make all territories roughly equal in sales potential.

Although territories were seldom physically realigned, accounts were occasionally reassigned; e.g., when an account relocated or added a branch. Whereas salesmen wanted to follow their accounts, particularly those they had converted from prospective to actual, company executives wanted to avoid inefficient routing. The division manager was given authority to transfer accounts within his division. Mr. Hartley, to whom the four division managers reported, adjudicated account transfers between divisions, an even more infrequent occurrence.

The typical Masco salesman was between 35 and 40 years of age, was married, owned his own home, and had two or three children. The average level of education among the sales force was equivalent to two years of college.

Because all Masco outside salesmen had had counter experience, formal sales training was nonexistent except for occasional "seminars" which emphasized the technical aspects of the product lines rather than selling techniques. Each outside salesman had a sales handbook which included sections on company policy; details of the product lines; operating policies; descriptions of Masco marketing support facilities, such as advertising; and a detailed outline of the outside salesman's authority and responsibility.

Every two weeks each outside salesman submitted his planned itinerary for the next two weeks to his division manager. The itinerary was planned by account, and included the purpose of each call. In addition, each outside salesman was required to submit a weekly sales and prospect call report.

In October of each year, each division manager was expected to prepare an evaluation sheet for each of his salesmen and to review each evaluation with the person rated. One copy of the evaluation was forwarded to Mr. Hartley, one was given to the salesman, and one was kept by the division manager.[2]

Counter salesmen were paid a straight salary of $12,000 a year to start.

---

[2]The factors, rated on a scale of 1–poor to 5–excellent, were: cooperation, enthusiasm, initiative, dependability, judgment, appearance, product knowledge, customer relations, work organization, and expense control.

Outside salesmen earned from $16,000 to $24,000 in salary annually, were reimbursed for normal business and automobile expenses, and could receive as much as 50 percent of their salary in an annual bonus. This bonus was calculated by taking 90 percent of the salesman's previous year's sales as his quota and paying him 1 percent of his salary for each 1 percent he was over quota, to a maximum of 50 percent. Thus, if a salesman sold 120 percent of his quota, and his base salary was $20,000, his annual bonus would be $4,000. Although the quota was apportioned by product group, the achievement of product quotas was not considered in determining the bonus payments.

TWO COMPENSATION PLAN PROPOSALS

The director of marketing, Mr. Stanley James, was required to submit annually to Mr. Hartley, a fiscal plan. An important part of this plan was the sales forecast, by product line, prepared from economic indicators, such as forecasts of industrial production and other regional and national economic data. Sales of each territory were then forecasted based on their share of Masco's market as a whole. These territory percentages were derived from information in industry journals and indices of local area marketing activities, such as the Rand McNally figures. Experience had proved these data to be highly accurate. Thus, if Masco sales were forecasted to be $18 million, and if a given territory were forecasted to represent 4 percent of the Masco market, that territory forecast would be 4 percent of $18 million, or $720,000. Territory forecasts were further divided into fiscal quarters, into months, and by product line. Each outside salesman received a monthly report showing him his dollar orders by product line, his potential by product line, and the variance of his orders from his potential. These territory forecasts were *not* currently used, however, in determining salesmen's bonuses. As mentioned above, salesmen's quotas were based on prior year's actual results.

One of the division managers wanted to take advantage of the forecast data prepared by the director of marketing by substituting for the current quota—90 percent of last year's sales—a quota based on the forecasted figures, and pay commissions and bonuses more frequently than once a year. His idea involved:

1. Continue to administer salesmen's salaries as is, i.e., award raises on qualitative merit factors, such as those included in the evaluation form.
2. Pay commission monthly equal to .5 percent of monthly sales if monthly sales exceed monthly territory forecast.
3. Pay bonus quarterly equal to 4 percent of all sales in excess of quarterly territory forecast.

According to the proponent of this plan:

It would stop giving a free ride to our weak salesmen who are getting a bonus for doing a few percent better than the lousy job they did last year. And it would keep *every*body hustling *every* month.

Mr. James, the director of marketing, agreed that the forecast data would be an improvement over what he called "the ratchet effect" of historical quotas. His idea, however, was to reward salesmen for selling the profitable or harder-to-sell items. Accordingly, he suggested the following:

1. Continue to administer salesmen's salaries as is, i.e., award raises on qualitative merit factors, such as those included in the evaluation form.
2. Pay commission quarterly equal to

    .5 percent on all cutting tool sales
    .2 percent on all fastener sales
    .3 percent on all portable electric tool sales
    .4 percent on all machinery sales

    if the quarterly territory forecast *for all four product groups* is made or exceeded. All four territory product sales forecasts must be made or exceeded before any commission payment is made.
3. Pay bonus annually equal to 4 percent of all sales in excess of the sum of the four annual territory product group forecasts. All four territory product sales forecasts need *not* be made to earn this bonus as long as the sum of the four is exceeded.

According to Mr. James:

> My plan rewards the profitable sale and the salesman who is selling what we want him to sell. Since the company makes more money from machinery and cutting tool sales, my plan won't cost as much.

To help him decide among the current compensation plan and the two proposals, Mr. Hartley prepared Exhibit 1, which compares the financial impact of the proposals on Parsons, who ranked 10th in sales volume last year with sales of $628,100, and on Smith, who ranked 20th in sales volume last year with sales of $518,000. Parsons earned $21,000 in salary and $2,730 in bonus last year; Smith earned $19,000 in salary and $3,230 in bonus.

Exhibit 1
Financial Impact of Compensation Plans

Salesman: Parsons

	Sales		Plan 2		Plan 3				
	Forecast ($000)	Actual ($000)	Monthly Commission at .5 percent	Quarterly Bonus at 4.0 percent	Cutting Tool Commission at .5 percent	Fastener Commission at .2 percent	Portable Tool Commission at .3 percent	Machinery Commission at .4 percent	Annual Bonus at 4.0 percent
January	$ 52.2	$ 52.4	$262						
February	50.0	57.6	288						
March	66.0	40.2	0						
quarterly total	168.2	150.2		$ 0	$ 0	$ 0	$ 0	$ 0	
April	59.2	49.4	0						
May	41.4	41.2	0						
June	53.2	53.4	267						
quarterly total	153.8	144.0		0	0	0	0	0	
July	49.4	48.4	0						
August	53.2	55.6	278						
September	41.6	48.8	244						
quarterly total	144.2	152.8		344	0	0	0	0	
October	47.4	52.6	263						
November	51.2	62.0	310						
December	49.2	66.4	332						
quarterly total	147.8	181.0		1,328	272	149	81	107	
year total	$614.0	$628.0	$2,244	$1,672	$272	$149	$81	$107	$560

Compensation	(Current) Plan 1	Plan 2	Plan 3
Salary	$21,000	$21,000	$21,000
Commission	0	2,244	609
Bonus	2,730	1,672	560
Total	$23,730	$24,916	$22,169

Salesman: Smith

| | Sales | | Plan 2 | | Plan 3 | | | | |
	Forecast ($000)	Actual ($000)	Monthly Commission at .5 percent	Quarterly Bonus at 4.0 percent	Cutting Tool Commission at .5 percent	Fastener Commission at .2 percent	Portable Tool Commission at .3 percent	Machinery Commission at .4 percent	Annual Bonus at 4.0 percent
January	$ 48.0	$ 49.8	$249						
February	46.5	50.2	251						
March	61.4	56.5			—	—	—	—	
quarterly total	155.9	156.5		$24	$0	$0	$0	$0	
April	55.2	40.3							
May	38.4	36.2							
June	49.4	40.7			—	—	—	—	
quarterly total	143.0	117.2		0	0	0	0	0	
July	45.8	43.1							
August	49.4	42.7							
September	38.7	35.7			—	—	—	—	
quarterly total	133.9	121.5		0	0	0	0	0	
October	44.0	35.8							
November	47.5	40.0	235						
December	45.7	47.0			—	—	—	—	
quarterly total	137.2	122.8			0	0	0	0	
year total	$570.0	$518.0	$735	$24	$0	$0	$0	$0	$0

Compensation

	(Current) Plan 1	Plan 2	Plan 3
Salary	$19,000	$19,000	$19,000
Commission	0	735	0
Bonus	3,230	24	0
Total	$22,230	$19,759	$19,000

Case 14
Austin Fibre Corporation

Early in February 1973, executives of the Austin Fibre Corporation of Chicago, Illinois, were discussing some proposals to modify the company's sales force compensation plan. The discussion had been prompted by the recent broadening of the product line and by widespread disenchantment with the current compensation plan, a straight salary system with an annual bonus set by means of subjective evaluations. Furthermore, Austin executives had recently reorganized the sales force and the marketing department. They believed that, if changes in compensation were to be made, now was the most appropriate time to make them. Accordingly, they wished to present the details of any new plan to the sales force at the annual sales conference scheduled for later that month.

COMPANY AND INDUSTRY BACKGROUND

Austin produced synthetic fibres, yarns, and fabrics. The company was founded in 1955 to serve the carpet manufacturing industry in new-product research and development. Subsequent to its founding, the firm made several major breakthroughs in fibre technology and production. These advances enabled Austin to become a significant supplier of carpeting materials and also to make competitive entries into related fields.

Austin's three major product lines were synthetic carpet fibres, yarns, and industrial fabrics. Its synthetic carpet fibres (monofilament) were used by leading carpet mills to produce both tufted and needle-punch carpets for industrial and residential carpeting. In synthetic yarns, the company manufactured a complete range of multifilament and ribbon styles for a variety of applications, including webbing for aluminum lawn furniture, grilles on high-fidelity speakers, and automobile seatcovers. In industrial fabrics, the company manufactured a material used as bagging for seeds, beans, fertilizer, minerals, and similar products, and also used to make tents, swimming pool covers, and tarpaulins.

The Carpet Market

Until the 1970s the dominant material used in carpeting was natural fibre, mainly wool and cotton. During the 1960s, synthetic fibres began to take a larger share of the market. In the belief that the cost of wool and cotton would continue to rise, and that the carpet industry would continue its rapid growth rate, Austin and its competitors moved quickly to increase their capacities for manufacturing synthetic fibre. In 1971 the synthetic fibre industry was operating at capacity. Using 1971s capacities as a base of 100, Austin officials calculated that they had increased plant capacity to 150 by the end of 1972. Planned commitments to additional machines would place this figure at 250 by the end of 1973 and 300 by the end of 1974. (There were also planned increases in fibre capacity to serve Austin's needs in yarn and fabric.) Selected market estimates, forecasts, and sales data for carpet fibres and other Austin products are given in Exhibit 1. Most carpet fibre customers (with a few notable exceptions) were located in the South.

Exhibit 1
Selected Market Estimates and Forecasts

	1971	1972	1973	1974	1975
Carpeting (million square yards):					
Estimated total market	550.0	680.0	775.0	868.0	971.0
Estimated natural fibres* ..	337.0	320.0	318.0	304.0	291.0
Estimated synthetic fibres..	213.0	360.0	457.0	564.0	680.0
Austin sales	47.0	72.0	117.0†	140.0†	157.0†
Austin share of total (percent).............	8.5	10.6	15.0	16.1	16.2
Austin share of synthetic (percent).............	22.1	20.0	25.6	24.8	23.0
Yarn (million pounds):					
Austin sales	6.2	6.4	7.2†	7.7†	8.3†
Industrial Fabric (million square yards):					
Estimated total market	n.a.	120.0	130.0	140.0	150.0
Austin sales		2.0	9.2†	27.0†	37.0†
Austin share of market (percent).............			7.9	20.0	25.0
Austin Sales Volume ($000):					
Carpet Fibres ....$ 9,822‡		$14,408‡	$18,500†	$25,800†	$34,300†
Yarn .... 4,015‡		4,385‡	5,300†	5,700†	6,000†
Industrial fabric		285‡	1,200†	3,500†	4,700†
Total $13,837		$19,051	$25,000	$35,000	$45,000

* Square-yard equivalents of pounds.
† Forecast.
‡ Actual.
Source: Company data.

The Yarn Market

Because of the many potential applications for synthetic yarn, company executives could not estimate potential sales volume or Austin's share of the synthetic yarn market. Company executives believed that Austin's sales were limited only by its ability to create customers and by available machine time. Currently, the company's backlog of firm orders extended into the middle of 1973. What little data there were indicated to company executives that Austin enjoyed perhaps 5 percent of the total applicable market for synthetic yarns in 1972, with an estimated 20 percent of the grille cloth market, 30 percent of the automobile seatcover market, and 20 percent of the market for lawn furniture webbing. Many of Austin's potential yarn customers were located near Chicago or other Midwest cities.

The Industrial Fabric Market

Because executives had waited to develop a truly superior product, the firm was late in entering the industrial fabric market. Austin fabric products were introduced during the last quarter of 1971. Demand for this material was so great in 1972 that the company was able to sell all of its limited production. There was no discernible geographic pattern among potential fabric customers.

Because monofilament fibre was the base material for both yarn and fabric, companies competing in any one of the above markets tended to compete in the others as well. Austin executives estimated that competitive pressure from overcapacity could become intense by the end of 1973. Their estimates of domestic manufacturing capacity for the major firms in the synthetic fibre industry indicated a 1973 equivalent capacity of 650 million square yards for carpeting, compared to a projected consumption of 457 million square yards.[1] Company executives ranked Austin fifth among its competitors in manufacturing capacity and estimated that the largest firm in the synthetic fibre industry deployed four times Austin's capacity to the manufacture of carpet fibre.

AUSTIN'S MARKETING ACTIVITIES

Austin was organized into four departments: marketing, finance and administration, operations, and research and development. Each department was headed by a vice president who reported to the company president. Three of the departments employed fewer than 30 people; operations employed more than 200.

Reporting to the vice president for marketing were a customer service

[1] Fibre and yarn was sold by the pound. The square-yard figures were based on pound equivalents. Industrial fabric was sold by the square yard.

manager, a sales manager, and three product development managers (one for carpet fibres, one for yarns, and one for industrial fabric).

The *customer service manager* handled telephone contacts with customers, solving customers' billing and delivery problems and their easier technical problems. He or she also served as an inside salesman, referring sales leads and requests for product information to the appropriate salesmen. These inside sales activities, however, were always credited to the salesman assigned to the account.

The *sales manager* developed sales plans by product, territory, and account, and also directed the sales force. The current sales manager had been promoted to his present position in January 1972, after two years as an Austin salesman. He was 32, a college graduate, and he earned about $25,000 a year in salary and management bonus.

The *product development managers* helped customers solve technical problems; analyzed the current and potential market for their product; suggested product development or line extension opportunities; developed specifications for new and proposed products; and forecasted demand for new, existing, and proposed products by making appropriate economic and profit analyses. The product development managers were expected to be technically expert with regard to customers' manufacturing techniques, as well as familiar with the marketplace and likely prospects for new and existing product offerings. Unlike a typical "brand manager," the product development managers had no responsibility for sales volume or profits.

Because the machinery used to manufacture synthetic fibres, yarns, or fabric represented a substantial capital investment, the company's basic business strategy was to attempt to operate at full capacity (normally two shifts) at all times. By and large, the company had kept its machinery occupied on a full two-shift basis since the company's inception. In some years, however, production had been severely undersold, because of competitive or technological developments. In other years, fluctuations in consumer's demand for carpeting caused under- or overselling.

These problems made Austin's executives realize that such a heavy reliance on one industry could prove dangerous. Accordingly, they decided in 1970 to broaden research and development in fibre and yarn for other industries. In 1971 Austin diversified into industrial fabric and began a marketing strategy to increase the proportion of sales of products other than carpet fibres.

In the carpet fibre market, Austin's strategy was to increase its share of business with major high-volume accounts, and to reduce the number of smaller accounts whose positions in the marketplace were marginal and therefore less desirable from the standpoints of credit and potential growth.

In the yarn market, the strategy was to find applications that would appeal to manufacturers with high poundage or high square-foot requirements. Such firms included manufacturers of furniture, automobile seatcovers, and grille cloth. Applications that would not generate significant volume were not attractive because of their low margins.

In the industrial fabric market the company's strategy was to provide improved material for volume applications by customers who were using or were likely to switch to synthetic fabrics in some of their end products. Examples of such products were bagging (sacks, bales, bags), swimming pool covers, tenting, and tarpaulins. Many of these synthetic fabric applications were competitive with products made with cotton or jute fibres, commodities that were subject to price fluctuations. Management estimated that much of the domestic market was concentrated in 60 large potential accounts. Major marketing efforts were to be undertaken at first, however, with only the largest potential customers with high-volume applications.

SALES AND SALES MANAGEMENT ACTIVITIES

The job of the Austin salesman was multifaceted. First, he or she was expected to service Austin accounts and obtain orders for all Austin product lines. By virtue of personal acceptability and technical competence, he or she was expected to assist customers in determining appropriate inventory levels, to monitor and correct possible problems with regard to the quality of delivered products, to monitor and correct Austin's delivery service, to handle complaints, and generally to serve as a troubleshooter on the spot.

Second, the salesman was expected to increase the proportion of business that Austin was obtaining from each account. Since most larger companies, particularly those purchasing carpet fibres, preferred to purchase from several sources, it was important that the salesman penetrated past the customer's purchasing office and became influential with the decision makers within the customer's operation.

Third, the salesman was expected to work closely with the product development managers in seeking new applications for existing products and extensions of the product line, and in introducing new products to potential customers. In effect, between the work with accounts and the close liaison with the product development managers, a good part of the salesman's job was to manage relations between the Austin plant and its customers.

Fourth—and increasingly important, given the company's efforts to reduce its dependence on carpet fibre customers—the salesman was expected to prospect for new accounts for fibres, yarns, and fabrics. He or she was responsible for generating leads through observation, listening, and looking at such sources as the *Thomas Register*, as well as by following up inquiries forwarded to him from the customer service manager.

Thus, the salesman was required to call upon many different kinds of customers, ranging from large carpet manufacturers to small grille cloth weavers. The salesman could experience considerable difficulty in determining who and where the likely prospects were for a number of quite different product applications. Finally, the company's marketing strategy was still in process of evolving, forcing the salesman to tailor his or her activities by industry and by geographic area.

Late in 1971, the sales organization had been reduced from two regional managers supervising eight Austin salesmen and three commissioned agents, to a single sales manager supervising four district salesmen and a national accounts representative. This action had been taken after a detailed study of the salesmen's activities had revealed that the sales force was underutilized. As a consequence, each territory had been studied to determine the optimum number of calls per day from a well-planned itinerary. Each current account was analyzed to determine how many calls per year were required to offer the desired amount of service and selling time. A similar procedure was undertaken with regard to current and potential prospects. This analysis produced the current territory assignments and a concomitant increase in the number of required and actual sales calls per week.

As Exhibit 2 shows, the dollar sales for 1972 were similar among the Eastern, Central, and Pacific districts. Because of the concentration of carpet manufacturers in the South, the Southern territory contained more high-volume carpet fibre accounts but, according to the company executives, offered somewhat less potential for yarn and industrial fabrics. The national accounts representative handled 11 major carpet fibre accounts that required little selling but a great deal of service work and "hand-holding."

The current sales force of five people had been with Austin from 4 to 10 years. They had been hired as experienced salesmen and their ages ranged from 43 to 52. The company had no formal training program beyond a two-

Exhibit 2
Sales Force Individual Results and Earnings—1972

Name	Age	Territory	Number of Actual and Potential Accounts*	Sales ($000)	Salary	Bonus
Walik	43	East	95	$ 2,333	$17,400	$1,400
Huston	50	South	91	3,282	16,900	1,000
Beebe	44	Central	89	2,266	16,600	1,000
Gould	52	Pacific	97	2,285	16,800	1,400
Johnson	52	National accounts	11	8,885	16,400	1,500
Total				$19,051	$84,100	$6,300

Sales ($000) by Major Product Line—1972

Name	Carpet Fibre	Yarn	Industrial Fabric	Total
Walik	$ 783	$1,540	$ 10	$ 2,333
Huston	2,519	697	66	3,282
Beebe	1,360	793	113	2,266
Gould	1,305	911	69	2,285
Johnson	8,441	444	0	8,885
Total	$14,408	$4,385	$258	$19,051

Potential accounts referred to identified customers that the salesman intended to call upon or had called upon.

week tour in the plant to gather technical knowledge and a two-week tour in the field with an experienced salesman to "learn the ropes."

In 1972 three control forms were instituted to monitor the field activities of the sales force. The first was a weekly itinerary submitted by the salesman to the sales manager. It listed by account and by day the salesman's planned calls. It was mailed in on Thursday to cover the following week. The second form was a trip report, which the salesman filled out after each call. The salesman listed the accounts's name, persons contacted, purpose of the call, results of the call, whatever marketing intelligence he or she had gathered, and whatever follow-up action should be taken by the salesman or by the Austin plant. This trip report was filled out in triplicate, with one copy kept by the salesman, one copy sent to the sales manager, and a copy kept in the accounts file in Chicago. For a serious complaint, the salesman was required to fill out a complaint report in seven copies, which were routed to various departments within Austin, depending upon the nature of the complaint. This form was used to request price adjustments and to advice other Austin departments of problems with service, billing, pricing, delivery, and quality control. The form included a description of the complaint and the salesman's suggested disposition. The actions taken on the complaint were recorded before the form was filed.

The sales manager also maintained personal contact with each of the five salesmen by telephone at least three times a week. The sales manager spent two and one half to three days a week in the field working with the salesmen and calling on customers with them. This schedule permitted the sales manager to work with each salesman for two or three days in the field every five weeks. An annual sales meeting, usually held in February, brought all the marketing and sales personnel together in Chicago. This meeting, a combination of social and business activities, was the company's major opportunity to inform the sales force of technical developments in the Austin product line.

The sales manager conducted a formal performance review with each salesman at the end of the year. The review took place either in the field or during a salesman's visit to the Austin plant. The vehicle for performance appraisal was a two-page sheet that provided space for the sales manager to write a subjective appraisal and developmental action plan in each of six areas: technical knowledge, quality of work, quantity of work, initiative, relations with Austin personnel, and office procedures. These criteria were used throughout the company, and the form was standard for all departments and for all nonmanagerial employees.

The current compensation plan for the sale force involved straight salary plus a year-end bonus ranging from $1,000 to $1,500 per person. The size of the bonus depended on the collective subjective judgments of the sales manager, the marketing vice president, and the president. Seldom, according to the sales manager, was the size of the bonus related directly to sales dollars produced. In addition to earnings, the salesman received all normal fringe benefits, plus a company car. He or she was reimbursed for all normal business expenses after submitting a monthly expense report. The sales manager believed that reported expenses were accurate and that no salesman took advantage of the company.

THE COMPENSATION ISSUES

The first problem that senior executives had to deal with was the appropriate amount of compensation. Austin executives estimated that the average salesman's earnings in the industry were approximately $18,000 a year, (including company car), although salesmen for two of Austin's larger competitors probably averaged about $21,000 a year. Earnings for top salesmen in the industry appeared to be in the neighborhood of $25,000 to $26,000 a year.

The sales manager recognized that Austin salesmen's earnings were close to the industry average. But he argued that, because Austin was a small company relative to its major competitors, Austin should pay more than average compensation in order to attract and keep the best possible salesmen. The controller argued that, since turnover was almost nonexistent, there was no need to pay Austin salesmen more than they were already getting.

The second issue was the method of compensation. The industry showed considerable variety in methods of compensating salesmen. Two of the large firms paid straight salary only. Some smaller companies used commissioned agents, who were paid 1.5 percent commission only. Most of Austin's competitors, however, used a straight salary system with some form of bonus payment. Each of these methods had its adherents within Austin.

The president indicated that the decision as to how the salesmen were to be compensated would be left up to the sales manager, the marketing vice president, and the company controller. He placed two constraints on their decision, however. First, no salesman doing a good job should suffer financially from a change in the pay plan; second, if a bonus system was instituted, no salesman could earn more than 50 percent of his salary in bonus, because the Austin managerial bonus plan had the same limit.

Accordingly, the marketing vice president, the sales manager, and the controller met to discuss the alternatives that they had developed during a six-month study. The five alternatives are discussed below.

Straight Salary

The controller advocated paying the salesmen a straight salary and basing future salary adjustments on past performance. He argued that the straight salary would give managers tight control over the salesman's order-taking and servicing of accounts. Since much of the salesman's success depended upon his ability to bring the internal resources of the company to bear on the solution of customer problems, the credit for the sale belonged to everyone in the Austin organization. Furthermore, much of his business was "handed to him on a silver platter" and was not a direct consequence of his individual initiative.

The sales manager disagreed. He maintained that straight salary gave salesmen no incentive to develop new business or to increase business with current customers, and that these objectives were the real focuses of the sales force's efforts. He added that both these activities were critical to the success of the company's strategic shift in product and customer emphasis. Furthermore, he maintained that salary adjustments such as the controller favored would still be set by the same kind of subjective evaluations which made Austin executives uncomfortable in determining bonuses under the current system.

Continuation of Current Plan

The major argument for continuing the present plan was based upon the marketing vice president's idea that "the devil you know is better than the devil you don't." He maintained that the current system had the advantage of familiarity and control over unexpected events. He recognized, however, that the current plan was favored neither by the salesmen, who had been complaining about the subjectivity of the bonus determination, nor by the sales manager, who was particularly uncomfortable in this situation because he had to explain the subjective judgments.

Straight Commission

Straight commission was the plan favored by the five salesmen. The commission rate under discussion was .5 percent of sales, paid monthly. The salesmen argued that they would be inclined to work harder if they were treated "as if they were in business for themselves," and that their efforts to maximize their own incomes would maximize the achievement of company objectives. The controller pointed out to the sales manager and the marketing vice president that straight commission meant that the firm could never improve its ratio of sales to cost of selling, if the company grew and increased its efficiency. The marketing vice president expressed the opinion that he did not want the salesmen "in business for themselves," he wanted them "working for Austin." The sales manager sympathized with both of these reservations. But he thought that straight commission might make his managing job easier in that he would have to do less "booting them in the tail."

Salary Plus Annual Bonus Based on Product Line Sales

The sales manager proposed an annual bonus based on product line sales over quota. He favored establishing quotas for each salesman for each major product line—carpet fibres, yarn, and industrial fabric. At 100 percent of quota for each product, salesmen would receive no bonuses; for each 3 percent in excess of quota for each product line, a salesman would receive a bonus of 1 percent of his salary. Thus, if a salesman exceeded his personal quota for each of the three product lines by 9 percent, his annual bonus would be 3 percent + 3 percent + 3 percent or 9 percent of his salary. The maximum bonus would be 50 percent of salary. The annual bonus would be supplemented by a one-time award given for each new account, to equal .1 percent of the new account's first-year sales, with a maximum payment of $100 per account. This payment would be made as soon as possible after the anniversary date of the new account's first order.

The controller was less than enthusiastic about his plan, maintaining that the quotas might be set too low with a resulting overpayment to the salesmen. He also wondered about the effects of windfall sales. The marketing vice president wanted to know how the sales manager planned to make the quotas fair, since sales had in the past been limited by plant capacity.

Salary Plus Quarterly Bonus Based on "Capitalized Sales Expense"

One of the product managers had passed along to the marketing vice president an article describing the "capitalized sales expense" approach to compensation. This method required that managers first determine the sales expenses that they were willing to incur. This expense was expressed as a percentage of sales. The salary and controllable expenses incurred by a salesman was then divided by this percentage. The resulting amount, called a bogey, was to be used as a dollar sales quota. The salesman would receive a bonus for sales in excess of bogey. The bonus would be set at a fixed percentage of these excess dollar sales. (The fixed percentage, of course, would be smaller then the figure initially chosen as the desired sales expenses, expressed as a percentage of sales.) No bonus could exceed 50 percent of a salesman's salary.

The marketing vice president was intrigued enough by this idea to calculate some percentages illustrating it. He set desired sales expenses at 1.5 percent of sales and set the bonus at .5 of sales in excess of bogey. He then figured a quarterly bonus for a salesman who earned a salary of $4,500 for the three-month period, made $500,000 in sales, and incurred $1,650 in expenses during the same period.

$$\frac{\text{3 month's salary } + \text{ 3 month's controllable territory expenses}}{.015} = \text{Bogey}$$

$$\frac{\$4,500 + \$1,650}{.015} = \$410,000 = \text{Bogey}$$

$$(\text{3 month's sales} - \text{Bogey}) \times .005 = \text{Bonus}$$

$$\$500,000 - \$410,000 = \$90,000 = \text{Sales in excess of bogey}$$

$$\$90,000 \times .005 = \$450 = \text{Bonus for the quarter}$$

The marketing vice president felt that this system would appear too complicated to the sales force, although he recognized that the bogey derived from capitalizing sales expense seemed less arbitrary than a quota "plucked out of the air." The controller felt that the system would be too complicated to administer, although he realized that the cost of sales would decline as the salesmen exceeded bogey. The sales manager noted that this plan did not emphasize sales by product line, nor necessarily motivate salesmen to open new accounts. But he acknowledged that the system would encourage salesmen to keep their expenses down, since spending less than budget would lower the bogey.

Case 15
Dynamic Products Corporation

Early in 1978 sales executives of Dynamic Products Corporation (DPC) in Dallas, Texas, were reviewing their system for evaluating the performance of individual sales representatives in the Consumer Tool Division. Such reviews were commonplace at DPC, for executives continually strove to improve a company that most industry observers acknowledged to be outstandingly successful. But this particular review seemed crucial for two reasons. First, many sales reps and management personnel believed that the current system did not adequately motivate sales personnel or communicate corporate objectives to them. Second, company executives had recently modified their marketing strategy in an effort to broaden DPC's distribution. Good motivation and communications would be essential to the strategy's success.

COMPANY BACKGROUND

DPC manufactured and marketed a wide line of electrical power tools and accessories for consumer and industrial uses. Domestic sales volume in 1977 exceeded $340 million, double that of 1972. Aftertax profits in 1977 exceeded $12 million, again nearly double those of 1972.

Research and development at DPC continually improved and diversified the power tool line. Thus, both consumer and industrial purchasers regarded DPC as a leading producer of quality power tools. Aggressive advertising had further enhanced the company's reputation. According to company executives, advertising was largely responsible for the company's rapid growth in sales and profits. All DPC consumer products and accessories were marketed under the Dynamic brand name.

INDUSTRY BACKGROUND

The home power-tool market had grown rapidly during the 1970s, both because of rising consumer income and because of heavy promotion of a host of new products and features.

According to industry estimates, some 70 percent of all U.S. homeowners owned one or more power tools in 1975. These tools ranged from very inexpensive ¼″ drills up to very expensive lathes and bench drills. According to DPC estimates, electric bills represented more than 50 percent of total consumer power tool purchases in 1975. Some 60 percent of home power tools were purchased for personal use; some 30 percent were purchased as gifts; and the remainder were received as prizes, premiums, or in return for trading stamps. Because of the importance of gift-giving, power tool sales were seasonal. November and December typically accounted for over 50 percent of total annual retail sales. The second most important selling season (May, June, July) accounted for nearly one fourth of annual sales.

CONSUMER TOOL DIVISION: THE PRODUCT LINE[1]

The major items in the Consumer Tool Division's product line were

Portable Power Drills.   Chuck capacities of ¼″, ⅜″, or ½″; single-speed, 2-speed, or variable-speed. Typical suggested retail prices were $24.95 for a ¼″ single speed; $79.95 for a ⅜″ variable speed. Accessories included drill bits; grinding, sanding, and buffing wheels; polishing pads; paint mixer; vertical and horizontal bench stands; and carrying cases.

Portable Power Saws.   Circular saws with blade capacities from 6½″ to 8¼″ in diameter. Typical suggested retail prices were $79.95 for a light power saw; $179.95 for a heavy-duty saw. Jig and saber saws with single-, 2-, or variable-speed; typical suggested retail price for a single-speed jig saw was $29.95. Accessories included saw blades, ripping guides, and carrying cases. Chain saws with 10″ to 14″ cutting bars; suggested retail price for the 10″ cutting bar chain saw was $129.95.

Portable Sanders.   Belt, orbital, vibrating, or rotary sanders; typical suggested retail price for a medium-duty orbital sander was $39.95.

Stationary Power Tools.   Circular saws, jointers, drill presses, scroll saws, band saws, lathes, radial saws, and grinders; typical suggested retail prices ranged from $399.95 for the economy-model drill press to $749.95 for the heavy-duty bench saw.

CONSUMER TOOL DIVISION: MARKETING STRATEGY

The Consumer Tool Division sold most of its products directly to 12,000 retailers, primarily to hardware and building supply stores, department

---

[1] For the sake of simplicity, this case does not discuss industrial, lawn-care, and other DPC products and marketing operations.

stores, general merchandise discount stores, and the buying offices of large chain stores. Some sales, however, were made to wholesalers servicing smaller retail outlets.

DPC did not publish sales figures for individual products. Trade sources, however, estimated that the division's products sold through retail outlets accounted for approximately 50 percent of DPC's 1977 sales volume, and that these sales represented approximately 20 percent of the home power-tool market (at manufacturer's selling prices). The division's competition included such well-known brand names as Craftsman (Sears), Black & Decker, Skil, Wen, Porter-Cable, and Stanley.

DPC emphasized national advertising. According to trade estimates, the company's advertising expenditures were approximately 7 percent of sales, with about 65 percent of this figure devoted to television, about 30 percent to magazines, and less than 5 percent to newspapers. The company's advertising announced new product features, such as cordless electric models, and publicized the availability of lower-priced units.

DPC set suggested retail prices, but dealers were free to set their own resale prices. The suggested prices provided gross margins for retailers of about 40 percent on more expensive items, declining to about 35 percent on less expensive items.

Because larger retailers saw Dynamic-branded products as attractive items to feature in discount promotions, prevailing retail prices were often well below suggested levels. During 1975, for instance, consumers in large metropolitan areas could buy a Dynamic single-speed ¼" drill with a suggested retail price of $24.95 at a discount price of around $19.95; and an orbital sander at a suggested retail price of $39.95 for around $25.95. The smaller conventional hardware stores sold Dynamic products at smaller discounts and sometimes at full list price.

In fact, discounting by the larger and more aggressive stores was making it difficult for the smaller conventional stores to carry the Dynamic line and promote it profitably. Partly for this reason, a large proportion of total retail sales were made by a relatively small number of dealers. Thus, 10 percent of the Division's retail accounts handled 40 percent of sales, and 20 percent of the retailers handled 60 percent of sales.

DPC executives were beginning to think that future sales growth must come in part from broadened distribution. Marketing plans would now have to take the smaller retailers into account.

In the past, the Division's sales force had been directed to increase sales volume through existing retail accounts, by convincing retailers to spend their own money on local advertising and promotion for Dynamic products. Company lore at that time maintained that if sales reps were asked, "What do you do?" they would reply, "I sell advertising space." Most sales programs had been designed to get DPC sales reps to sell the retailer on the idea of building volume, a goal that benefited discounters and chain stores. But these programs had less appeal to buyers in smaller stores, who were less interested in volume and not at all interested in selling at a discount.

Thus, many of these retailers were not sure what the benefits were of carrying Dynamic products.

DPC executives believed that sales volume could be increased if smaller stores and stores in more remote areas could be persuaded to carry the Dynamic line and to promote it more aggressively. Consequently, executives had started developing new promotional programs, materials, and display racks for smaller retailers. Executives also hoped to shift the sales rep's current emphasis on short-run volumes to an emphasis on longer-term dealer relationships. The sales reps would come to see themselves as "merchandising consultants" building stable relationships with their dealers. This perspective—a new one for most reps—would ensure a steadier sales base in the long run, without jeopardizing sales volume from the existing large accounts.

THE CONSUMER TOOL DIVISION'S SALES FORCE

The sales representative was responsible for setting up in-store displays, training retail sales personnel, assisting retailers in planning local advertising of Dynamic products, and introducing new products. From time to time, the sales rep conducted special in-store promotional campaigns, offering special sales prices on low-end products. DPC provided the display and advertising materials for these campaigns.

The 40 members of the division's sales force were characterized by one executive as "a bunch of young, hard-chargers who want to become managers, *fast!*" The company tried to hire college graduates in their middle or late 20s who had had two or three years' sales experience with well-known consumer products firms. After a brief indoctrination period in Dallas, which concentrated on product features and promotional activities, the new sales reps were turned over to their district managers for further training. Once or twice a year the sales training manager conducted two- or three-day training programs for new and experienced reps. These varied from general how-to-sell sessions to specialized programs, such as workshops in advertising copy layout.

A typical territory included as many as 300 regular dealers. Call frequency depended upon the dealers' sizes and locations. Small dealers located in remote areas were visited only once every four to six months. Large dealers in major metropolitan areas were visited weekly.

The sales force also included three national account managers who were stationed in Dallas and reported to the division sales manager. These senior sales reps were responsible for selling consumer tool products to the buying offices of large chain stores. Merchandising activities for these stores were assigned to the sales reps servicing the territories in which the chain store outlets were located.

Each of the 40 sales reps reported to one of six district managers. The district managers reported to the division's sales manager, who reported to the company's general sales manager. In addition to these line management personnel, the division employed several product managers and a sales training manager responsible for sales training and sales management development. These staff personnel also reported to the division sales manager.

District managers, almost without exception, had risen from the ranks of the sales force. District managers were expected to spend at least two days a week in the field training their sales reps. Depending on the time of year and the district's training needs, this figure could rise to as much as four days a week. Administrative duties took up the rest of the manager's time. These tasks included interviewing and hiring sales reps; maintaining liaison with regional warehousing personnel; supervising office personnel; fostering community relations; and furnishing headquarters' personnel in Dallas with a wide variety of reports on sales activity, market conditions, and retail promotional activities. A few district managers also had direct account responsibility for major chain stores not handled by a national account manager.

SALES QUOTAS AND PERFORMANCE EVALUATIONS

The general sales manager and the division sales manager jointly set the division's national sales quota, after considering economic conditions, historical sales trends, market research, current products, and prospective product introductions. The two managers developed three sales estimates: minimum, best, and maximum.

After considering the three-year historical trend in each district's share of national sales, the division sales manager assigned to each district a share of the national quota. Each district manager, using the same data for each sales territory, further subdivided the district quota among the territories. These quotas were assigned to individual sales reps at a January sales meeting.

Each individual's quota included a quota for total dollar volume, plus quotas for unit volumes in three tool categories: electric drills, all other portable tools, and standing tools. The quota for a fourth category, accessories, was expressed in dollar volume. The sales reps received monthly reports on their quota achievements. If national sales during the year fell considerably below the national best estimate, these individual quotas were revised.

The quotas were used to develop an objective evaluation, in the form of a point score, of each sales rep's performance. Volume achieved in each category contributed a designated percentage of the total point score. For each category, this percentage was multiplied by the percentage of the quota achieved; the results for each of the four categories were then totaled. The division manager compared the total point scores of all sales reps to establish an objective ranking for each sales rep. However, the division manager adjusted these rankings to accommodate extenuating circumstances, such as unexpected store openings or strikes.

In addition to this objective evaluation, a yearly subjective evaluation was made of each rep's performance by his or her district manager. The evaluation form allowed each rep one to five points for each of 51 characteristics spread over five categories: self-management, job knowledge, selling techniques, job attitude, and personal attributes (see Exhibit 1 for this evaluation form). The district manager discussed these evaluations with the division sales manager before reviewing them with the reps themselves. At that time, usually in March, the district manager discussed the subjective evaluation, point by point, and required the rep to sign the evaluation form. The objective evaluation was also reviewed at this time, and plans were made for improved performance. District managers were evaluated by the division sales manager in much the same way and at the same time.

Exhibit 1
Performance Evaluation Form

SALESMAN PERFORMANCE EVALUATION FORM

District Manager _____   Date _____

Salesman _____   Evaluation Period _____

	Rating				
Attributes to be Rated *Self-management:*	5 *Excellent*	4 *Good*	3 *Average*	2 *Fair*	1 *Poor*
Plans his work					
Uses time efficiently					
Files reports promptly					
Keeps accurate and up-to-date records					
Controls expenses					
Maintains sales tools and equipment					
Answers correspondence regularly					
Requires little supervision					
Total points: _____					
Job knowledge:					
Technical knowledge of company product					
Knowledge of company policies and procedures					
Knowledge of competition					
Knowledge of product application					
Customer and prospect knowledge					
Territory knowledge					
Accuracy of problem analysis					
Total points: _____					

Exhibit 1 *(continued)*

	Rating				
Face-to-face salesmanship:	5 Excellent	4 Good	3 Average	2 Fair	1 Poor
Can locate and see buying authority					
Handles opening gracefully					
Speaks in customer's terms					
Delivers organized and persuasive presentation					
Handles objections well					
Stresses benefits, not features					
Controls the interview					
Listens carefully					
Asks pertinent questions					
Uses sales aids effectively					
Employs showmanship					
Speaks with confidence and authority					
Maintains pleasant manner					
Asks for action					
Remembers names and faces					
Knows when to stop selling and ask for action					

Total points: _____

Attitude toward job:

Interest in selling					
Competitive spirit					
Industriousness					
Confidence in company					
Ability to pull out of slumps					
Persistence					
Self-confidence					
Cooperativeness					
Receptivity to suggestions					
Creativity					

Total points: _____

Personal attributes:

Judgment					
Personal hygiene and grooming					
Attire					
Grammar and language					
Health					
Patience					
Reliability					
Social sensibility					
Manners and etiquette					

Total points: _____

Final total of all points: _____

Both evaluations were used to determine the sales rep's yearly bonus (base salaries were about $2,000 per month). The rep's nationwide objective ranking was combined with his subjective ranking (on a weighting of 80 percent objective, 20 percent subjective) to produce an overall nationwide ranking. The top 20 to 25 sales reps received bonuses ranging from $500 to $2,000, depending upon their national rankings. The bonuses were shares of a yearly bonus pool, which was an amount equal to 5 percent of the monthly field sales payroll. In 1977, this pool was $60,000. District managers received slightly larger shares of this pool. The field bonus was usually paid in the first quarter at the time of the annual performance review. Salary increases were announced at the same time, but the effective dates were usually April 1 or July 1.

In 1976, DPC executives engaged a consulting firm to recommend a new system for evaluating sales force performance. This consulting firm had been working with the consumer tool division sales force on several projects over a three-year period. DPC executives considered this organization to be familiar with the company's sales and marketing operations, as well as experienced in designing performance evaluation programs. Below is the consulting firm's report, entitled "DPC Performance Evaluation Programs." In early 1978, company executives were trying to decide whether to adopt, modify, or reject these recommendations.

DPC PERFORMANCE EVALUATION PROGRAM

This report suggests a method for evaluating consumer tool division sales personnel. The objectives of this method, which we call Performance Evaluation Program (PEP) are

1. To clarify for supervisor and subordinate the job to be done.
2. To ensure that individual performance fulfills organizational goals.
3. To measure performance for equitable salary, bonus, and promotion decisions.
4. To enhance communication and teamwork between supervisor and subordinate.
5. To stimulate the subordinate's motivation and professional growth.

Before describing PEP in detail, we must address the constraints placed on the program by your manner of doing business. Product line quotas are currently set on a top-down basis. Given this procedure, management by objectives in its pure form will not work at DPC, because the sales reps do not *participate* in setting these quota figures. On the other hand, if sales reps were allowed to set their own quotas independent of corporate sales objectives, their quotas would probably be higher than those of the previous year, perhaps even higher than quotas that would normally be set for them. Once these quotas were approved by sales supervisors, the quotas would become the supervisors' objectives. All persons concerned would have committed themselves. They would therefore be subject to being hoist by their own petards.

Our proposal, then, sets a median course between pure management by objectives and pure top-down management. It would be unreasonable for us to suggest sweeping changes in your quota system or overall managerial philosophy. Instead, we suggest small but key changes in your current evaluation system that will produce substantial benefits.

To maintain control, we recommend that quotas as well as sales activities be designated from the top down. Quota achievement will be considered satisfactory performance, although each sales representative should aspire to exceed quota. To motivate the representative, we recommend that annual bonuses be made dependent upon the rep's quota achievement relative to that of the division's other representatives. Quotas must be set fairly—both in the aggregate and for individuals—if PEP is to work as a system for performance measurement and control.

To introduce management by objectives gradually at DPC, we recommend that salary adjustments and promotions be based jointly on (1) the representative's performance of sales activities designated by management, and (2) the representative's fulfillment of professional goals outlined by the representative himself.

We believe that measuring and rewarding the representatives partly on the basis of corporate objectives and partly on the basis of individual professional goals offers the best compromise: DPC can maintain organizational control while enhancing motivation by allowing representatives to set some of their own goals.

The Performance Evaluation Program is administered in five segments:

1. Job Description.
2. Field Observation Report.
3. PEP Results Review.
4. PEP Activities Review.
5. PEP Development Review.

1. Job Description (Exhibit 2)

All performance evaluations should be based on the job description, which is, in effect, the contract between employer and employee. Note that the format of the job description is followed in most subsequent PEP documents, and that the three parts of the description correspond to the three performance reviews discussed below. In making evaluations, the supervisor should use the job description as a guide; in reviewing performance with the subordinate, the supervisor should use this document as the basis for discussion.

At the beginning of the year, supervisor and subordinate meet to review the job description and to agree on expected performance. By this time, quotas assigned by Dallas have been posted by the supervisor on the appropriate lines in the "Results" section of the document. If quotas have to be changed—and we argue that they should not be except in the most dire circumstances—the subordinate should be issued a superseding quota, also posted on his job description. Copies of each individual job description with quotas posted should be provided for the subordinate, the supervisor, and the national sales manager in Dallas.

198

Exhibit 2
Job Description

DPC PERFORMANCE EVALUATION PROGRAM

JOB DESCRIPTION

Name _____ Job Title _____ Date _____

As a Sales Representative, Consumer Products, you are responsible for the sale of consumer products through approximately 300 retail dealers of all types in your assigned territory. (*All types* meaning outlets who are controlled by a home office National Account Manager plus other dealers who buy and merchandise on a local basis.) You operate sales programs, achieve your quota, run promotions, and perform other functions as assigned. You are the front-line representative of Dynamic Products Corporation to the dealer and consumer and you are responsible for dealer relations in your territory.

Report to: District Manager

I. *Results:* During 19 ___ , you are expected to achieve the following assigned quotas:

	Weighting	Quota
Total dollar sales		$
Portable drill units		
Other portable units		
Standing units		
Accessory products	_____	$
	100%	

II. *Activities:* During 19 ___ , you are expected to:
A. *Manage your territory*
   1. Demonstrate efficient call routing.
   2. Prepare specific objectives for each major account.
   3. Prepare specific plans for each major account.
   4. Engage new dealers when desirable.
   5. Upgrade or terminate weak dealers.
   6. Generate and transmit recommendations to improve territory business.
B. *Manage your dealers*
   1. Prepare specific call objectives for every dealer visit.
   2. Prepare specific call strategy for every dealer visit.
   3. Have sales materials well organized.
   4. Be well received by dealer and his personnel.
   5. Show understanding of dealer's problems.
   6. Be respected by dealer for your sound business knowledge.
   7. Handle his complaints and questions effectively.
   8. Train dealer and his personnel in DPC policies.
   9. Train dealer and his personnel in DPC product knowledge.
   10. Train dealer and his personnel in DPC selling skills.

Exhibit 2 *(continued)*

---

11. Gain dealer's cooperation in DPC merchandising activities.
  a. Local newspaper and radio advertising.
  b. Special advertised promotions.
  c. Special unadvertised promotions.
  d. In-store display.
12. Introduce new products effectively and enthusiastically.
  C. *Manage your company relationships*
  1. Service branches of national accounts who do not buy from you.
  2. Report pertinent marketing intelligence to management.
  3. Submit required reports promptly.
  4. Expedite orders when necessary.
  5. Assist administrative staff in solving problems (e.g., credit).
  6. Perform special assignments as directed.
  7. Take physical or verbal inventories as directed.

III. *Development:* During 19__ , you are expected to:
  A. Develop objectives, plans, and timetables relative to achieving your personal career development goals and implement these plans with the assistance of your supervisor.
  B. Develop objectives, plans, and timetables relative to achieving improvement in your job activities and implement these plans with the assistance of your supervisor.

_____   _____
(Division Sales Manager)   (Supervisor)

                                    _____
                                    (Received by)

---

2. *Field Observation Report* (Exhibit 3)

The Field Observation Report (FOR) is to be completed each time that a supervisor observes and coaches a subordinate. One copy is given to the subordinate, one copy kept by the supervisor, and one copy forwarded to headquarters.

The FOR is almost identical to the job description, except that activities are given ratings of "professional," "satisfactory," or "needs improvement." Activities are not rated if the supervisor has insufficient observation to make a careful judgment.

The FOR should be discussed at length with the subordinate at the conclusion of the observation/coaching period. It is highly desirable that the subordinate concur with the supervisor's rating and plans for improvement. To help achieve this agreement, the subordinate should complete an FOR independently and compare these ratings with those of the supervisor.

The national sales manager can use the FOR to (1) pinpoint overall training needs, (2) "red flag" representatives in difficulty, and (3) keep track of supervisors' field training.

Exhibit 3
Field Observation Report

DPC PERFORMANCE EVALUATION PROGRAM
FIELD OBSERVATION REPORT

Name _____ Job Title _____ Date _____

Rater _____ Time Spent _____ Calls Made _____

Rating Code: (P) Professional (S) Satisfactory (N) Needs improving (X) Not applicable or insufficient evidence for judgment.

I. Results: Was he informed of his *current* standing in regard to quota achievement?   Yes _____   No _____

II. Activities: Rating:

   A. *Manage your territory*
      1. Demonstrate efficient call routing.   _____
      2. Prepare specific objectives for each major account.   _____
      3. Prepare specific plans for each major account.   _____
      4. Engage new dealers when desirable.   _____
      5. Upgrade or terminate weak dealers.   _____
      6. Generate and transmit recommendations to improve territory business.   _____

   B. *Manage your dealers*
      1. Prepare specific call objectives for every dealer visit.   _____
      2. Prepare specific call strategy for every dealer visit.   _____
      3. Have sales material well organized.   _____
      4. Be well received by dealer and his personnel.   _____
      5. Show understanding of dealer's problems.   _____
      6. Be respected by dealer for your sound business knowledge.   _____
      7. Handle his complaints and questions effectively.   _____
      8. Train dealer and his personnel in DPC policies.   _____
      9. Train dealer and his personnel in DPC product knowledge.   _____
     10. Train dealer and his personnel in DPC selling skills.   _____
     11. Gain dealer's cooperation in DPC merchandising activities:
        a. Local newspaper and radio advertising.   _____
        b. Special advertised promotions.   _____
        c. Special unadvertised promotions.   _____
        d. In-store display.   _____
     12. Introduce new products effectively and enthusiastically.   _____

   C. *Manage your company relationships*
      1. Service branches of national accounts who do not buy from you.   _____
      2. Report pertinent marketing intelligence to management.   _____
      3. Submit required reports promptly.   _____

Exhibit 3 *(continued)*

4.	Expedite orders when necessary.	———
5.	Assist administrative staff in solving problems (e.g., credit).	———
6.	Perform special assignments as directed.	———
7.	Take physical or verbal inventories as directed.	———

Major strengths observed and acknowledged:

_____

_____

Major areas for improvement discussed:

_____

_____

_____

_____   _____
(Supervisor)   (Received by)

3. *PEP Results Review* (Exhibit 4)

If supervisor and subordinate have secured agreement with one another over the job description and the quotas, it is possible and desirable to hold each responsible for year-end results, if these results are evaluated in relation to those of other employees. (Corporate windfalls and catastrophes presumably affect everyone equally).

The PEP Results Review form is similar to the Results portion of the job description, except that:

1. Percent-of-quota achievement has been posted by Dallas personnel.
2. A relative ranking has been calculated and posted by Dallas personnel.

Each sales representative, then, has been ranked by percent of quota achieved in comparison with all others. The resulting ratings are as follows:

Outstanding (top 5 percent)

Professional (next 28 percent)

Satisfactory

Unsatisfactory

One copy of this completed form remains at headquarters; two copies are sent to the supervisor, who gives one to the subordinate. The subordinate initials the supervisor's copy.

There can be no argument between subordinate and supervisor about ratings in the first three categories. These ratings are based strictly on *relative* results. Sales representatives are competing for the *outstanding* or *professional* ratings. It might be possible for an individual to earn an *outstanding* rating with, say, an 85 percent quota achievement if this figure was within the top 5 percent. By the same token, a quota achievement of 150 percent might not earn an *outstanding* rating if more than 5 percent of the sales representatives achieved similar or better results.

202

Exhibit 4
Results Review

DPC PERFORMANCE EVALUATION PROGRAM
RESULTS REVIEW

Name _____ Job Title _____ Date _____

Degree of achievement of assigned quotas:

	Weighting	*Quota*	*Actual*	*Percent of Quota*
Total dollar sales		$	$	
Portable drill units				
Other portable units				
Standing units				
Accessory products	____	$	$	____
	100%			

	Outstanding (top 5%)	*Professional* (next 28%)	*Satisfactory*	*Unsatisfactory*
Rating	____	____	____	____

The above rating is based on your weighted percent of
Quota achievement during 19__ relative to all other Consumer Tool Division Sales Representatives.

_____   _____
(Division Sales Manager)   (Supervisor)

_____
(Received by)

Because of the small size of the division's bonus pool, we suggest that
substantial bonuses (say, $5,000) be awarded for *outstanding* performance;
token bonuses (say, $2,000) for *professional* performance; and no bonuses for
satisfactory performance.

The line between *satisfactory* and *unsatisfactory* will vary according to the
judgment of the immediate supervisor and the national sales manager. For
instance, mitigating circumstances may explain one representative's performance falling in the bottom 10 percent but not explain another representative's
performance falling in the bottom 20 percent. Problems like these, however,
should occur rarely. Most individuals would have been terminated before receiving an *unsatisfactory* rating.

Because bonuses are not determined by the immediate supervisor, the supervisor does not "play God" but rather helps the subordinate to achieve the bonus. We also recommend that the supervisor's bonus be determined by the total bonuses earned by his or her subordinates. This system gives supervisor and subordinate a common goal and should enhance their communication and teamwork.

Exhibit 5
Activities Review

DPC PERFORMANCE EVALUATION PROGRAM
ACTIVITIES REVIEW

Name _____ Job Title _____ Date _____

	Outstanding	Professional	Satisfactory	Unsatisfactory
Results rating	☐	☐	☐	☐

Activities rating

A. *Manage your territory*
1. Demonstrate efficient call routing. ☐ ☐ ☐ ☐
2. Prepare specific objectives for each major account. ☐ ☐ ☐ ☐
3. Prepare specific plans for each major account. ☐ ☐ ☐ ☐
4. Engage new dealers when desirable. ☐ ☐ ☐ ☐
5. Upgrade or terminate weak dealers. ☐ ☐ ☐ ☐
6. Generate and transmit recommendations to improve territory business. ☐ ☐ ☐ ☐

B. *Manage your dealers*
1. Prepare specific call objectives for every dealer visit. ☐ ☐ ☐ ☐
2. Prepare specific call strategy for every dealer visit. ☐ ☐ ☐ ☐
3. Have sales materials well organized. ☐ ☐ ☐ ☐
4. Be well received by dealer and his personnel. ☐ ☐ ☐ ☐
5. Show understanding of dealer's problems. ☐ ☐ ☐ ☐
6. Be respected by dealer for your sound business knowledge. ☐ ☐ ☐ ☐
7. Handle his complaints and questions effectively. ☐ ☐ ☐ ☐
8. Train dealer and his personnel in DPC policies. ☐ ☐ ☐ ☐
9. Train dealer and his personnel in DPC product knowledge. ☐ ☐ ☐ ☐

Exhibit 5 *(continued)*

10. Train dealer and his personnel in DPC selling skills.	☐	☐	☐	☐
11. Gain dealer's cooperation in DPC merchandising activities:				
a. Local newspaper and radio advertising.	☐	☐	☐	☐
b. Special advertised promotions.	☐	☐	☐	☐
c. Special unadvertised promotions.	☐	☐	☐	☐
d. In-store display.	☐	☐	☐	☐
12. Introduce new products effectively and enthusiastically.	☐	☐	☐	☐

C. *Manage your company relationships*

1. Service branches of national accounts who do not buy from you.	☐	☐	☐	☐
2. Report pertinent marketing intelligence to management.	☐	☐	☐	☐
3. Submit required reports promptly.	☐	☐	☐	☐
4. Expedite orders when necessary.	☐	☐	☐	☐
5. Assist administrative staff in solving problems (e.g., credit).	☐	☐	☐	☐
6. Perform special assignments as directed.	☐	☐	☐	☐
7. Take physical or verbal inventories as directed.	☐	☐	☐	☐

(Supervisor)   (Received by)

4. PEP Activities Review (Exhibit 5)

Most performance appraisal systems fail because they require supervisors to judge subordinates' personality traits, such as mental alertness, integrity, and initiative. Even trained psychologists are unable to do this well, and most supervisors are extremely uneasy when asked to make such judgments. The primary concern in performance review should be counseling subordinates—showing them how to improve performance. We recommend that supervisors observe and measure specific selling activities, advising subordinates on specific actions that would improve their performance of these activities.

The PEP Activities Review form is similar to the Job Description and the Field Observation Report. The Results portion of the Job Description is summarized (to agree with the rating posted on the PEP Results Review form). The activities listed in the Job Description are rated by the supervisor as *outstanding, professional, satisfactory,* or *unsatisfactory.* This form is completed in triplicate by the supervisor and signed by the subordinate, one copy forwarded for filing in Dallas, one copy kept, and one copy given to and discussed with the subordinate.

Note that in preparing the PEP Activities Review form the supervisor has two guides to the ratings. First, the PEP Results rating should be the major indicator for the overall pattern of individual activity ratings. The pattern of the individual activities ratings should be consistent with, but not necessarily individually identical to, the PEP Results rating determined by Dallas.

Second, the collective FOR's should provide the supervisor with solid evidence for ratings of individual activities. Thus, since the subordinate has a file of his own FOR's, the PEP Activity Review rating should:

1. Come as no surprise to the subordinate.
2. Show the subordinate how his activities specifically have contributed to results.
3. Pinpoint for the subordinate and supervisor those areas where the subordinate is strong and where he needs to improve.
4. Serve as a basis for plans to improve the subordinate's performance.
5. Reduce, if not eliminate, rancor, argument, unsupported judgments, and other elements of ill-will that are so often created when one person is required to make subjective judgments about another.

The FOR rating categories are slightly different from the PEP Activities Review rating categories. This open-endedness in the FOR form prevents the supervisor from getting locked into favorable or unfavorable ratings developed in field visits and perhaps contradicted by year-end results.

5. *PEP Development Review* (Exhibit 6)

The subordinate and supervisor are now ready to prepare the PEP Development Review form, based on the PEP Activities Review form. Each should do this work independently. The final document is the responsibility of the *subordinate*, the supervisor lending advice only. The supervisor's independent review ensures that the supervisor has given careful thought to the subordinate's individual situation and is thus able to provide useful counsel. Final signed copies go to subordinate, supervisor, and national sales manager.

The PEP Development Review form has two sections: personal goals and corporate goals (performance improvement). Placing personal goals first does not minimize DPC's goals, but merely recognizes that people are best motivated by personal goals. The review form will help subordinates to understand their personal objectives and to assess how these objectives can be reached within the framework of DPC's goals.

Personal goals stated on the PEP Development Review form might be:

"Work with less supervision."

"Become a district manager."

"Win a sales award."

To avoid general statements that merely sound good and to provide a firm basis for personal development, all such goals should be accompanied by:

1. Specific plans for accomplishment (such as courses, readings, and activities).

206

Exhibit 6
Development Review

```
┌─────────────────────────────────────────────────────────────────────┐
│            DPC PERFORMANCE EVALUATION PROGRAM                         │
│                    DEVELOPMENT REVIEW                                 │
│                                                                       │
│  Name _____ Job Title _____ Date _____       │
│  Personal Career Goals: _____          │
└─────────────────────────────────────────────────────────────────────┘
```

Plans to Accomplish	Timetable and Checkpoints	To Be Measured by:	Supervisor to Assist by:

Job Improvement Goals: _____

Plans to Accomplish	Timetable and Checkpoints	To Be Measured by:	Supervisor to Assist by:

(Supervisor)   (Completed by)

2. Timetable and checkpoints.
3. Method of measuring achievement.
4. Nature and timing of supervisor's required assistance (such as discussions, and field visits).

Corporate (job improvement) goals to be stated on the PEP Development Review form might include:

"Increase total ad lineage for ABC Corporation by x percent."
"Add x number of new dealers."
"Improve relations with LMN Company."

Again, all such goals should be accompanied by plans, timetables, checkpoints, measurements, and required assistance. *Which* corporate (job improvement) goals are listed on the PEP Development Review form should be determined by the subordinate's ratings on the PEP Activities Review form. *What* those goals are quantitatively should depend jointly on what the subordinate sees as reasonable and on what the supervisor sees as reasonable and desirable from DPC's point of view.

The more the subordinate participates in this process, the more likely he is to feel (a) that the superior is helpful and constructive, (b) that some current job problems are being cleared up, and (c) that reasonable future goals are being set.

In this system, hitting the target is not the measure of success. A person who sets meager targets and always hits them is of little value to the organization. Our goal is to get people to make substantial improvements on their past work. The total process of performance evaluation—setting targets and analyzing what intervenes between planned and actual performance—is the major benefit to the individual and to the organization. DPC management has assumed all too often in the past that it alone has the prerogative to set objectives and to reward and punish. As long as this assumption exists in any organization, the appraisal process is certain to fail as a device for performance improvement.

TIMETABLE

Our recommended timetable is based on several of our axioms of performance appraisal.

1. Subordinates need frequent opportunities to discuss their performance with their supervisor.
2. Comprehensive annual performance appraisals are of questionable value because the mix of praise and criticism. The praise has little effect because subordinates dismiss it as merely the bread surrounding the raw meat of the criticism sandwich.
3. Separate appraisals should be held for different purposes. A supervisor cannot be both a counselor helping a subordinate improve performance and at the same time a judge over the subordinate's salary action case.

We suggest the following timetable.

January. Dallas prepares job descriptions with new quota figures, calculates quota achievements and overall ratings, and posts these on the PEP Results Reviews. These are forwarded to supervisors who prepare PEP Activities Reviews. Reviews are then conducted with subordinates who are (1) given bonus checks (or notified that they did not get one), (2) given full and candid evaluations of the PEP Activities Review, and (3) asked to prepare PEP Development Review forms.

February–March. Subordinates and supervisors complete PEP Development Review forms.

April. Subordinates are advised by their supervisors of salary adjustments to be effective July 1. Salary adjustments are based on the supervisors' recommendations to Dallas. Supervisors base their recommendations on overall subjective evaluations that combine PEP Activities Review ratings and PEP Development activities.

May–June. Subordinates and supervisors hold three-months PEP Development review sessions to discuss progress toward goal achievement.

August–September. Subordinates and supervisors hold six-months PEP Development review sessions.

November–December. Subordinates and supervisors hold nine-months PEP Development review sessions.

Throughout the year. Field Observation Report forms are completed, and discussed by subordinates and supervisors. Subordinates are advised of their performance compared to quota during each field visit.

SUMMARY

The positive advantages of PEP are: (1) subordinates know in advance the basis on which they will be judged; (2) the supervisor and subordinate agree on what the subordinate's job really is; (3) PEP takes place within the supervisor/ subordinate relationship and should strengthen this relationship; (4) PEP has self-correcting characteristics that help people set targets that are both challenging and reachable; (5) PEP provides a method of spotting training needs; (6) PEP treats as a total process the ability to see an organizational problem, devise ways of attacking it, translate these ideas into action, incorporate new information as it arises, and carry these plans through to results.

In order for PEP to work, (1) individual quotas *must* be fairly set and perceived as such by the subordinate; (2) subordinates must realize that bonuses are based on results relative to all others in their job class; (3) subordinates must realize that salary adjustments are based in large measure on their ability to set, plan for, and achieve intelligent personal and job-related targets; and (4) supervisors must realize that their job calls for, and their ultimate reward is based on, their ability to improve the performance of their subordinates. And that is what PEP is designed to do.

CONCLUSION

Executives at DPC were now evaluating the proposal, trying to decide whether to adopt it, modify it, or search for an entirely different evaluation system. Would PEP enhance communication and motivation among sales representatives and management personnel? And would the appraisal system help to promote the division's new marketing strategy, aimed at broadening distribution and strengthening relationships with small dealers?

Part Four
The Marketing Executive

The primary responsibility of the marketing executive is to formulate marketing strategy and develop marketing plans to implement that strategy. Without a soundly conceived strategy, based on a thorough understanding of customer wants, the sales force will not get to first base. Put another way, the best sales force in the world will find it almost impossibly difficult to sell a product which is poorly conceived, poorly designed, poorly manufactured, poorly distributed, poorly priced, and poorly promoted.

MARKETING AND CORPORATE STRATEGY

Marketing strategy is but one facet of a firm's overall strategy. Formulating marketing strategy is an activity performed within the context of a firm's overall strategic planning. The latter involves (1) identifying the nature of the business by selecting specific objectives from the many possible objectives, (2) plotting the course of the business by forming plans to achieve those objectives, and (3) determining the character of the business by describing the policies that will support those plans. This sort of planning ensures that short-term decisions advance rather than hinder long-range goals.

Formulating corporate strategy begins with identifying risks and opportunities in the environment. This assessment requires data on current economic, social, and political conditions, as well as reasonable predictions about these conditions 2, 10, even 20 years in the future. Corporate executives try to answer such questions as, Will interest rates continue to rise? Will skilled labor be available? Will workers prefer shorter hours to higher salaries? Will local governments become more active in regulating businesses? Will the federal government's policies foster economic growth?

In addition to predicting general economic and social conditions, executives try to forecast factors that are particularly pertinent to their business. For example, will the predicted increase in retired persons in the United States offer new product opportunities? Will increased leisure time bring similar opportunities? Will our current competitors remain strong? Will our technologies be rendered obsolete by new processes? Will our competitors spend more of their funds on advertising, or on expanding their distribution networks?

After analyzing the risks and opportunities in the environment, senior executives project the resources that the company will need to seize these opportunities and minimize these risks. The company's internal resources must be evaluated and plans made to secure or develop additional resources, as needed. Such resources include personnel, finances, facilities, the firm's reputation, and its relationships with suppliers and customers.

To develop marketing strategy, marketers follow the same basic format as do corporate strategists. The marketer's first step is to match the environmental opportunities—potential customers—with the firm's resources—current and future product offerings. (The term *product* comprises both goods and services.)

CUSTOMER BEHAVIOR

For every product, the marketer must identify potential groups of customers so that marketing efforts can be directed toward these groups. Identifying potential customers requires first that one understand what motivates consumers to buy the product. How do people decide what goods and services to buy?

One useful theory about consumer decision making holds that customers are guided by their perceptions of the *functional* and the *symbolic* qualities of the product. A customer chooses a product not only for the product's intrinsic value, as the customer perceives it, but also for the product's ability to enhance the purchaser's feeling of self-worth. The functional aspect of buying a carpet, for instance, might involve an assessment of product durability: Will it wear well? The symbolic aspect might involve an assessment of style: What will the neighbors think of this shade? Similarly, in industrial marketing a purchasing agent might be concerned with a functional attribute: Will this lathe be easy to service? The agent might also be concerned with a symbolic attribute: How will the user feel about operating a lathe manufactured overseas?

How do customers evaluate the functional and symbolic characteristics of a product? Some rely entirely on their own judgments. Most people find such independence too risky, however. To temper the risk of making incorrect choices, some people rely on certain brands, some rely on certain vendors, others rely on the previous selections made by social reference groups. These groups may subtly determine, for example, the success of an L. L. Bean chamois-cloth shirt or a Brooks Brothers gray pin-striped suit. Successful marketing then, gains customers by developing their brand and vendor loyalties, by providing functional information, and by offering symbolic reassurance.

MARKET SEGMENTATION

Once the marketer has determined the most likely functional and symbolic needs that the product fulfills, the second step in developing marketing strategy is to isolate groups of customers that are most likely to have these particular functional and symbolic needs. The process of defining customer groups is called *market segmentation.*

Demographic analysis is the most common means of segmenting the market. Groups are isolated by sex, age, residence, income, and so on. Objective data, however, are often insufficient to determine consumer buying habits. Many executives supplement demographic data with an analysis of buyers' motivations. This kind of analysis had become known as psychographic segmentation and includes such criteria for isolating customer groups as: the customer's perception of value, his or her susceptibility to change, the purpose in purchasing the product, aesthetic preferences, consumption behavior, and general self-confidence and familiarity with the product class.

The beer industry contains many opportunities for illustrating psychographic segments. Beer drinkers can be distinguished by their purposes in drinking the product—refreshment, stimulation, or sociability. They can be distinguished by their aesthetic preferences for "light" or for "full-bodied" beer. Another criterion is the consumer's perception of value. Some people want to pay the lowest possible price for their beer; others are willing to pay more for "premium" beer. And some will pay even more for the unusual flavor or snob-appeal of an import. The market can also be segmented by consumption habits. Beer drinkers may drink occasionally, frequently, or both frequently and in large quantities.

Miller Brewing Company researchers in 1973, shortly after the company acquired the Lite trade name from Meister Brau, Inc., discovered that Meister Brau Lite was popular in certain industrial cities in the Midwest. This observation encouraged them to think that targeting marketing efforts to the urban, blue-collar, television-sports-watching segment would produce a large number of beer drinkers who would consume on a frequent basis a large quantity of a less filling beer. Thus was born Miller Lite, "Everything you always wanted in a beer, and less."

Industrial products lend themselves to psychographic segmentation as well. Consider the market for air freight. In 1965 Emery Air Freight Company was the largest air freight forwarder in the world. Emery picked up freight from the customer, selected the most advantageous air carrier, and delivered the freight at the other end of the flight. Since Emery was not limited to a few routes and a few schedules, it could use any equipment, route, and schedule operated by any airline or by any surface carrier.

One of the major marketing problems in this industry was the market's heterogeneity: almost every business was a potential customer. After several years of trying to be everything to every business, Emery executives decided to tailor their services to particular market segments. After analyzing customer scheduling habits, Emery divided its market into three segments: emergency users of air freight, frequent but unplanned users, and planned users. Deciding that planned users offered the greatest potential for profits, Emery conducted studies to identify the conditions under which regular planned use of air freight could reduce a customer's costs for inventory, warehousing, and distribution. The studies also identified industries in which these favorable conditions were most likely to be present. Thus, without ignoring the emergency and erratic users, Emery concentrated its marketing activities on a select and highly profitable group of customers.

PRODUCT POSITIONING

Matching the characteristics of the product to a particular market segment is known as *product positioning*. By product positioning, Emery promoted the advantages of planned freight use to customers most likely to benefit from Emery's services. Another example of product positioning is offered by Kellogg's marketing of its Special K cereal, the first "nutritional" ready-to-eat cereal to be marketed nationally in the United States. Special K was introduced in 1956. In 1961 Quaker Oats and General Foods introduced their own nutritional cereals, Life and Total. Despite these competitors, Special K maintained its dominant share of the market, largely because Kellogg's marketing executives had targeted the market segment most appropriate to the product. Special K was the least filling, least fattening, and least sweet of the three new cereals. Kellogg's executives decided that these characteristics would suit adult purchasers. Kellogg's advertising consistently aimed at this market segment. One famous campaign was the Lean Animal series. Some of these ads featured a virile-looking man and a prancing stallion; others depicted a slender, satin-clad woman and a sleek panther. By contrast, the initial advertising campaigns for Life and Total were inconsistent. Some were aimed at adults, others at children. Some stressed taste, some nutrition, and some economy. Credit for Kellogg's success must certainly be shared with its advertising agency, but advertising people find it easier to be creative for clients who know exactly what their goals are.

Customer analysis, market segmentation, and their end result, product positioning, are a marketing executive's most important activities. The advantages of good product positioning are numerous. The company's manufacturing resources are committed to salable products. Decisions to abbreviate or to extend the product lines are based on the needs of identified groups of customers, and not merely on manufacturing ease or research and development breakthroughs. Advertising copy appeals to the pertinent attributes of potential customers. Advertising media are selected to reach specific consumer groups. This is more effective and inexpensive than choosing media at random. Pricing decisions are based partly on the prices that customers are willing to pay. Distribution decisions are based on customers' vendor preferences and service expectations. Sales executives can identify likely customers in advance and can offer their salespeople more effective sales aids and training programs.

STIMULATING DEMAND

Having positioned the product accurately, whether it is a new introduction or an old model, the marketing strategists must now stimulate demand for the product. Using the right tactic to stimulate customer demand at the right time requires an understanding of the *product life cycle.* Some products have extremely short sales lives. The life of the hula hoop, for example, was measured in months, although nostalgia for the 1950s has allowed the product a recent comeback. Other products have long sales lives. The guitar, then already several hundred years old, began edging out the lute in the 18th century and shows no signs of slackening. The functional improvement of electrification gave it a new sales boost.

The sales life of every product generally includes four successive stages—an introductory phase followed by phases of growth, maturation, and eventually, decline. In the introductory stage, competition is limited to one or two innovators, and customers are unfamiliar with the product's functional and symbolic benefits. Product differentiation and increased competition emerge in the growth stage, and broader customer interest develops as adapting firms market variations on the original idea. The mature stage is characterized by great similarity among products offered by competing firms, which fight intensively for market share—customers have become sophisticated about the product. In the declining stage, competing products are nearly identical. Competition continues among a few dominant survivors. Customers view the product with the boredom suited to a commodity's lack of novelty.

The life cycle of the ball-point pen illustrates these phases clearly. During the mid-1940s, the ball-point pen made its commercial appearance in selected stationery and department stores. The pens leaked and left blotches of ink wherever they renewed contact with a writing surface. Despite their defects, the first ball-points were priced at about $15. The pens were heavily advertised and promoted. By the late 1940s, ball-points were no longer owned solely by the affluent and adventurous few. Their prices had dropped to about $2, the same price as that of a medium-quality fountain pen. Ball-points no longer leaked, although they still blotched the paper occasionally. Product features proliferated—some models offered retractable points and multibarreled ink supplies.

By the middle 1950s, the price of a typical ball-point had dropped to less than $1. Quality was assured, refills had been standardized, and ownership was so widespread that sales of fountain pens had declined sharply. Today, ball-points can be purchased by the gross for much less than the unit price of the original model. Although the product still offers a range of prices and features, the ball-point has become essentially a commodity that stirs little consumer interest. Just as the ball-point captured the fountain pen's market share, now the fabric-tip threatens to edge out the ball-point.

Each phase of the product life cycle has its own marketing requirements. To stimulate consumer demand for the product, the marketing executive must adjust product policy, distribution, pricing, and advertising according to the product's stage in its life cycle. Each of these aspects of stimulating demand is discussed below.

Product Policy

Product policy refers to the choice of features and associations that are secondary to the basic product. Forming product policy includes determining the product's design, appearance, and packaging; choosing the variations to be offered within the product line, such as various styles, colors, and sizes; and determining whether or not the product will be branded to link it with other products marketed by the firm.

When the product is in its *introductory phase*, its novelty is often the key impediment to consumer acceptance. In some cases, novelty causes customers to question the product's functional value. Power brakes and power steering, for example, required that drivers learn new driving habits, and many drivers complained that the innovations were unnecessary and dangerous. Word processors were initially resisted by many secretaries. Microwave ovens also seemed risky and unlikely to work as well as old-fashioned ovens. For other new products, symbolic attributes are uncertain. Molded plastic furniture initially seemed of questionable aesthetic value. Generally, marketers are best advised to choose for the initial introduction the model that is most likely to provide customers with a favorable first experience with the product.

In addition to selecting features and variations for the product introduction, product policy in the introductory stage includes determining the proper fit between the new product and others already marketed by the firm. The key question is whether or not the sales of both old and new products will be helped or hindered by the association. Giving the new product an already established brand name may help its sales. On the other hand, if the new product has quality control problems, the new product may hurt the established brand's reputation. And if the new product's use is similar (or will be perceived as similar) to that of an older product, one of the two products may draw sales from (cannibalize) the other product. If the marketer believes that cannibalization is a significant risk, he or she may choose product features to minimize the similarity between the two products. The advertising, pricing, and distribution methods may also be varied for each product to reduce the risk of cannibalization.

The *growth stage* begins once the innovator's product is accepted in the marketplace. Success attracts adaptors, firms that develop variations on the original model. Accumulated product variations and improvements, and the sheer mass of promotional spending and sales force effort combine to produce rapid growth in per capita consumption (also known as "primary demand"). The new competitors capitalize on the innovator's marketing and production efforts, and may profit by the innovator's technical and marketing mistakes. To survive in this stage, the innovator must offer more and better variations on the original product. The innovator can then take advantage of the increased demand caused in part by competitors' advertising dollars and sales force efforts. The key product-policy decision, then, is to choose the product features and variations that offer the best functional improvements over competitors' products.

For example, General Foods Corporation sustained the early sales of its JELL-O brand gelatin dessert by increasing the number of flavors. Don Wilson's famous "six delicious flavors" was soon augmented by half a dozen more. Marketers also promoted JELL-O as a base for gelatin salads and developed several vegetable-flavored variations. By increasing the number of flavors and promoting varied uses of the product, marketing executives increased the frequency of consumption.

Executives of 3M (Minnesota Mining and Manufacturing) Company have used similar methods to lengthen the product life cycle of Scotch tape. To raise sales among current users, they developed a variety of dispensers that made the product easier to use. Product variations included colored, patterned, water-proofed, invisible, and write-on Scotch tapes. 3M introduced Rocket Tape, a product much like Scotch Tape but lower in price, and developed a line of commercial cellophane tapes of various widths, lengths, and strengths and developed products such as double-coated tape and reflecting tape, which used the basic material in new ways.

In the *mature stage*, the growth rate in per capita consumption has begun to slow. This stage is not as profitable as the growth stage, primarily because marketing expenses increase. Product variations with genuine functional benefits have been adopted by all competitors, now seen as "gladiators" for market share points. Because the products are now essentially similar, customers are quite sophisticated in making judgments about the relative functional value of competing brands. Marketers generally use two product policies to interest customers in their products in this stage. One policy is to augment the product's auxiliary services—offering longer warranty periods or more comprehensive service packages, for example. A second policy is to emphasize the symbolic differences between one's own and the competing products. For example, the Virginia Slims cigarette offers a modest functional variation—a somewhat smaller diameter than that of the average cigarette. But this product variation supports an advertising campaign that has produced powerful symbolic associations for the product as a feminine cigarette. Who can confuse the "You've come a long way, baby" cigarette with any other? In a similar move, marketing executives at General Foods began advertising Jell-O brand gelatin as a low-calorie dessert. The product remained the same; only its symbolic associations were changed.

In the *declining stage,* per capita consumption is falling, usually because of competition from a new technology (e.g., the slide rule falling prey to the hand-held calculator). Because products made by the survivors are nearly identical in function, image, and price, the only way to maintain profits is to cut costs through mass production and mass distribution. Thus, the key product-policy decision in this stage is to determine the features and associations that will allow the product to be mass produced and mass distributed at the lowest possible cost.

Distribution Policy

Distribution policy is the marketers' second key means of stimulating demand. Distribution marketing generally includes both moving the product from point of manufacture to point of purchase and selecting and managing the channels of distribution, collectively known as the trade. The former activity, known as physical distribution or logistics, involves choosing basic units of shipment, methods of transport, and storage systems. Once the physical distribution system has been set up, buying patterns may show the need for changes in material handling, inventory levels, stocking points, data processing, and transport methods. Then the physical distribution or marketing manager must weigh the costs of making such changes against the anticipated gains in customer satisfaction and trade cooperation.

Because physical distribution is influenced by many nonmarketing factors, such as plant location and manufacturing technology, detailed discussion of this function is beyond the scope of this book. In fact, in many firms physical distribution is assigned to the manufacturing group, rather than to the marketing group. Our focus here is on the channels of distribution: Where and under what conditions do we offer our product for sale?

In selecting distribution channels and policies, the marketer should keep in mind two basic premises. First, customers seek dealers whose physical facilities or business practices are congruent with the customers' self-images. (For simplicity's sake, the term *dealer* refers to wholesalers, distributors, jobbers, retailers, and other types of middlemen.) Having identified potential customers in order to position the product, the marketer attempts to select dealers who fit the image preferred by these customers. The second major premise behind distribution selection is that the dealers must match the particular product—regardless of whether or not these dealers handle the firm's other products. For example, the new product may require special promotions or services that cannot be delivered by the firm's usual channels. If the product represents an unusual degree of purchasing risk to the customer, then the firm must choose dealers who can educate customers and reduce the perceived risk. Similarly, if the product requires extensive promotion to make its claims heard above those of competitors, or if it requires special installation or postsale services, the outlets chosen must be equipped to perform these activities. If the product's cost is high, or if large volumes must be held in the dealer's inventory, the marketer must choose dealers with the requisite financial resources.

Having matched the dealer to the customers and the product, the thoughtful marketer comes to view dealers as extensions of the firm, not as outsiders, enemies, or even as customers. If the marketer, in arrogance or carelessness, provokes or allows the dealer to gain greater strength in the local market than the marketer has, then the marketer will lose control over that dealer and that market, and, eventually, the firm's brand. The rise of the so-called generics is a good example, a phenomenon which has spread from pharmaceuticals to household food staples.

Like product policies, distribution patterns must be altered to fit the varying phases of the product's life cycle. In the *introductory stage* dealers should be selected for their abilities to perform certain key functions. They must be able to guide the customer to a favorable first experience with the product, to monitor the customer's experience with the product, and to provide postsale service, if necessary. Usually, the best distribution system for the introductory stage is *direct* and *exclusive*, for several reasons. Middlemen are not yet necessary, because the small volumes moving from point of production to point of sale do not require sophisticated logistics. Direct distribution gives the innovator greater control over the customer's first experience with the product and more rapid, accurate information about that first experience. Direct contact with the reseller also enables the innovator to explain the product and its use.

Exclusive distribution—using one or two dealers in a given trading area or market—is desirable for both the dealer and the innovator. Dealers can support the product more fully when other dealers carry no competing items or product lines. In return for this service, the marketer helps the dealers to promote the product, to train sales and service personnel, to carry adequate inventory, and to react quickly to customer inquiries and complaints.

In the *growth stage*, competitors race for additional dealers. Exclusively in distribution gives way to selectivity. Adaptors try to get their product lines carried by the "best" dealers, whether or not these carry competitors' lines. Eventually, selective distribution is replaced by intensive distribution, as adaptors try to have their products carried by all dealers that customers consider appropriate vendors for the product.

The original innovator now faces a dilemma. Does the marketer keep the promise of "protected sales territories," thereby risking loss of market share and perhaps double-crossing from dealers who finally agree to take on competing lines? Or does the marketer break the promise, jettison the policy of exclusivity, and join the adaptors in the scramble for broader distribution?

Some companies handle this dilemma by introducing additional lines under a new brand name, preserving the original brand for the original dealers and using the new brand for the additional dealers. Sometimes the new brand is identical in quality, appearance, and price to the original brand. More often, the new brand is lower in price and quality, as may befit a less-exclusive dealer network.

In the *mature stage*, lack of product differentiation and increasing customer sophistication mean that dealers' service and sales capabilities are no longer so useful nor so cost-effective. The marketer's focus now shifts from intensive distribution to mass distribution. The gladiators try to have their products carried by all possible dealers, whether or not customers may initially have considered those vendors to be appropriate. Inexpensive cameras are sold in supermarkets, phonograph records in drug stores, and clock-radios in bookstores. Mass distribution means *indirect* distribution. Middlemen proliferate, for intermediate stocking points are needed to ensure quick responses to dwindling inventories. The marketer no longer has much control over the vendor. Only for the most complex or high-priced products is it still necessary or cost-effective for the marketer to control the channels.

In the *declining stage,* mass distribution reaches its extreme limits. If the product's characteristics permit, even salespeople may become unnecessary, replaced by vending machines.

Pricing Policies

What price to charge for the new product? The easiest pricing technique is to apply a uniform markup on costs. But this process does not allow firms to charge premium prices in good times, or to charge low prices to stimulate volume during hard times.

In the *introductory stage,* the innovator enjoys a pricing latitude that will never recur. The customer has no experience with the product. No competition exists. And, to the degree of the product's novelty, its benefits have not been translated into a specific price range. Thus, the innovator may choose a high price relative to costs. This pricing policy, known as skimming, has some obvious advantages. Skimming allows the firm to recoup its investment more quickly. It also allows the innovator to minimize the loss if demand falls short of expectations, or to maximize profits if the product's life cycle turns out to be short. High prices are particularly useful for products with patent protection (such as the early Xerox copiers), or long production lead times (such as commercial jet aircraft). Skimming is also effective with products that are drastic departures from current offerings and whose pricing may require experimentation before the most acceptable long-run price level can be determined. The innovator can always reduce the price as soon as adaptors enter the market.

On the other hand, offering the product at an initially low price has other advantages, particularly if the firm has the financial resources to ride out a long period of losses or marginal profits. This pricing strategy, called penetration pricing, uses low prices to build market share while discouraging adaptors from entering the market. By the time that adaptors realize the potential profits of the new market, promotional efforts by these late entrants only expand a market now dominated by the innovator. Penetration pricing makes particular sense when the product's life cycle is expected to be long (Henry Ford knew what he was doing when he priced the Model A). It is also useful when unit costs are expected to drop considerably with increases in volume, and when it is desirable to protect one's hold on the market against anticipated strong competition. The firm producing the most units usually enjoys the lowest cost of value added per unit. This phenomenon, called the experience curve, means of course that the firm with the largest market share should be the low-cost producer. The experience curve is a strong argument for building market share rapidly through penetration pricing.

Whether the innovator decides to price high or low, the key pricing consideration in the introductory stage is to have the product accepted in the market. Novelty often means ambiguity. If the targeted audience can readily evaluate the product's benefits, then a high price is easier to justify. On the other hand, if the product's features, benefits, and uses are difficult for customers to grasp, then a high price may only further deter consumers' acceptance of the new product.

In the *growth stage*, the adaptor begins to lose pricing latitude. As competition focuses on product features, customers begin to weigh the benefits of these features against their costs. The question in the customer's mind changes from "Should I buy a trash compactor?" to "If I buy a trash compactor, is the easy-open feature worth an extra $20?" At this point, product differentiation develops consumers' brand preferences—preferences that the adaptor hopes will carry over into the mature stage, when the differentiation is less marked.

The adaptor's pricing latitude is now restricted not only by consumer sophistication but also by the increasing complexity of the channels of distribution. The longer the chain—agents, wholesalers, jobbers, distributors, retailers—the more the margins that must be paid to these agents mount up. These accumulating margins lock the adaptor into a narrow price range.

Thus, in the growth stage, price emerges as an important element of the brand's identity and of the product's identity. The overriding pricing criterion in this stage is to set price ranges that can be justified by functional improvements.

In the *mature stage*, products are fairly similar. The gladiator must now decide whether or not to make the product's price the basis of competition. Can the marketer increase market share and/or profitability by reducing prices relative to those of competitors? Or would other marketing tactics be more effective, strategies such as increased advertising, broader distribution, or better customer service?

In some cases, conditions within the industry as a whole will determine whether or not the marketer chooses to compete by price. Price competition in the mature stage is usually not marked if (1) product differentiation is still feasible (as with cameras); (2) symbolic values can still be created (as with cosmetics); (3) customers cannot easily gauge the benefits of a particular brand (as with dog food); or (4) customers cannot easily compare brands (as with prescription drugs). On the other hand, price competition becomes intense under the following conditions: (1) one or more firms can offer customers a clear choice between low price and brand reputation (as with

Econocar and Hertz); (2) the trade becomes more powerful than the manufacturers and can offer low-priced, private label brands; or (3) the industry faces competition from substitute products (aluminum competing with steel).

The decision on whether or not to compete by price also depends on the marketer's perceptions of future conditions in the marketplace. How will general economic conditions, such as interest rates and consumer confidence, influence demand? How many gladiators will enter or leave the market? Will a price leader emerge?

Determining whether to compete on the basis of price depends as well on consumer attitudes to the firm's products. Is there enough differentiation in the product to warrant a price premium, or at least to ward off any need to reduce the price? Does a residue of loyalty exist from previous marketing activities that will insulate the firm from competitors' pricing tactics? Are customers' choices in this product class determined solely by price, or are customers influenced by other factors?

Finally, the decision to enter price competition depends on the firm's corporate objectives. What role is this product expected to play among the firm's other lines? Has the product been selected to promote some image of quality or price for the line as a whole? Is the product expected to generate profits to support other products? Or is it a "loss leader," priced for volume sales in order to attract customers to more profitable lines?

Whether or not price competition becomes the dominant pricing strategy for this product, the gladiator may decide to use tactical pricing—temporary price changes made to achieve specific marketing objectives. One type of tactical pricing is "trade loading"—offering dealers special discounts (called buying allowances) to purchase specified quantities within a specified time period. To move products out of the stores, the marketer may try "trade unloading," offering dealers discounts to display the product prominently or offering advertising allowances for products featured in the dealer's advertising. "Consumer loading" is often used simultaneously with trade unloading. Common forms of consumer loading are the "cents-off" deal and the "one free with five" deal. Once the products have been purchased, "consumer unloading" encourages immediate consumption. For example, marketers may insert cents-off coupons *inside* the package. All of these tactical pricing maneuvers are used most often in the product's mature or declining phases.

The common tactical pricing equivalents in industrial marketing are "push money," also called PMs and spiffs, and a variety of dealer incentives in the form of contests and special promotions to dealers and their salesmen. Push money is generally paid to dealer salesmen on a per-unit-sold basis to encourage them to sell one brand over another.

In the *declining phase*, the competing products are all equivalent, if not identical, and survivors are rarely able to charge price premiums. Nor are firms able to reduce prices significantly. Prices are already so low as to allow only the barest margin over costs. The keys to success in this stage are low-cost production, mass distribution to increase sales volume, and minimal expenditures on advertising and other marketing supports. In the declining stage, then, the key pricing criterion is to find the lowest price that will allow reasonable profitability.

Advertising Policy

Advertising is the marketer's fourth means of stimulating demand. Advertising provides potential customers with information and reassurance about the product's functional and symbolic qualities.

The *effectiveness* of the advertising message on the consumer is heavily dependent on the talents of the creative people, guided by the marketer's information about market segmentation, product positioning, and the campaign's goals. The *efficiency* of an advertising campaign refers to its benefits to the company—that is, the campaign's ability to increase sales at reasonable costs.

Advertising Effectiveness.   Advertising is most likely to be effective if the consumer perceives both the functional and symbolic risks of product adoption to be relatively minor. If, on the other hand, the consumer is particularly anxious that the product fulfill its promises, then he or she is likely to run from advertising to a more credible source of information and reassurance.

Consider two products, similar in composition and use, but differing in their consumers' perceptions of risk. The first product is an athlete's foot powder, the second a medicated baby powder used to control diaper rash. The customer for the first product may prefer not to pay for information from a physician, and he or she may be too embarrassed to ask a pharmacist or a friend. And the risk that the product will not work may not be significant to the customer. Thus, the customer is willing to rely on information conveyed by advertisements. On the other hand, the purchaser of a medicated baby powder is anxious that the product relieve the baby's pain. This purchaser will probably rely on information from a pediatrician or another trusted source, such as the child's grandmother. For this customer, advertising will have little credibility.

Advertising's effectiveness is also determined by characteristics of the product and of its stage in its life cycle. In his classic work, *The Economic Effects of Advertising*, Neil H. Borden identified five conditions under which advertising is most likely to be effective. First, advertising is more likely to be effective if there is growing primary demand for the product. But if consumers have lost interest in the product category as a whole, advertising campaigns are unlikely to turn the tide. If men stop wearing hats, no single hat-maker's advertisements will generate much business.

Second, advertising is more likely to be effective if the product allows high gross margins that can pay for large dollar investments in advertising. The third condition for effective advertising is that the product's qualities are difficult to assess at point of purchase; for example: mattresses, power drills, and packaged goods. The customer is forced to rely on the manufacturer's or the brand's reputation—which usually has been communicated through advertising. Fourth, advertising is more likely to be effective if the product can be easily associated with a symbol central to the potential customer's self-image. Recall the husky sailor of the Old Spice cologne ads, and the sophisticated Lauren Hutton of Revlon's Ultima II cosmetics. Finally, product differentiation is essential to effective advertising. Creative people can compose more stimulating advertisements for products with truly distinctive features than they can for products with only symbolic advantages.

One reason industrial marketers tend to rely more on "push" strategies—reliance on personal selling efforts to move products through the channels of distribution—than on "pull" strategies—reliance on advertising to create consumer demand to draw products through the channels of distribution—is that many industrial products do not conform well to Professor Borden's notion of advertisability. Many industrial products are "big ticket" and are of keen interest to purchasing agent *and* user (who may not be the same individual). Second, these big-ticket items seldom have the high gross margins characteristic of many consumer package goods. Third, the technical specifications of many industrial products allow the prospective buyer a means of comparing and contrasting vendor's features at point of purchase. Fourth, it is difficult for many industrial products to be invested with a symbol "central to a customer's self-image." Finally, the kinds of product differentiation activities common in industrial marketing are usually better and cheaper to explain and communicate via salesmen than via advertisements.

Nevertheless, advertising can and does play a role for many industrial products, particularly when they have characteristics similar to packaged goods. Moreover, industrial marketers find advertising messages an effective means for establishing a favorable image for the company and its sales force, for making announcements about new products, for reaching executive levels beyond those ordinarily reached through normal sales call patterns, and for achieving a wide variety of *specific* communications objectives related to the product line. Examples here include the use of advertising by Federal Express to expand the use of overnight letter and small-package delivery beyond that dictated by the customer's traffic department.

Advertising Efficiency. The key to advertising efficiency is clear-cut objectives. For example, an advertising objective could be to "increase the proportion of potential buyers who are aware of our unconditional guarantee from the current 30 percent to 50 percent by the end of the year." The objective chosen should be achievable within the chosen time limit and market segment, and it should fit into the firm's overall marketing objectives. The objective must also have a built-in criterion for measuring the campaign's performance. And here is where efficiency and effectiveness become intertwined. The same objective outlined above uses the effectiveness of *customer awareness,* which can be measured by assessing consumer's memories of information presented in advertisements. Two other common measures of advertising effectiveness used in setting advertising objectives are *consumer attitudes* and *consumer behavior*. Changes in consumer attitudes are assessed by determining changes in consumers' stated preferences or in their images of the product. Attitudes and awareness are both generally studied through telephone surveys, questionnaires, or marketing study groups. Consumer behavior, on the other hand, is generally measured by counting such indicators as store visits, requests for brochures, and use of coupons.

Few sophisticated marketers believe that advertising effectiveness should be measured by changes in sales volume. Advertising is essentially a means of communication. Thus, it should be evaluated according to its ability to deliver a message. Advertising shares the responsibility for sales volume with product policy, distribution, pricing, product quality, and the sales force. Consider an advertising campaign that had made large numbers of people aware of and favorably disposed toward a product. But once the customer gets to the store, he or she may settle for a competitor's product if the product originally sought is poorly displayed, difficult to find, or out of stock. Even if the product is readily available, the customer may choose the competitor's product for its more attractive package, special features, lower price, or promotional offer. If the sale goes to the competitor, most thoughtful marketers would agree that advertising alone was not responsible.

Advertising efficiency, like advertising effectiveness, is aided by sound market segmentation, which allows good media selection, and by sound product positioning, which allows good advertising copy creation. Once the market is segmented and the product is positioned, the key to advertising efficiency is again that the campaign have clear-cut objectives. For example, having established the purpose of increasing consumer awareness of the unconditional guarantee from 30 percent to 50 percent, the marketer can ascribe a dollar value to the achievement of that objective. The marketer can also determine the preferred maximal cost of achieving that objective. When the year is over the marketer can test consumer awareness and can calculate the costs of that change. If the marketer does not know what the objective is, the advertisement will merely be an expense, not a business tool.

Advertising's emphasis varies with the stage of the product's life cycle. In the *introductory stage*, advertising must first make consumers aware that the product exists and secondly educate them about its use. In the *growth stage*, when firms vie for customer preference by offering functional variations, advertising naturally stresses the advantages of the product's particular cluster of features. In the *mature* and *declining stages*, as competing products become more similar, advertising stresses image rather than function. Appeals are based on the product's symbolic qualities and on the brand's reputation. It is in these latter two stages that advertising may be criticized for influencing consumers with irrational appeals. But such advertising is often necessary to sustain sales among very similar products and generate sufficient profits to enable the launch of new products. In the *declining stage*, when the products are essentially similar and the customers are sophisticated, if not bored, advertising is often designed to keep the trade enthusiastic about the product. In this stage, the trade often needs to be reassured that the firm still supports the product.

CONCLUSION

While the marketer's advertising, pricing, distribution, and product policies are usually dictated by the product's stage in its life cycle, these policies must also be chosen so that they complement one another. For example, one key issue facing marketers is whether these policies should be combined in an effort to stimulate *primary demand* (demand for the product class) or *selective demand* (demand for the firm's own product). Consider the market for light aircraft. Cessna Aircraft Company has long held an enviable 50 percent share of this market. Cessna could reasonably try to stimulate primary demand, because half of all the new users would become Cessna customers. Should Cessna then spend its marketing funds to encourage people to learn to fly, in the hope that 50 percent of all new pilots will eventually buy a Cessna? Or should Cessna try to increase selective demand by advertising particular product features and services? A corollary issue is whether to build distribution networks intensively or selectively. Should Cessna expand distribution in the hope that, as new airfields open up, Cessna dealers will be available to all pilots? Or should Cessna use its money to improve selling and servicing capabilities among its present dealers, in the hope that these dealers can convince prospective buyers to buy a Cessna instead of a competing aircraft?

Marketers must also decide whether to emphasize marketing tactics which stimulate demand through more aggressive vendor activity—"push," or through more aggressive appeals directly to consumers—"pull." Push marketing pressures the channels of distribution so that they in turn will apply pressure to prospective customers. Typical push tactics include aggressive personal selling, high dealer margins that encourage the channels to stock and to promote the product, protected trade territories that make it worthwhile for dealers to invest their time and efforts in selling the product, and attractive factory service offerings and point-of-sale promotional efforts to help the dealers sell the product. Pull marketing aims to get consumers to seek the product. Typical pull tactics include aggressive consumer advertising to stimulate consumers' interest and broad distribution to assure that consumers will find the product once they decide that they want it. Pull tactics are usually correlated with limited manufacturers' service offerings and with lower dealer margins, because minimal dealer selling activity is required.

Most companies' marketing strategies are a hybrid of push and pull tactics. Advertising aimed directly at the consumer can help the sales force; at the same time, an effective sales force can ensure that a nationally advertised product is stocked and promoted by retailers. Developing marketing strategy is a delicate balancing act. The marketer must match the firm's products with its potential customers. The marketer must also coordinate advertising, pricing, distribution, and product policies with one another and with the various stages in each product's life cycle. Finally, the marketer must ensure that the firm's product offerings allow the financial needs of new products to be satisfied by funds generated by older products, while consumers' boredom with older products is compensated for by the interest stirred by new models.

Case 16
Scott-Air Corporation

Ben Millar, marketing manager of the Central Air Conditioning (CAC) Division of Scott-Air Corporation, settled back in his luxury Mercury Montego and moved the speed up to 70 MPH. With one finger of his left hand on the steering wheel and his right hand vigorously cutting the air in determined support of his words, he explained to the casewriter the strategic and tactical decisions he had to make within the next few days.

> For 1972, we have to decide whether or not to spend more money and, if so, which products we should promote, how we should promote them, and at what level in the marketing chain the dollars should be spent. For example, should I spend $160,000 in regional TV advertising, or concentrate in the big cities with regional print media, or redo all my catalogs, some of which are out of date and unattractive, at a cost of $120,000? Alternatively, should I reduce the advertising and sales promotion and spend some money on market research? We really know so little about the ultimate customer and about what makes a successful distributor and dealer.
>
> Since my marketing plan and budget have to be ready within the month, I have to get straight in my mind the big picture, too. It seems to me that we have really got to start again and rethink our basic policies. We have to decide what markets we are going to attack, what products will be required and how they can be developed, what strategy we should use and what this strategy means in terms of tasks to be performed by dealers, distributors, territory managers, advertising, sales promotion, and training programs, and finally, how all of these decisions will affect our terms to the trade, our incentives to buy, and our commission scheme for salesmen. A tall order, but I really think it is the only way.

Mr. Millar's deliberations on a marketing plan for 1972 were complicated by several problems. First, the company had just doubled central air conditioning capacity at its plant, bringing capacity to $64 million (factory sales value, two shifts). But "teething" troubles in the new facility had caused CAC to miss delivery dates. This tardiness and, in some cases, outright failure to supply customers had lost goodwill and lowered morale among distributors, dealers, and the division's sales force. Second, the new plant had a $28-million break-even, which Scott-Air executives wanted to surpass rapidly. Third, the division's market share had declined: from 3 percent on 1970s sales of $26 million to less than 2 percent on 1971s sales of $18 million. Fourth, although the central air conditioning market was growing at about 15 percent per year, CAC was not keeping pace with the growth rate, and senior managers were pressuring Mr. Millar to step up sales growth.

COMPANY BACKGROUND

Scott-Air Corporation had been founded around the turn of the century in Kansas City, Missouri, as a manufacturer of meat lockers and display cases for butcher shops. During the 1930s, company executives, fearing a stable demand for meat lockers, diversified into other refrigerating technologies and products. The survivors of these diversification moves were room air conditioners and central air conditioners. Large industrial air conditioning products had been dropped as unsuccessful in 1963; the locker and display case division had continued as part of the company's heritage.

Scott-Air sales by division in 1971 were expected to be as follows:

Division	Sales ($ millions)
Room air conditioning	$35
Central air conditioning	18
Lockers	2
Total..........................	$55

The company confined its marketing to the southern part of the United States—roughly, the area south of an imaginary line running from Baltimore in the East to San Francisco in the West. Although the company's three divisions were autonomous in marketing and manufacturing, all manufacturing took place within the same plant in Kansas City. Corporate staff handled all other functions, including personnel, research and development, finance, and legal counsel.

Scott-Air executives believed that the company and its products had developed an excellent reputation for quality. In particular, the Room Air Conditioning division's products—the Scottie, the Huskie, and the St. Bernard—were considered the luxury models within their respective BTU classifications.

THE CENTRAL AIR CONDITIONING INDUSTRY

The term *air conditioning* signified managing the air's temperature, humidity, purity, and circulation. Central air conditioners controlled all four

228

Exhibit 1
Selected Industry Statistics

A. Unit shipments of cooling-only and year-round systems

	Total	Cooling-Only		Year-Round	
		Package	Split System	Package	Heat Pumps
1960	350,422	97,680	190,773	14,468	47,501
1962	467,719	85,565	297,890	22,451	61,813
1964	701,569	85,321	489,606	49,857	76,785
1966	958,546	105,724	689,434	81,171	82,217
1968	1,234,611	120,136	910,597	115,378	88,500
1969	1,635,025	135,380	1,255,585	146,742	97,318
1970	1,616,018	157,599	1,210,741	150,031	97,687
1971	1,876,579	195,737	1,415,000	183,561	82,281

B. Dollar value of shipments at manufacturer's net prices

	Cooling-Only and Year-Round ($000)
1968	$ 617,000
1969	817,000
1970	808,000
1971	943,000
1972*	1,100,000
1974*	1,300,000
1976*	1,550,000

*Forecast.
Source: Air Conditioning and Refrigeration Institute and Bureau of Census.

factors. Three basic types of units were produced: cooling only, heating only, and year-round (heating and cooling).

Central air conditioners had been introduced in the 1930s, but sales grew slowly until 1953, when they began to mount steadily. (Selected industry sales statistics are shown in Exhibit 1.) Demand for central air conditioning in the home was constantly stimulated by the widespread use of air conditioning in offices, factories, schools, shops, and cars. Sales seemed to be closely related to personal income. A regression of total unit shipments from 1949 to 1970 on disposable income had an R^2 of .95.

Manufacturers' fixed costs were about 20 percent of factory selling prices. Materials could run as high as 60 percent of total variable cost, but parts standardization, efficient tooling, and materials substitution could lower this percentage significantly. A well-managed manufacturing operation could expect to lower unit variable costs by 10 percent with each doubling of unit cumulative production.

Distribution

Most manufacturers sold to independent distributors or to factory branches. These in turn sold to dealers for ultimate sale to homeowners. Air conditioners for residences under construction, however, were usually sold directly from the factory branch or distributor to the building contractor. Some companies also sold through mass-merchandisers, such as Sears. A few companies did not market directly, but sold their output to manufacturers that wanted to carry a full line, or to companies that concentrated on marketing central air conditioners.

Distributors typically suffered from undercapitalization. For example, a distributor who represented a manufacturer with a 10 percent market share could have sales of about $1.2 million at wholesale. Assuming a stock turn of four, the capital requirement for inventory alone amounted to $125,000, a substantial sum to many small businessmen.

Using factory branches to supplement independent distributorships alleviated the problem of finding enough distributors with adequate financing. Factory branches also gave the manufacturer more control over inventory service and dealer training. Despite these advantages, many firms preferred independent distributors, believing them more aggressive.

Terms of trade varied widely. Distributors' markups ranged from 15 to 20 percent. Distributors could increase this markup by taking advantage of 90-day terms and by selling to dealers on 30-day terms. (In 1971, distributors' receivables were estimated at 48 days.) Typically, distributors received a discount from the factory of 3 percent for orders placed before December 31, 2 percent before January 31, and 1 percent before February 28. Most distributors ordered 25 percent of their annual requirements by February 28. These discounts provided distributors with a fund out of which they awarded free trips, organized and sponsored by the manufacturers, to dealers who ordered a minimum amount in the winter.

The distributors' markup could also be reduced. Large dealers buying in volume could often command significant quantity discounts. In the new construction market, for example, distributor's markup could be reduced to as low as 5 percent because units were usually shipped directly from manufacturer to building contractor.

Dealers' markups ranged from 20 to 25 percent. A few dealers had kept pace with market growth. These dealers generally employed 10 to 15 salesmen (each making $20,000 to $25,000 per year), had sales of 3,000 to 7,000 units per year, and gave full installation and postsale service. Many dealerships, however, were small and grossly undercapitalized; many were owned by former merchants of limited ambition. To these dealers, sales growth was a problem, not an opportunity.

Competition

In 1971, the Air Conditioning and Refrigeration Institute listed 71 companies selling central air conditioners. Twelve manufacturers held 69 percent of the market. These firms and their market shares are listed below. The balance was divided among regional manufacturers such as Scott-Air.

Carrier (including Bryant and Payne/Day & Night)	20%
General Electric	8
Lennox	8
Westinghouse (including Luxaire)	6
Sears	6
Fedders	5
American Standard	5
Chrysler	3
Air Temp	2
York	2
Williamson	2
Trane	2
Total	69%

Some industry observers predicted that a shakeout would occur in the near future and that three or four large companies would dominate the market. Other observers claimed, however, that, since central air conditioning manufacturers were really nothing more than assemblers of components made by other companies, the market would support many manufacturers. A third view was that the costs of shipping inevitably favored regional manufacturers, and thus the industry would remain fragmented.

The marketing strategies of these companies varied quite widely. Carrier relied on national advertising to compete in the room, central, and industrial air conditioning markets. Carrier's sales to various end-users were as follows:

New homes and apartments	20%
Existing homes and apartments	18
Commercial	27
Industrial	20
Institutional	8
Defense, space, and transportation	7

Carrier also manufactured industrial machinery and heaters, but air conditioning accounted for 80 percent of its sales. Carrier used both factory branches and independent distributors to sell to its dealers.

Fedders was the leading company in room air conditioners. In 1971 it was making a determined and successful effort to penetrate the central air conditioning market. The company's major tactics were low prices, aggressive distribution, and generous incentives to dealers, such as luxury trips to the Amazon and Tahiti. Fedders sold through 70 independent distributors to 2,500 dealers.

General Electric concentrated heavily on selling to building contractors because these offered the potential of high volume and repeat business. To date, GE had showed little interest in the existing residential market. GE advertised heavily in national and local media. Distribution was through factory branches to 3,000 dealers.

BEN MILLAR'S CAC MARKETING ANALYSIS

Ben Millar, 40, had joined Scott-Air as a territory manager in the CAC division in 1961 after a successful retail sales career with Sears. In 1968 he was promoted to field sales manager of the Room Air Conditioning (RAC) division and in September 1971 to marketing manager of the CAC division. His first act as marketing manager was to call his sales and marketing personnel together to ask them to evaluate the marketing department's performance in five key areas: market segmentation, product line and pricing, sales force, distributors and dealers, and marketing communications.

MARKET SEGMENTATION

The responses that Mr. Millar received indicated to him that the market for units of 1½ to 10 tons could be segmented according to end-users. Millar described four segments: new residential, modernization of existing residences, replacement, and light commercial.

The new residential market accounted for 55 percent of total market unit sales, modernization for 18 percent, replacement for 20 percent, and light commercial for 7 percent. Of CAC's total sales 20 percent were in new residential, 75 percent in modernization, and the remainder in replacement.

The New Residential Market

Traditionally, CAC had not committed itself to the new residential market for several reasons. First, this market was price competitive, with prices sometimes only 15 percent above direct product costs. Builders were interested, furthermore, in availability of the product, low inventory requirements, and service. A second problem with serving this market was that the manufacturer had to sell to both the builder and the heating contractor simultaneously, consulting closely with them on specifications and bids. A third obstacle was that some executives considered this market "messy" because builders might be here today and gone tomorrow. Long and fruitful relationships with builders were difficult to sustain, and service problems often became the manufacturer's responsibility by default.

Mr. Millar acknowledged these problems, but stressed that the new residential segment offered the greatest sales potential. He also addressed the problem of builders' transience:

> You have to remember that when new home starts are down, the builder becomes a modernizer. Therefore, he can offer a valuable entry into the modernization segment. Also, I wonder if some builders will become dealers by developing their own air conditioning contracting companies. After all, the

builder is a man who will promote, who is invariably hungry, and he could take over a dealership. If you look at it this way, then, it seems to me you have to be in the builder business. I have to admit, however, that it would not be easy to accomplish.

Mr. Millar had some suggestions for getting builders' attention:

One idea for promotion is to offer the builders cooperative advertising arrangements similar to our dealer co-op plans. Also, we think that builders might be similar to dealers in their love of trips, and we might include them in Scott-Air dealer trips in return for some minimum order size.

The Modernization Segment

The modernization segment had margins often much higher than those in the new residential segment. The dealer seemed particularly important in this market. Since the installed cost to the customer could range from $700 to $1,500, central air conditioning represented a major investment in an area in which consumers were not very knowledgeable. In addition to advice on the product and its installation, consumers needed reassurance on reliability, maintenance, and service. Although CAC had 80 percent of its business in this segment, Mr. Millar believed that the division's share was but a fraction of the potential market.

Marketing staff believed that purchasers of central air conditioning lived in homes valued $25,000 or more, could be either white- or blue-collar workers, and already owned a room air conditioner for the bedroom. Marketing staff also believed that the decision on whether to buy central air conditioning was made jointly by husband and wife, but that the choice of brand was made by the husband.

Two broad alternatives were available for increasing sales in this segment. CAC could (1) go directly to the consumer via regional and local advertising or (2) use the money to raise dealers' interest and expertise in selling the product. CAC had traditionally relied on the latter tactic. Mr. Millar had to decide whether this strategy was still valid. If so, he needed to decide whether to allocate more money to this strategy.

The Replacement Segment

The replacement market was as profitable as the modernization segment. Mr. Millar commented on this market:

We have made penetration here, but it is not significant and this really worries me. Do you realize that this segment could well be 45 to 50 percent of total sales by 1977?

The decision maker in the replacement market was clearly the homeowner. Little was known about his or her buying behavior. But division executives assumed that, after seven years or so, the household head began to think of replacement and asked the air conditioning dealer, "What's new?" It seemed to Mr. Millar that the promotional alternatives open to him were similar to the two options in the modernization market.

The Light Commercial Segment

This segment included restaurants, schools, and churches. Like the new construction market, this segment presented a specialized selling task, and CAC had made little headway to date.

In addition to choosing a promotional strategy for each segment, Mr. Millar had to allocate marketing funds among the segments. The new residential market offered volume but low profitability; the modernization and replacement markets offered superior profitability but lower volume.

THE PRODUCT LINE AND PRICING POLICY

CAC marketed about 40 products of two basic types: cooling-only systems and year-round (cooling and heating) systems.

Cooling-Only Systems

These products were sold either as packaged or as "split" systems. The advantages of packaged systems were that all components were contained in one container and that better performance could be expected because much of the control work was performed in the factory. The main advantages of the split system were reduced costs per ton and flexibility of installation, because the evaporator and compressor could be separated from the other units by up to 50 feet.

Sizes of cooling-only units ranged from 1½ to 10 tons in split systems and 1½ to 30 tons in packaged systems. For the 3-ton size, a split system might cost $385 factory, $620 retail, plus $300 for installation in an existing house with good ducting or $250 in a new construction. A 3-ton packaged system might cost $460 factory, $740 retail, plus $300 installation. Cooling-only systems represented 70 percent of CAC's 1971 sales and supplied 64 percent of gross margin.

Year-Round Systems

CAC produced two packaged year-round systems and one split system. The two packaged systems were the Waverly and the Ivanhoe. The Waverly used electricity for cooling and gas for heating. It was made for outside installation—an advantage because the combustion and the operating noises remained outside the house. The main disadvantage was that slightly longer duct work might be involved which could increase installation costs. The Ivanhoe used electricity for both heating and cooling. Again, this style had the advantages of the one container plus the flexibility of being able to provide supplemental heating in extreme areas (Colorado, for example). The Waverly's sizes ranged from 2 to 10 tons, and the Ivanhoe ranged from 1½ to 3 tons. The split system, called the Kenilworth, offered the same flexibility of installation as did split-system cooling-only units. Kenilworth's sizes ranged from 2½ to 5 tons.

Typical prices for a 3-ton Waverly were $537 factory and $860 retail; for a 3-ton Ivanhoe, $494 factory and $793 retail; for a 3-ton Kenilworth, $775 factory and $1,245 retail. Installation costs were somewhat higher than those of cooling-only systems. Year-round systems represented 30 percent of CAC's 1971 sales and 36 percent of gross margin.

Before evaluating pricing policies, Mr. Millar wanted to learn how the line's quality and breadth were perceived by CAC personnel, by dealers and distributors, and by consumers.

CAC personnel compared the line's quality and breadth to that of competing products. Their conclusions were as follows:

	Westinghouse	Carrier	GE	Lennox	Scott-Air
Cooling only	3d	1st	2d	5th	4th
Year-round	2d	4th	3d	5th	1st

Ken Dallas, CAC's product manager, explained these rankings:

> We are first in Year-Round because, without doubt, we have the best heat pump in the business. In Cooling Only systems we rank fourth primarily because we do not have the multiplicity of models per size group that Carrier, GE, and Westinghouse have. In general, our product line is as broad as that of York and Lennox, but narrower than our other major competitors'.

A brief marketing survey had indicated that consumers viewed CAC products as superior to competitors' in reliability and breadth of the product line, but inferior in price and innovation. Consumers seemed to find Scott-Air equal to other brands in appearance and style. Dealers and distributors shared these perceptions for the most part. However, dealers and distributors serving the new residential and light commercial segments felt that CAC's product line was much narrower than competitors'.

To address potential problems with quality and breadth of the product line, Mr. Millar asked corporate research and development personnel to review the line and to suggest a system for making product development a regular feature of marketing and divisional planning.

Mr. Millar's next step was to consider pricing policy. CAC prices were usually higher than competitors'. Mr. Millar explained:

> Manufacturers in air conditioning make great use of the Chinese feint trick: to announce a price increase in the trade press and not implement it in the field. CAC, however, actually implemented the price increases and, of course, we lost competitiveness. Overall, I would say that we are between 6 to 10 percent

high on our prices to distributors. This means that the sales force is not making much money. Neither, of course, are the division or our distributors.

Mr. Millar's executives reasoned they had three pricing alternatives—to stay at a premium, to equal competition, or to undercut competition. Each option applied to each of the four market segments.

Furthermore, Mr. Millar believed that three specific pricing decisions were particularly important. The first concerned the price for split system cooling-only units, which accounted for 62 percent of the division's sales and 54 percent of its gross margin. One executive had suggested undercutting the competition in the construction market and maintaining the premium or equal prices in the modernization market.

The second decision involved the price for the Kenilworth. Although Scott-Air held a patent on the Kenilworth's heat pump and customers had paid a premium for it, unit sales of the heat pump had begun to decline. In 1971, the Kenilworth accounted for 15 percent of the division's sales and 18 percent of its gross margin. Millar estimated the price premium at 10 percent. He had to decide whether to maintain the 10 percent premium, drop it to 5 percent, equal competition's price, or undercut them.

The third decision was the price for the Ivanhoe. This product had a number of exclusive features. In 1971, it accounted for 10 percent of sales and 12 percent of gross margin. Just recently, a regional competitor had produced something close to the Ivanhoe and sold it about 15 percent cheaper. Ivanhoe's sales had subsequently declined. Millar had to decide whether to hold his price and push the superior product features more heavily, or to drop the price to equal competition.

THE SALES FORCE

The current sales force included 2 zone managers, 13 territory managers, 6 service representatives, and 2 customer service agents. Mr. Millar believed that more service personnel were needed for 1972. Total salary and administrative costs for a zone manager amounted to approximately $40,000 per year; for a territory manager, $35,000; for a service representative, $30,000; and for a customer service agent, from $15,000 to $25,000.

Comparing his sales force to those of competitors, Mr. Millar believed that it was superior in selling skill and responsiveness to supervision, inferior in morale and motivation, and about the same in account coverage, product knowledge, and opening up of new accounts. To decide how to deal with the low morale, Mr. Millar asked Alice Harker, corporate director of personnel, to investigate its causes. Ms. Harker outlined these factors:

1. CAC's high prices.
2. Lack of new products.
3. Inability to fill customer's orders in full.
4. Constant complaints from distribution about order handling.

5. Inappropriate incentive system.
6. Lack of marketing direction.

The inability of the division to develop new products had two consequences, Mr. Millar believed. First, the sales force believed that Scott-Air was behind in product innovation. Second, the sales force came to distrust division marketing personnel.

The sales force's complaints about product availability arose from the lack of inventory and the start-up problems in the new plant. In Millar's words, "you cannot sell from an empty wagon, and that is what we have tried to do." He also concurred with the complaint about order handling:

> I was sure that Alice would find this. Our customers phone CAC orders and are unable to get answers on the phone. Not only were we unable to help the customer get his goods, but often we did not even know how to pacify him. Even if we have the stuff in stock, it takes about a week to process it. We should have orders out in a day.

Mr. Millar also agreed that the compensation system had drawbacks.

> The territory managers' commissions are based on gross margin. Thus, volume is very important to them, and management has attempted to compensate for the low volume by increasing territory size. This is the wrong way 'round, and it is not surprising there is poor morale. We have to turn this compensation scheme around somehow so that it is related to territory potential, ensures a decent wage, and then rewards an individual for performance on as many aspects of his or her job as possible.

Mr. Millar commented on the territory managers' feeling that they received little direction from the marketing department.

> They told Alice—and I'm not surprised—that they never knew for sure where CAC wanted to compete, that they could not understand why we seemed to have little interest in the valuable new-construction residential market, and that we failed to give them clear job definitions and goals.

Mr. Millar complained, though, that many territory managers felt that their job was to manage relations with existing dealers, not to sell. He exploded, "Regardless of our eventual strategy, they must sell—and I'll have to change their minds very quickly!"

DISTRIBUTORS AND DEALERS

CAC had 55 distributors who provided warehousing, finance, and service, but did not sell. It seemed to Mr. Millar that selling was the very thing they should be doing, although this deficiency tended to be industry-wide. Mr. Millar believed that his distributors were equal to competitors' in their community reputations. But he could see no area in which his distributors or dealers surpassed competitors', and they were inferior in financial strength and selling ability. He also believed that CAC had far too few distributors.

Steven Quinn, the distribution manager, outlined the problems of selling through independent distributors.

> How do we make distributors realize the great potential of central air conditioning? How do we find distributors who can finance this growth? How can we help distributors overcome the lack of glamour in wholesaling and air conditioning, so that they can attract and keep good people? How can we train distributors, so that they can in turn train dealers to sell and to give good customer service?

Mr. Millar felt that the key problem was to find enough distributors with adequate financing. Many current distributors had told him that they would not allow Scott-Air to amount to more than 50 percent of their business, and several had said no more than 30 percent. (All CAC distributors and dealers also handled Scott-Air's room air conditioners; three fourths of the room air conditioner distributors and two thirds of the dealers also handled central air conditioners.) To find more well-heeled distributors, Mr. Millar considered taking on large successful distributors carrying another line of air conditioners, if the volume potential for CAC looked attractive enough. The ultimate objective would be for CAC to replace the distributor's other air conditioning suppliers. Mr. Millar knew that nonexclusive distributorships were common in other industries, and he wondered if they might be the answer to distributor selling problems in central air conditioning. About six months were needed to get a new distributor on his feet. Thus, increasing the number of CAC distributors would have to be considered a long-term project.

A second option was to open factory branches. However, CAC executives felt that factory branches tied up corporate finances and forced the division to assume credit responsibility. Mr. Millar felt that factory branches would not market aggressively:

> Have you ever tried to get urgently needed parts from a factory branch on Saturday? For me, the most important wholesale job is to make inventory available at any time. The independent does that best.

A third alternative was to sell to mass-merchandisers. Mr. Millar was concerned, however, that this move might anger distributors and dealers. Also, mass-merchandisers' prices were unattractive.

Mr. Millar faced problems with his dealers, too. CAC had about 800 dealers, considerably fewer than Carrier or GE had in Scott-Air's markets. He considered CAC's dealers to be inferior to competitors' in selling, financial strength, and use of in-store promotional material. Also, CAC dealerships tended to be smaller and less aggressive than other local businesses. For their part, both dealers and distributors complained that CAC's advertising and public relations were inferior to its competitors, as was its customer service—a broad category including stock and parts availability, ordering procedures, and delivery.

Mr. Millar believed that, if he decided to put his emotional emphasis on dealers, a program to improve their effectiveness would have to include (1) identifying existing dealers who could benefit from training; (2) a county-by-county analysis to pinpoint where new dealers were required; (3) comprehensive training programs in selling and business management; (4) more training and sales supervision from distributors; and (5) more frequent visits from CAC territory managers (such visits were rare at the moment, because distributors did not like manufacturers' salesmen to visit their dealers).

Thus, increasing dealer training would require increasing the sales force budget to hire additional territory managers. On the other hand, analysis of dealer training needs and preparation of training materials would be considered part of marketing communications. Thus, any changes in dealer training would have to be planned in conjunction with possible changes in the marketing communications budget.

MARKETING COMMUNICATIONS

Marketing communications included advertising, sales promotion, dealers' product brochures, and distributor/dealer training. In 1971 the total marketing communications budget was $680,000. Of this figure, more than half went to cooperative advertising with dealers. Other advertising accounted for $25,000; sales promotion, $161,000; training, about $80,000. (See Exhibit 2 for further breakdowns of these figures.)

This budget reflected several kinds of marketing policy decisions. For example, a decision to push a particular product line or market segment would require additional product brochures for dealers—such materials already accounted for about three fourths of the sales promotion budget. An attempt to increase the number of dealers or to make them more efficient would require added allocations for training and for product information materials.

In addition to allocating funds to accommodate these ripple effects, Mr. Millar was considering several other specific changes in the communications budget. First, he wondered whether CAC should increase its noncooperative advertising. Carrier, Fedders, American Standard, GE, and some regional manufacturers did heavy national advertising. CAC traditionally did little national advertising, spending only $10,000 in 1970 on ads in business and trade journals. In 1971, this allocation had been split among these journals and regional editions of men's and women's magazines. Both male and female audiences had been chosen because executives believed that the decision to buy central air conditioning was made jointly by husband and wife. Mr. Millar wondered whether such advertising should be increased. Another option was local TV advertising in conjunction with dealers and distributors, a tactic that some competitors had already used.

Mr. Millar was also concerned about his lack of information about consumers' reasons for buying air conditioning and for choosing a brand. Some

Exhibit 2
Marketing Communications Expenses and Budget 1969–1971 ($000)

	Actual			Budget
	1969	1970	1971	1971
Advertising:				
Newspaper				
Television...............................				
Radio				
Outdoor................................				
Business and trade magazines	10	4	4	13
General magazines..........................	—	–	6	12
Total advertising.......................	10	4	10	25
Sales promotion and literature:				
Telephone directory Yellow Pages..............	38	44	36	48
Permanent signs...........................	15	17	13	16
Booklets, folders, and brochures..............	80	43	118	136
Exhibits and trade shows	20	16	4	8
Warehousing and shipping	1	1	1	1
Recoveries from sales of materials.............	(40)	(20)	(39)	(48)
Total	114	101	133	161
Surveys and research.........................	—	—	—	—
Cooperative advertising	294	374	273	354
Training and special merchandising:				
Customer meetings and material..............	20	16	8	20
Sales training (in-company)....................	—	—	—	—
Sales training (distributors and dealers)	40	56	45	57
Prizes and contests	1	1		
Publicity (agency)...........................	—	1	—	3
Total	61	74	53	80
Departmental operations	80	100	44	60
Grand total	559	653	513	680

executives claimed that the dealer influenced the consumer more than the manufacturer did. In effect, the consumer did not care about the manufacturer's reputation but bought whatever a good dealer sold. Other executives argued that the manufacturer's reputation was all-important. Still others claimed that the dealer's recommendation created the manufacturer's reputation. Other factors believed to influence brand selection were advertising, prices, ease of installation, friends' recommendations, manufacturers' guarantees, special product features, and the brand of room air conditioner currently owned.

Any consumer research would have to come from the communications budget. Such a study would cost about $20,000, as would a study of the number of dealers needed before any dealer training program could begin. Although these studies might give Mr. Millar some valuable information, the results would not be available in time to affect his 1972 planning. Also, these expenditures would be made at the cost of some additional advertising or promotion activity.

Mr. Millar also had to decide whether to adopt two specific promotional plans. One had been suggested by the Nielsen Corporation. Owners of CAC units might recommend Scott-Air central air conditioning to their friends in exchange for free gifts. The costs of collecting friends' names and addresses from warranty cards, of promotional materials for mailing to new owners, and of gifts for those who sent in names of friends prepared to receive a personal sales call were expected to be $40,000.

The second proposal had been made by *Sports Illustrated* magazine. The magazine had suggested that CAC sponsor a competition for distributors, dealers, and territory managers, the winners to be guests of the magazine at the Super Bowl and the Indy 500 in 1972. The cost was $35,000 a page and $15,000 per event for premiums and direct mailings for the trade. Transportation and lodging for the winners would be additional costs.

CONCLUSION

Mr. Millar's marketing plan and his sales force and marketing communications budgets were due in one month. He realized that he had begun to lose sight of the forest for the trees, and needed to refocus on the overall costs of his plans. Although manufacturing cost information from the new plant was unreliable, fixed manufacturing and marketing costs of $600,000 a month seemed certain. At $28 million in sales, a sales force budget of $755,000 and a communications budget of $680,000 would amount to break-even, as far as the division's contribution to corporate overhead and profit was concerned. On the other hand, $40 million in sales and doubled budgets for the sales force and communications would produce a contribution of 6 percent of sales. Senior executives had targeted the CAC division's 1972 contribution at 15 percent of sales.

Case 17
Avon Products, Inc.

In mid-1974, executives of Avon Products, Inc., were discussing the impact of changing economic and social conditions on the company's longtime marketing strategy—a selling approach that relied primarily on some 680,000 independent door-to-door saleswomen who used their own initiative to develop sales within their assigned territories.

In 1973, Avon had held 85 percent of the door-to-door market for cosmetics and toiletries and 20 percent of the total $5 billion market for these products. Net earnings were $135.8 million on sales of $1.2 billion. This sales volume was twice the combined sales volume of Revlon and Max Factor, Avon's largest competitors. (Selected financial data for Avon in recent years are shown in Exhibit 1.)

Exhibit 1
Selected Financial Data ($000)

	1973	1972	1971
Sales (net)	$1,150,659	$1,005,316	$873,153
Cost of goods sold	413,006	355,886	315,948
Gross profit	737,653	649,430	557,205
Selling and administrative expenses	470,005	394,603	336,011
Earnings before taxes	267,648	254,827	221,194
Earnings after taxes	135,750	124,929	109,137
Total assets	711,448	598,647	506,607
Long-term obligations	31,696	37,529	36,076
Shareholder's equity	447,126	379,070	317,083

Operations in the United States and Canada accounted for the following sales and profits:

	1973	1972	1971
Sales (net)	$ 736,064	$ 675,375	$599,826
Earnings after taxes	98,628	97,499	87,591

Source: 1973 and 1972 annual reports.

Recent changes in the industry and the markets, however, posed possible challenges to Avon's position. In the industry, large outsiders had begun during the early 60s to buy up smaller, independent cosmetic firms. By 1973 many of the major cosmetic firms had been purchased: Max Factor by Norton Simon; Helena Rubenstein by Colgate-Palmolive; Elizabeth Arden by Eli Lilly. Firms selling door-to-door were not immune to acquisition. Vanda Beauty Counselor was purchased by Dart Industries, Luzier Cosmetics by Bristol-Myers, and Viviane Woodward Cosmetics by General Foods. Referring to this last acquisition, James L. Ferguson, president of General Foods, commented to *Business Week* magazine:

> The whole field of door-to-door selling and other direct marketing in the home (estimated to be a $50 billion-a-year business) promises to be a big growth area of the future. And we feel we have a lot we can bring to it.[1]

The second challenge was to Avon's key marketing technique: door-to-door selling by "Avon ladies." As *Business Week* recognized, the cheerful "Avon calling" slogan had "become one of the most widely recognized calling cards in consumer marketing." But the article questioned the future of Avon's door-to-door selling.

> Today's housewife is far more mobile than her counterpart of a few years ago. Now when Avon calls, she may be out visiting, playing tennis, or more often, working. At the same time, the Avon representative, like her customer, has more outside interests. And many are less willing to spend the time that it takes to develop a territory and bring it up to the exacting standards that Avon demands.

Now Avon was considering how best to use the Avon lady under these new conditions. David W. Mitchell, Avon's president, stated the issue thus:

> Over the last 15 or 20 years, much of our marketing thrust in the United States has been toward adding representatives and filling in sales territories. Now we have pretty well completed that phase. The next big step is to take this distribution machine we have created and do more fine-tuning to meet today's needs.

AVON'S MARKETING HISTORY

Avon Products had been founded by D. H. McConnell in 1886 as the California Perfume Company. The business was originally designed as a service to women in rural communities who had little access to retail stores. In the late 30s Avon began selling in cities with populations of 75,000 or more. City offices were established, each with a city manager who was to attract new sales representatives and give them selling information, methods, and materials. The program proved so effective in cities that in 1943

---

[1] *Business Week*, May 11, 1974.

Avon extended it to rural areas by establishing rural districts, each with a permanent district manager.

After World War II, Avon expanded into large metropolitan areas. The number of representatives increased almost threefold from 1950 to 1963. This increase in representatives was the dominant force in Avon's sales growth. Operating from a low base and capitalizing on untapped geographical areas in the United States and Canada, Avon increased its sales by an annual rate of 16 percent during this 13-year period.

From 1964 through 1973, sales in the United States and Canada grew at an average annual rate of 13 percent. The continued sales growth was due partly to increased numbers of representatives but primarily to increased productivity among the representatives.

During this 10-year period, the numbers of representatives increased by 5 percent per year. Avon achieved most of this gain by paring down sales territories. Executives had discovered that in some districts large blocks of homes were not being served by any Avon ladies. Marketing executives decided that the average territory of 300 homes was too large for the Avon lady to cover adequately. Thus, in the late 60s and early 70s, Avon executives gradually reduced territory sizes from 300 to 200 homes, trying not to disturb existing client relationships in the process. At the same time Avon increased the number of territories and representatives. By 1973, more than 290,000 active representatives worked in the United States and Canada.

Also during this 10-year period, Avon executives moved to improve the productivity of the Avon lady by increasing the number of sales campaigns per year from 18 to 26, thereby giving the representatives more frequent opportunities to call on customers. Productivity increased by about 5 percent per year during this period, and Avon executives credited this increase with domestic sales gains of 18 percent, 15 percent, and 15 percent in the years 1968, 1969, and 1970. Executives were confident that further productivity gains could contribute to sales growth in future years.

Although Avon's sales growth in the United States and Canada had slowed during the last 10 years when compared with previous periods, international sales kept Avon's consolidated sales growth at an annual rate of 17 percent. At the end of 1973, Avon had operations in 16 countries outside North America: Argentina, Australia, Belgium, Brazil, England, France, Ireland, Italy, Japan, Mexico, The Netherlands, Puerto Rico, Spain, Sweden, Venezuela and West Germany. The remainder of this case focuses on Avon's marketing in the United States and Canada.

THE MARKETING ORGANIZATION

Avon's marketing activities were organized by function rather than by product. The four marketing departments were Field Operations, Product Marketing, Campaign Planning, and Sales Promotion and Advertising. Each department had equal voice in Avon's marketing plans, a condition designed to ensure that the departments cooperated with one another and reviewed each other's plans.

Field Operations

Field operations in North America were divided geographically among seven distribution branches, each supervised by a branch manager. Within each branch were 10 regions, supervised by regional sales managers. Each regional manager oversaw 8 to 10 divisional managers. All of these supervisors operated from the branch headquarters.

Each divisional manager supervised about 18 district managers. The district manager operated from her home and had direct contact with the 150 Avon ladies in her district. Most district managers had been recruited from the ranks of the Avon ladies. The district managers were full-time Avon employees, in contrast to the Avon ladies, who were independent contractors. Avon executives considered the group of 2,300 district managers to be one of the company's key assets, an asset that few competitors had been able to duplicate.

The main duties of district managers were to recruit the Avon ladies, to motivate them, and to help them with their sales problems. The average district manager spent about one half to two thirds of her time in recruiting Avon ladies. Most of her leads came from existing Avon ladies, who received a fee or a merchandise prize for each person recommended who became an Avon lady. The district manager also recruited representatives through classified advertising.

When interviewing a prospective representative, the district manager typically inquired about her schedule and other elements in her daily life that might affect the amount of time she could spend selling Avon products. The district sales manager relied heavily on a booklet, *The Story of Avon*, as her primary selling tool in the interview. The booklet explained the history of the company, its selling philosophy, and the benefits of selling Avon products.

At the completion of this initial phase of the interview, the district manager decided whether the prospect was acceptable. If so, and the prospect was favorably impressed, the district manager immediately proceeded with the training phase of the interview. Again, she relied heavily on a short, pictorial sales technique brochure published by the company. The brochure explained policies and procedures and contained information about approaching and selling to prospects. The district manager discussed this manual with the new Avon lady and then encouraged her to start making calls. This entire interview and training process took about 45 minutes to one hour.

Once the new Avon lady accepted her appointment, she was given primary responsibility for a specified territory of approximately 200 homes, and she reached an informal understanding with her district manager as to the number of hours she was willing to spend calling on homes in her area. She also received at the time of appointment an Avon beauty showcase with an assortment of merchandise and promotional pieces. The new Avon lady paid $10 (less in some inner-city areas) as an "appointment fee."

Following the appointment, the district manager telephoned the new representative at intervals of one, two, and four weeks to assist her sales efforts. The district manager was, of course, always available to the representative by phone. Most district managers held conferences at a central location and invited representatives to attend to obtain more information about Avon products and selling techniques.

The selling cycle was as follows. Each Avon lady called on her regular customers and canvassed new prospects for two weeks. At the end of the period, she sent in her orders to the branch headquarters and started the next two-week campaign. Within a week she received the merchandise and a bill from the Avon branch. The better representatives then called their customers to tell them that the merchandise had arrived, thus ensuring that the customer would be at home and able to pay for the ordered merchandise. The Avon lady then delivered and collected payment for the merchandise ordered during the first campaign and solicited additional orders for the second. After delivering the merchandise, she sent in the orders for the second campaign with the payments for the first. Thus, accounts receivable to Avon were always a campaign behind, but the cycle perpetuated itself. In most instances, the cost of merchandise to the Avon representative was 60 percent of the suggested retail price.

Avon's basic promotional approach was to encourage the Avon ladies to call on households every two weeks, but not to pressure prospective customers to place large orders. Executives wanted to sustain and build Avon's image of offering friendly, low-pressure expertise. Avon executives believed that the Avon lady's relaxed friendliness and capability helped to direct the customer's whole attention to the Avon line as she examined it in her own living room, free from the distraction of competing products.

To carry out this promotional approach, Avon directed its district managers to elect women who would "wear well," as opposed to those who were aggressive or high-powered. The Avon lady was also expected to have a neat personal appearance and a manner sufficiently mature to inspire faith in her judgment.

Although Avon ladies came from all age groups and income brackets, typically they were between the ages of 25 and 44, married, had two children, and were in the lower- to middle-income brackets ($8,000 to $17,000). About 45 percent of all Avon ladies had been with Avon a year or longer, and 65 percent of this group had been with Avon for over three years. The "active representative" count was the number of Avon ladies from whom the company could expect to receive an order in any given campaign. The "activity rate" was the active representatives as a percentage of the total number of Avon ladies. Depending upon the campaign and season, the activity rate varied from 70 percent to 90 percent.

Avon managers believed that most of the Avon ladies devoted from two to four hours a day, four to six days a week to the job. A woman who worked effectively for 15 hours a week could expect to make about $2.50 an hour. She probably would have developed about 75 to 100 customers on whom she called and from whom she received orders, although in a single campaign she would probably receive orders from about 30 of these customers.

The Avon lady received no company benefits and paid for most of her promotional material and samples. The cost to the Avon lady for promotional materials and samples usually ranged from $5 to $10 a campaign, an amount that covered Avon's cost for them. Since the Avon lady was an independent contractor, no reports were required of her except her orders. The company did not maintain records regarding the number of calls made, hours worked, or sales interviews gained. According to several Avon ladies, a satisfactory sales interview ran from 20 minutes to a half-hour, and in that period the typical customer might spend $5 or $6 on Avon products.

Product Marketing

Avon executives considered the Avon product line to be one of the most important assets in their business. They believed that Avon's 700 products (not including makeup shades) made the Avon line the broadest of any cosmetics and toiletries company. The present size of the line was considered maximum, and executives did not anticipate any increase in the future. In the last several years, the company had averaged about 250 new product introductions each year. These were prominently displayed in brochures, and many new products were specially priced, giving the Avon lady an opportunity to show something new and different to her customers in every campaign.

The Avon product line by category and contribution to sales volume was as follows: fragrance and bath products for women, 40 to 45 percent; makeup, skin care and other products for women, 25 to 30 percent; men's products, 10 to 15 percent; and other products, such as teens' and children's products, other personal care products, and costume jewelry, 15 to 20 percent.

New-product concepts were developed within the product marketing department, which worked closely on the concept with the research and development department and the package design department, and sometimes with outside fragrance suppliers. After the initial study of the concept, which might take one year, the concept required approval by a central marketing board on which all marketing departments were represented.

Following this approval, the product marketing department prepared a profile describing the product, its value to consumers, date of introduction, pricing, and expected sales volume. The actual development of the product then proceeded for a year or more. During this period, major new-product lines were usually subject to a consumer test to determine the acceptability of the fragrance and the product.

After final approval of the product, the other marketing departments planned brochures and sales campaigns featuring the new product. The entire process, from concept to sales introduction, normally took two to three years.

Avon executives considered the product line's high quality to be an essential ingredient in the firm's success. All Avon products were sold with a money-back guarantee, but returns were few. The company was considered a leader in providing consumer product information, having been the first cosmetics and toiletries manufacturer to list ingredients on product labels. The firm was also recognized as one of the first in the industry to recognize the relationship between attractive packaging and sales.

All Avon products carried the Avon brand name. Since Avon did not have to compete for shelf attention, the Avon signature was generally subordinate to the product name. For many product items, packaging quantities followed the industry's practice. For example, both Avon and Revlon packaged liquid eyeliner in ¼-ounce packages. However, enough diversity in packaging existed to make direct comparisons very difficult. Generally speaking, Avon products were less expensive per ounce than leading full-line cosmetic manufacturers' products, although a number of popular shelf brands offered lower per-ounce prices.

Campaign Planning

Planning for each of the 26 two-week campaigns started about nine months ahead of time. Plans were made final about six months before selling time, although prices could be changed in brochures for four more months. If changes in price or other features had to be made in the two remaining months before introduction, revisions could be arranged through correspondence with the representative.

Sales and gross profit objectives were established 12 to 18 months ahead of selling time. Campaigns were planned within the framework of these objectives by quarters and then by individual campaign. Because of the seasonal variations in Avon's business, information required to structure a selling campaign varied widely throughout the year. The campaign planning department first obtained statistics from field operations as to the expected number of active Avon ladies and customers for the campaign. The department then selected the products to be highlighted in the campaign and determined the pricing and incentives for the Avon ladies.

Incentives were considered by Avon executives to be particularly important to the success of the campaigns. Incentives fell into two categories—recognition and campaign support. In the area of recognition, special prizes were awarded to about 50,000 to 60,000 Avon ladies, top producers who were designated President's Club members. Also, in 1973 the company instituted a recognition program for years of service—a series of award plates for Avon ladies who had been with Avon from 2 to 25 years. Campaign support was designed to increase sales of a specific campaign or of a particular product. For example, product awards or prizes were given for meeting specific sales levels, specific levels of customer service, or specified sales levels for particular products.

Sales Promotion and Advertising

For each of the 26 sales campaigns held during the year, the Avon representative received a promotional kit. This kit contained (1) a brochure highlighting the theme of the campaign (e.g., "President's Campaign" or "Shop Early") and featured the particular price specials and newly introduced products; (2) the order forms to be used during the campaign; (3) the "Outlook," the Avon lady's house organ; and (4) announcements of special prizes, contests, or other incentives offered during the period. Each kit was attractive, if not glamorous.

The campaign brochure, which the Avon ladies used with their customers, was the major vehicle through which the campaign plan was communicated to the ultimate customer. One large-size copy of the brochure was included in each kit. Also, the representatives could purchase advance copies of the next campaign brochure, which they could leave with customers. Avon executives estimated that over 300 million of these brochures would be distributed by Avon ladies in 1974.

In addition to these brochures, the campaign planning department created approximately 175 different field pieces for district managers and representatives, including training materials, sales aids, and explanations of inactive programs.

Avon's media advertising was essentially institutional. Its primary purpose was to give the public a knowledge of Avon so that the representative would be welcomed when she called. Advertising was also geared, however, to current marketing strategies. For example, in 1974 advertising stressed value/price relationships, product quality, and convenience of shopping in the home. Avon's domestic advertising budget for 1973 was approximately $7 million, an amount somewhat less than in previous years.

The sales promotion department also made periodic marketing studies to determine the "profile" of the Avon customer. Typically, these data revealed that the Avon customer conformed closely to the U.S. Census data averages, with the exceptions that she was more likely to have a larger family and was more likely to be better educated. On the other hand, when compared to Revlon or Clairol customers, she was more likely to be older, with a lower income, to be a housewife as opposed to a career woman, and to perceive herself as less glamorous and less fashion-conscious than the average woman.

AVON'S DISTRIBUTION AND MANUFACTURING ACTIVITIES

Each general branch manager also had reporting to him an operations manager and a regional controller, who were responsible for handling orders, shipping merchandise, keeping track of representatives' accounts, and contacting representatives on any of these or other subjects via mail or telephone.

Avon's distribution practices were designed to increase marketing efficiency by speeding up order handling and product delivery. For example, at Avon's Monrovia (California) distribution center, a computerized system automatically dispensed and assembled high-volume items, which represented more than half the products ordered. This part of the order could be put together in only four seconds, an achievement that boosted productivity and raised shipping capacity dramatically. According to one executive,

> A key part of our marketing strategy has always been the return trip by the representative to deliver an order to the customer. That return call provides selling opportunity. So if we can shorten the cycle between the time the representative places her order and receives it—now averaging five days—we increase her contact with buying customers.

Manufacturing strategy was similarly designed to increase marketing efficiency. In Avon's Springdale (Ohio) plant, for example, a computer directed a forklift to a preappointed place, where it picked up empty containers and put them on a conveyor belt. These empty containers traveled to the basement of the warehouse, and then traveled on a belt for a quarter of a mile to a production line where they were automatically filled and capped. The containers were then sent back on a conveyor belt that ran through the attic of the manufacturing area to a warehouse, where a machine palletized the finished goods. The computer then gave the forklift operator a punch card that told him exactly where in this half-million-square-foot warehouse these finished goods were to be stored for quick retrieval.

PROPOSED CHANGES IN MARKETING STRATEGY

As stated in the 1973 annual report, Avon's major objective for the domestic market was to achieve greater penetration, with special emphasis on improving the effectiveness of the field sales organization. Of the 67 million dwelling units in the United States and Canada, according to a recent study, only 32 million had bought Avon products at least once in the previous year, and fully two thirds of those customers were only infrequent or occasional buyers. Of the 35 million nonbuyers, 9 million expressed interest in having a representative call. According to one Avon executive,

> The biggest reason that interested nonbuyers and infrequent and occasional buyers did not purchase more often was that a representative did not call frequently enough. So the business is there, and we intend to go after it.

In considering possible changes, Avon executives kept in mind that they did not wish to lose any of the advantages of the company's existing sales force and selling approach. The use of part-time sales representatives who were living in their territories allowed Avon to employ a friendly, dignified and low-pressure form of selling. This selling approach was also looked upon as a low-cost method of selling. In contrast with the standard retail and wholesale margins of 40 percent and 10 percent that were prevalent in cosmetics, Avon paid a 40 percent commission. Furthermore, in contrast with the usual advertising expenditure in the industry of 15 percent or 20 percent of sales, Avon spent less than 2 percent of sales.

However, Avon executives recognized that the practical problems of operating a part-time sales force did affect marketing coverage. Many representatives relied upon friends and neighbors for sales and were reluctant to cultivate additional customers through cold sales calls. If friends and neighbors made few purchases, the representative would quit, causing vacant sales territories.

To head off possible challenges to sales and profits, Avon executives had considered several diversification ventures as well as changes in marketing policies.

Diversification

Avon executives were currently testing and evaluating some diversification ventures. A test group of 16 Avon-operated beauty salons in Atlanta, Dallas, and Denver was currently in operation. Avon executives had already concluded that beauty salons were not profitable enough to justify further investment.

After a decision was made to enter into the sale of men's and women's apparel through direct mail, the company incorporated a subsidiary known as Family Fashions by Avon and conducted several successful test mailings during 1973. In the latter part of 1973, Family Fashions by Avon completed a shipping and service center in Virginia and began regular mailings throughout the United States. In addition to renting customer lists, Avon was also building up a list of customers among Avon ladies and then customers.

The third venture, Avon's plastic housewares, was just beginning to be tested across Canada. The housewares were sold by groups on a "party plan," rather than door-to-door. Avon executives would decide in 1975 whether to bring this venture to the United States market.

Marketing Changes

In addition to discussing these strategic alternatives, Avon executives were discussing number of marketing changes. Under consideration was altering Avon advertising to emphasize value, price consciousness, and other consumer concerns in an inflation-weary market.

Another executive suggested that the company should test the idea of reducing prices as much as 50 percent on 4 or 5 key products of the 300 or so offered in each campaign. He proposed that this alternative could be promoted as an "inflation fighter" program and would provide an immediate sales boost. One of the major advantages from such a program would be to preserve the Avon lady's earning opportunities during a period of sluggish sales. Another executive pointed out, however, that such a program might have a disadvantageous impact on gross margins and should be used sparingly.

This discussion provoked a reexamination of the 40 percent discount structure used in determining the cost of products to the representatives. As one executive pointed out, the current system limited merchandising mostly to the raising or lowering of retail prices. For instance, if a cologne was normally priced at $6 and Avon executives put it on sale for $3.99, the representative would receive her 40 percent discount on the $3.99. Thus, there was no way to target the Avon lady's work on higher-priced items that might return a bigger margin than the discounted cologne. Consequently, as one possibility, the discount might be pegged at 30 percent on toiletries where Avon faced heavy price competition; and raised to 50 percent on other items where the cost of manufacturing was low. One executive believed that this tactic would give Avon the flexibility to merchandise products at more competitive prices, simply by varying the discount. Mr. Mitchell cautioned that any change in the discount system must be profitable for the representative. He stated that he would approve no change if the Avon lady ended up with lower earnings.

Another alternative discussed was the reduction of the district sales manager's span of control from the present average of 150 Avon ladies to a lower average of 100. According to one executive,

> The average manager now spends two thirds of her time just recruiting and training new representatives. With smaller districts, managers could work more closely with representatives and help them build up their territories.

Another means of improving the productivity of Avon ladies was to have them use customer lists. One proposal was to provide newly appointed representatives with customer lists developed by former representatives. In addition, it was decided to explore a new system whereby a computerized list of customers in a specific territory could be made available to established representatives if they desired to receive it.

Another executive proposed that since sales were correlated with the number of sales representatives, quicker market development could be accomplished by merely accentuating efforts to attract more Avon ladies to the fold. Such action would probably require an eventual reduction in the size of the Avon lady's territory, perhaps from the current 200-family territory to 150 or even 100. Since the company in 1970 had already reduced the territories from 300 to 200, one executive stated that any further reduction might reduce the earnings of those women who really wanted to develop their current territories.

An opposite alternative was to reduce the size of the sales force and gradually replace those women who left with women who were interested in working full-time. This alternative would involve enlarging the size of the individual sales territories to provide each full-time representative with an opportunity to develop a large, regular clientele.

Avon executives believed that continuing programs of self-examination, as reflected in the above discussions, enabled them to understand better the conditions of present operations and to plan for continuing success. Avon executives planned to approach their new ventures and the job of tightening and refining the distribution system slowly and carefully. Noting that the top 10 percent of the Avon ladies accounted for 20 percent of the company's sales, one executive commented,

> They are just ordinary housewives who have come to us to make a buck. Yet, if we could raise the other 90 percent up to that same level of productivity, our sales in the United States and Canada would double. That's the kind of potential we have around here.

Case 18
Masonne Furniture Company

In February 1978, Mr. Douglas Shean, vice president of marketing of
Masonne Furniture Company, Danville, Kentucky, was wondering whether
to alter the compensation plan for the Masonne Furniture Company sales
force. A proposal submitted by Mr. Don Jamison, director of retail development, argued that a salary plus bonus plan was appropriate because of recent
changes in Masonne's marketing strategy. However, Mr. Tom Walker, vice
president of sales, thought that the present straight commission plan, standard for the furniture industry, was responsible for the company's past marketing success. Mr. Shean knew that any change in the compensation plan
must be included in the 1978 marketing budget proposal, due in less than
one month.

INDUSTRY BACKGROUND

From the close of World War II until the early 60s, furniture industry
sales grew at an average annual rate of 5 percent. Between 1964 and 1974,
the average annual growth rate was 7.5 percent; between 1969 and 1974,
this growth rate accelerated to 8.1 percent. Industry observers expected the
8.1 percent annual growth in sales to continue, leading to a market of about
$13 billion at manufacturer's prices in 1986. In 1977, total furniture sales at
manufacturer's prices were $6.3 billion.

Manufacturers

Despite projected growth in furniture sales, family-managed, regional
manufacturers dominated the furniture industry. In 1977, 1,200 furniture
manufacturers operated 5,000 facilities nationwide. Few manufacturers had
changed the handcraft furniture operations of the 18th century. Technological change was slow for several reasons: (1) the loyalty of manufacturers to

Copyright © 1978 by The Colgate Darden Graduate Business School Sponsors, University
of Virginia. Reproduced by permission. This case was prepared by Charlene LeGrand under
the supervision of Derek A. Newton.

the way that their "fathers and grandfathers manufactured furniture," (2) the tendency to equate furniture quality with the degree of hand labor used in production, and (3) the meager financial resources of most furniture manufacturing firms.

Although product bulk meant high costs in transporting furniture long distances, there was a trend toward consolidation in furniture manufacturing. Twenty years ago, the top 20 manufacturers accounted for less than 10 percent of total furniture sales; in 1977, the top 20 accounted for nearly 33 percent, and the top 10, 21 percent of total furniture sales. As in 1967, however, the leading manufacturer in 1977 held a mere 3 percent share of the furniture market. Masonne executives expected consolidation to continue because the cyclical nature of furniture purchases threatened the financial viability of small family-managed firms. Other industry observers thought that the products' bulk and the industry's fixation with hand labor would sustain the present fragmented structure.

Furniture was classified as either case goods, furniture made predominantly of wood, or as upholstery, fabric-covered furniture with wood frames. In case goods, a manufacturer could develop product traits difficult for competitors to imitate. For example, Masonne developed a wood finish and drawer construction that few firms could copy.

In contrast, differences in upholstery construction were invisible to the consumer, and imitation in fabric and design were frequent. Colors and fabrics were subject to consumer fads, even if the furniture's style remained unchanged. Many manufacturers maintained racks of fabric swatches at each retail outlet. From these fabric racks, the consumer could choose the fabric and color for a selected piece of upholstery.

Ease of product imitation and low overhead costs meant that numerous local manufacturers specialized in upholstery. These regional upholstery manufacturers shipped short distances and accepted margins as low as 15 percent. Masonne shipped long distances and seldom accepted margins lower than 30 percent. Traditionally, dealers bought Masonne upholstery as part of their Masonne selective dealership arrangement.

Numerous furniture manufacturers competed in Masonne's market segment, comprised of consumers with annual incomes over $15,000. The company's major competitors were Alex Hamil, Grandon, and Scholberts at the national level, as well as numerous companies at the regional level. Regional competition was characterized by severe price cutting and annual style changes. The following table shows selected financial data for several national furniture manufacturers from 1972 to 1976:

	Sales Growth	Average Pretax Return on Sales	ROI (1976)
Alex Hamil	16%	9%	15%
Grandon	17	18	26
Masonne	8	13	27
Scholberts	10	12	19

Alex Hamil, Masonne's major competitor, had sales of $170 million in 1977 compared to Masonne's volume of $36 million. Alex Hamil distributed furniture through franchised retailers with a complete line of medium- to high-priced furniture and accessories. Its sales reps were salaried employees trained in "program selling," or selling a package of merchandise and retailing aids. Alex Hamil had originated this concept in the furniture industry.

Most furniture manufacturers did little or no consumer research. Instead, manufacturers presented new designs each year at industrywide furniture markets and encouraged retailers to order the untested designs for their floor displays. The high costs of design, prototype construction, and short production runs caused by this marketing approach were eventually passed on to the consumer.

Retailers

The furniture retail market mirrored the fragmentation and family ownership of furniture manufacturing. Of the 50,000 furniture retailers in 1977, 30,000 averaged less than $100,000 annually in sales (sales equivalent to one sofa per day). Furniture retail outlets included mass merchandisers, department stores, traditional furniture stores, and decorator shops—cited in order of increasing specialization, expertise, and prices.

A typical furniture retailer chose furniture for floor displays from as many as 100 manufacturers each year. Because of the variety of styles offered by manufacturers, retailers seldom developed well-balanced floor displays. Most floor displays reflected the last truck of furniture unloaded rather than a conscious effort to place furniture in coordinated settings. Despite the recognized need to have furniture displayed to fit a range of consumer incomes, most retailers specialized in either low-to-medium, medium, or medium-to-high-priced furniture, using frequent price promotions to encourage a broad range of income groups to enter the store.

Competent retail personnel could encourage consumers to trade up to higher-priced lines. Most furniture retail personnel, however, lacked knowledge and experience in interior design and seldom stayed with a single retailer long enough to learn the retailer's lines. Their knowledge of wood, styles, and brands seldom exceeded that of the average consumer. Retail personnel with knowledge of competitive products and prices were even rarer.

In a recent study, furniture retailers ranked the following manufacturing services in order of importance: maintenance of stocks and fast delivery, selective distribution, catalogs, sales training, and cash discounts. The most common complaints from retailers were of late deliveries and merchandise damaged during shipping.

Consumers

Furniture was a big-ticket item; the average purchase was around $500. The average consumer bought a piece of furniture every 2.5 years. Many consumers wanted their new purchases to match the styles of previous purchases, but this desire was often frustrated by annual style changes from manufacturers and poor sales assistance from retailers.

Company executives believed that consumers had little brand awareness of furniture. One study showed that fewer than 40 percent of the consumers surveyed could name the brand of their most recent furniture purchases. Unaided awareness tests asked people in the survey to name a brand of furniture. In these tests 6 percent named Alex Hamil, 1 percent named Masonne, and less than 4 percent could name more than one brand. In aided awareness tests, in which the person was asked about a particular brand, 6 percent said that they had heard of Masonne and 22 percent had heard of Alex Hamil.

Industry observers blamed retailers for the lack of brand advertising. Retailers were more interested in promoting the name of the store than the name of the furniture manufacturer. Some retailers went so far as to tear furniture tags from the furniture to deemphasize brand recognition in the sale. Even if they chose to prominently display brand names, few furniture retailers knew the differences in the manufacturing processes for furniture brands. However, retailers did more brand advertising on upholstery than on case goods. Whereas case goods could be easily inspected, hidden frame construction in upholstery made inspection difficult and brand pull more important.

MASONNE FURNITURE DIVISION

Masonne manufactured and distributed a traditional American collection of quality home furniture. The Masonne catalog presented the entire collection in attractive home setting each year. As is shown in Exhibit 1, 85 percent of Masonne's total sales were to furniture stores and 15 percent to department stores in the United States. Masonne furniture was in the medium-to-high-priced segment of the market. Masonne's 1977 income statement (Exhibit 2) shows annual sales of $35.5 million, of which 75 percent were sales of case goods and 25 percent were sales of upholstery.

In the mid-60s, Masonne Furniture Company had become a division of a large corporation. The division received few directives from its parent com-

Exhibit 1
Masonne Furniture Retail Network

Account Type	Average Floor Space (square feet)	Percent Masonne Accounts
Mass merchandisers	500,000	0
Major department stores	250,000	15
Furniture stores		85
More than $1 million in sales	15,000	
Less than $1 million in sales	5,000–8,000	
Total Masonne accounts	10,000–12,000	

Exhibit 2

MASONNE FURNITURE COMPANY
Income Statement
January 1, 1977–December 30, 1977
($000)

	Case Goods	Upholstery	Total	Percent
Net Sales	$26,614	$8,899	$35,513	100.0%
Cost of sales	18,996	6,950	25,946	73.1
Gross profit	7,618	1,949	9,567	26.9
Less expenses:				
General and administrative.......			2,450	6.9
Selling			2,225	6.2
Commission			1,668	4.7
Total expenses			6,343	17.8
Pretax profit.....................			$ 3,223	9.1%

(handwritten: 28.6% 21.9%)

pany other than to achieve specific targets for annual sales growth and return on investment and to adhere to the corporation's image as a marketer of products appropriate to broad consumer tastes. Masonne's managers hoped that the company could achieve style leadership in the industry by staying abreast of consumer preferences and by maintaining close relations with selected distributors. Backed by the resources of its parent company, Masonne could pretest styles, wood finishes, and fabrics prior to trade introduction. To its retailers, Masonne offered pretested products and a complete package of dealer services, including floor layouts, sales training, and promotion aids.

Marketing Organization

The Masonne Division organized marketing in four departments: product development and design, styling and display, advertising, and sales. Exhibit 3 is an organization chart of the division showing the marketing organization in detail.

In addition to its research, the product development and design department forecasted sales for the division, because 80 percent of all sales were special orders made directly to the factory by the dealers. Mr. Shean used the sales forecasts prepared by this department to schedule production. Scheduling was important because efficiencies in production and shipping could be realized by proper scheduling. An average production run lasted 18 to 20 weeks and produced 75 pieces of furniture. Thus, interruptions in production were costly. Also, coordination of production and shipping schedules could increase the number of full shipments, thereby reducing overall shipping costs.

The styling and display department presented recommendations to Masonne's retailer accounts on floor layouts, fabrics, and accessories.

Exhibit 3
Organization Chart

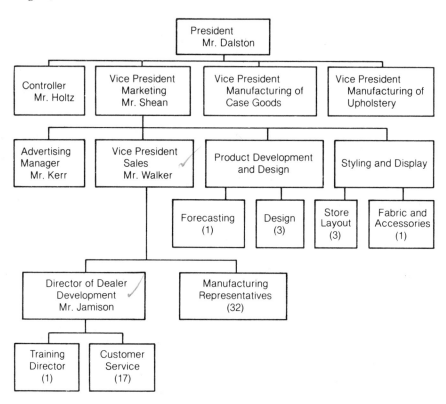

Masonne executives believed that this department was important because it offered services that retailers could not provide themselves.

Incorporated in the advertising budget were charges for promotional aids. Masonne advertised nationally in trade journals and magazines such as *Better Homes and Gardens, House Beautiful,* and *Reader's Digest.* Local promotions included tabloids sent by direct mail or distributed as newspaper inserts. Masonne paid design costs, and retailers paid distribution costs for local promotions. Potential uses for advertising funds included cooperative advertising and national brand advertising on television.

Reporting directly to Mr. Tom Walker, vice president of sales, were Mr. Don Jamison, director of dealer development, and 32 manufacturing representatives. Mr. Jamison's job, recently created, was to oversee retailer seminars and customer service, and to develop key retailer accounts.

Sales Force

In 1977 Mr. Walker retained the services of 32 manufacturing representatives, commonly called reps. Mr. Walker assigned each rep to an exclusive

Exhibit 4
Current Market Position (1977)

Total NAFM* volume	$6.3 billion
Total Masonne furniture volume	$35.5 million
Masonne furniture share of market	.0056
Number of Masonne territories	32
Average number of accounts per territory	24
Average Masonne sales per territory	$1,110,000
Average NAFM sales per territory	$196,875,000
Average Masonne commission per territory	$52,170
Total Masonne commissions (4.7%)	$1,668,000
Number of active Masonne accounts	768
Number of NAFM trading areas	300
Number of NAFM trading areas without Masonne distribution	101 (34%)

*NAFM is the National Association of Furniture Manufacturers.

territory. According to the data shown in Exhibit 4, sales averaged over $1 million per territory, and direct selling expenses averaged 4.7 percent of sales in 1977. Masonne reps sold to fewer than 1.6 percent of the 50,000 furniture retailers in the United States in 1977. Masonne's market share was less than three quarters of 1 percent. Because he was self-employed, a Masonne rep was entitled to carry auxiliary lines. Masonne reps, however, held a noncontractual agreement to sell Masonne furniture exclusively. Self-employment allowed the rep deductions in personal income taxes, and freed Masonne from employee obligations such as FICA payments, insurance payments, or pension plans.[1]

A brief history of changes in sales commissions since 1968 is shown in the following table:

Year	Commissions (regular case goods)
1968	8%
1970	7
1971	6
1972	5
1977	4

During 1977 sales commissions were paid as follows: closeout sales, 3 percent; discount sales, 4 percent; and regular sales, 5 percent. Closeout sales

---

[1] A bill was recently introduced to change the self-employment status of manufacturing reps who sold one product exclusively to company employees. If the bill passed, it would cost Masonne 4.8 percent on the first $20,000 earned by each rep, or $30,720. Pending legislation could increase the obligations to 4.8 percent of the rep's total earnings bringing Masonne obligations to $80,064, using 1977 as an example.

were infrequent, irregular sales used in isolated instances by Masonne marketing executives to clear excess inventory in a discontinued line. Closeout
sales offered 20 percent discounts to retailers. Discount sales were regular
semiannual promotions in winter and summer. During these promotions,
retailer discounts of 10 percent were offered. Regular sales were made at list
price. Masonne marketing executives varied the above commission plan to
adjust for higher travel expenses in less concentrated territories or lower
sales potentials in underdeveloped territories.

In the fourth quarter of 1977, Mr. Walker initiated a new commission
plan based on product type: case goods, 4 percent, and upholstery, 5 percent. This plan reduced Masonne's commission obligations to 4.2 percent of
sales.

The composition of the Masonne sales force had changed over the last
seven years. The average age of a rep had decreased from 55 in 1970 to 40 in
1977. During this time, four representatives over 70 years of age retired. In
1977, 10 reps had sold for Masonne for more than seven years. Mr. Walker
thought that Masonne reps had above-average qualifications for the industry
but needed better qualifications to help meet Masonne's long-term needs.

Selection criteria for Masonne reps included a track record in sales (pref-
erably not in furniture sales) and the ability to present a merchandising
program. The selling task demanded independence, patience, and persistence. Exhibit 5 gives the resume of an attractive candidate for the manufacturing rep position with Masonne.

Exhibit 5
Resume of Candidate for Manufacturing Representative with Masonne Furniture

EDUCATION: December 1973—Niagara University, Bachelor of Science
                        Major: Business Administration
                        Concentration: Management

EXPERIENCE:
October 1976   *Marketing Representative*
to
present   Assigned to one of Alex Hamil's largest volume territories,
                        working with the 6th and 8th largest dealers from Balti-
                        more, Md., to Norfolk, Va. Responsible for selling carpet,
                        draperies, lamps, accessories, case goods, and upholstery
                        through dealers. Also responsible for the professional
                        training of store personnel and the profitability of those
                        dealers. For Alex Hamil's 6-month fiscal period finished
                        4th in the country, obtaining 104 percent of sales objec-
                        tive. In addition, sold dealers on more than just product.
                        For example, sold dealers on instituting follow-up sys-
                        tems, replacing old signs, replacing floor samples, paint-
                        ing interiors and exteriors of buildings, cleaning and
                        replacing carpets, placing salespeople on commission,
                        and selling general furniture stores to become profitable
                        in Alex Hamil store. Given pay increase at end of this
                        period.

Exhibit 5 *(continued)*

June 1976 to present	Alex Hamil, Inc. Assigned to financially troubled account. Objective: to turn sales around, train, and motivate salespeople. Took charge in this account, training salespeople in product knowledge and selling techniques, placing all salespeople on commission, coordinating all departments, reassigning responsibilities of all personnel, increasing amount of deliveries to improve cash flow. Recommended areas to cut cost; obtained free publicity for account. Counseled manager on improving his effectiveness in motivating personnel. At the end of this period given one of Alex Hamil's largest volume territories and pay increase.
January 1976 to present	Alex Hamil, Inc. Hired as a marketing representative assigned to a company-owned store until a territory became available. Worked in all departments, becoming familiar with procedures in sales, warehousing, budgeting, credit, and operations. Worked closely with manager in setting up warehouse sale, training and motivating salespeople, collecting past due accounts, setting up budget.
April 1974 to present	Texaco Oil, Inc. Marketing representative in Boston territory. Assisted dealers in selling oil and service products through their stations. Accomplishments: Taken out of training and given special assignment of converting underground leaded tanks to lead-free. After one week on this job, increased the speed of conversion from 3 tanks a day to 4 by changing the process that the contractors were using. I was then transferred from Buffalo, N.Y., to Boston, Mass., receiving pay increase. On this assignment I increased sales in each category by at least 30 percent and as much as 120 percent.
Prior to April 1974	Winnet Furniture Company Grew up in family-owned business. Worked in all departments, including warehouse, deliveries, and selling. During college years, assumed full responsibilities for buying and advertising. Handled all advertising through various media. Initiated imaginative promotional activity that brought great exposure to the firm.
PERSONAL	Age: 26 Married: 1 child Health: Good Height: 6'1″ Weight: 180 Relocate: Yes
PROFESSIONAL ORGANIZATIONS:	Former Member: Massachusetts Petroleum Council (Speakers Bureau), Niagara Falls Junior Chamber of Commerce, Niagara Falls North End Businessmen's Association.

Once selected, a Masonne rep spent one week in the Danville plant learning the manufacturing process and the product, and two weeks selling with another rep. After three weeks, he worked alone, having infrequent contact with the Danville office and only brief affiliation with other reps at semiannual sales meetings. Because the reps worked for straight commissions, Walker saw no need for a formal reporting or appraisal system other than the reports provided by incoming orders from the territories. Only weak reps were requested to submit call reports to the Danville office.

Selling Task

Reps presented new products and catalogs to retailers, and helped retailers with display, personnel training, and advertising. One rep estimated the time spent on different tasks as follows: 20 percent prospecting for new accounts and 80 percent servicing existing accounts. Of the latter work, half the time was spent making sales presentations; one quarter on updating fabric racks, checking inventories, and handling miscellaneous problems; and one quarter in driving. Reps visited most accounts every month, spending about three hours per visit.

At Masonne, the selling tasks for case goods and upholstery differed. With case goods, the rep's job was to convince the retailer to keep a permanent display and to special-order directly from the factory any consumer purchases not in stock. Because all upholstery goods were sold directly from the retail floor, reps had to make frequent visits to maintain floor displays and fabric racks.

Selecting and opening a new retail account usually took six months. A new retailer either replaced a weak retailer or was the first Masonne retailer in an area. Reps looked for dealers with good locations, financial strength, and cooperation. The latter two characteristics were important because the rep wanted to get from the retailer 2,000 square feet of floor space to display Masonne furniture. This commitment required an investment of $35,000 in floor merchandise and inventory. Ideally, a new retailer would use Masonne's services to design a Masonne gallery, which required a large investment in addition to the investment in merchandise. A good Masonne rep learned regional consumer preferences and competitive products and prices before recommending a merchandise and promotion package to a retailer.

Retail Development

Mr. Jamison believed that retailers were loyal first to Masonne and second to Masonne manufacturing reps. He attributed this loyalty to Masonne's retailer services. As head of the retail development program, Mr. Jamison conducted training seminars in Danville and assigned to each retailer a permanent customer service agent. Customer service agents freed manufacturing reps from common problems best handled in Danville, such as late deliveries and damaged merchandise.

The newly created Model Store Program, also headed by Jamison, was another means of building a nucleus of retailers loyal to Masonne. In return for a floor space commitment of 4,000 square feet, the retailer received from Masonne's style and display department a complete gallery design incorporating specific merchandise and coordinated accessories such as wallpaper, draperies, and carpets. In addition to normal retail services, Masonne offered Model Store accounts high-priority shipping, prepaid freight billed as a fixed percentage of wholesale cost, and toll-free telephoning to the Masonne customer service department. To help retailers to launch the gallery successfully, Masonne offered credit on the opening order and a Gallery Opening ad campaign tailored to the store.

The Model Store Program was designed to help retailers to emulate Masonne's key accounts. A 1975 study of Masonne's most successful retailer accounts had revealed the following success variables: well-maintained displays, well-trained sales personnel, good catalog distribution, and frequent local advertising. The key retailers were community leaders with reputations for quality furniture in the medium-to-high price range. The following table shows that these retailers compared favorably to others in the industry.

	Industry Averages	Masonne Key Accounts Average
Sales per square foot	$40–57	$99
Annual inventory turn	2–3	3.9
Gross margin	43%	45%
GMROI*	1.5–2.3	3.2

$$* \text{ Gross margin return on investment—GM percent} \times \frac{\text{Sales}}{\text{Cost of inventory}}$$

The Model Store Program seemed to increase retailers' returns. Exhibit 6 shows the income statement for a sample Model Store account. The program also altered the rep's task. Instead of selling the program, the rep generated Model Store prospects, and Mr. Jamison or Mr. Walker sold the program if the prospect met their approval. Marketing executives expected the rep to assist the layout department and the advertising manager in presentations to the store. In addition to leading a full-day training session before the opening, reps were expected to attend the official grand opening of the new Masonne gallery.

Exhibit 6

MASSONE FURNITURE COMPANY
Sample Statement of Income and Expense
For Model Store Accounts

Sales...		$900,000	
Cost of sales:			
Opening inventory	$110,000		
Purchases	480,000		
	590,000		
Less closing inventory	95,000		
Total cost of sales......................		495,000	
Gross income from sales......................		405,000	45%
Operating expenses:			
Advertising	$ 50,000		5.6
Freight	41,000		4.6
Wages	124,000		13.7
Taxes—payroll	13,000		
Taxes—general............................	10,000		
Insurance	12,000		
Heat—light—power	6,000		
Telephone	3,000		
Stationery/office expense	2,000		
Travel.....................................	2,000		
Delivery expense...........................	12,000		
Depreciation...............................	4,000		
Interest	2,000		
Services...................................	5,000		
Maintenance/repairs	3,000		
Bank charges/miscellaneous expenses...........	2,000		
Rent......................................	24,000		2.6
Officers' salaries...........................	42,000		
Total operating expenses		$357,000	
Net income from operation		48,000	5.3
Other income/purchase discounts		9,000	
Net income pretaxes..........................		$ 57,000	6.3%

Notes on gross margin and inventory turn:

Opening inventory	$110,000
Closing inventory	95,000
	$205,000
Average inventory............................	102,500
Average inventory at retail	102,500 × 2.20 = 225,500
Inventory turn	900,000 ÷ 225,500 = 4
Gross margin	45%
Gross margin return on investment	$3.28

MR. JAMISON'S PROPOSAL

Mr. Jamison believed that the existing sales force could not adequately promote the Model Store Program. He also felt that Masonne reps were overpaid and that a younger sales force, given smaller territories, could give better sales coverage at lower cost. Exhibit 7 shows Mr. Jamison's cost calculations for 58 territories and an average salary plus bonus of $28,000 per sales rep. Mr. Jamison pointed out that salary-based compensation would give Masonne more control over sales activities, would compensate the sales reps for nonfinancial, long-term sales activities, and would reduce the rep's dependence on cyclical furniture sales.

The advertising manager, Mr. James Kerr, liked Mr. Jamison's proposal. Fewer marketing dollars allocated to direct selling could mean increases in his advertising budget.

On the other hand, Mr. Walker, vice president of sales, was not enthusiastic. Last quarter, Mr. Walker had initiated commission reductions to a sales force that had increased sales by 23 percent over the last year and had raised dollar sales from $14 million to $36 million in seven years. Mr. Walker maintained close relationships with many reps, who expressed faith that "anyone but Walker" had initiated the cut. The combined effects of reduced commissions and increased inflation on the reps' incomes and attitudes concerned Mr. Walker enough, without the severe change proposed by Mr. Jamison.

Mr. Walker also thought that Mr. Jamison's financial analysis was incomplete. Currently, reps paid for their own travel, food, and lodging. Masonne would incur these expenses for salaried sales reps, at an estimated $11,000 per rep. The proposal omitted costs for sales supervision and employee benefits. Mr. Walker thought that the new plan would require at least four

Exhibit 7
Comparison between Mr. Jamison's Proposal and Current Compensation Plan

	Present Plan	Proposed Plan
Number of territories	32	58
Average number of accounts per territory	24	13
Average NAFM volume per territory	$197 million	$109 million
Average Masonne volume per territory in 1977	$1,110,000	$ 612,300
Goal at 1 percent share of market	$1,970,000	$1,086,207
Average payment to salesmen per territory	$ 52,170	$ 28,000*
Total direct selling expenses	$1,668,000	$1,624,000

*Example of salary plus bonus plan:

Assume quota = $1,000,000 (sales)
Base salary = $20,000
Planned commission = .005 × Quota = $5,000
Assume actual sales per rep = $1,100,000
Additional commission = .03 × 100,000 (amount over quota) = $3,000
Total compensation = $28,000

Exhibit 8
Revised Calculations for Salaried Sales Force by Mr. Walker

Costs per salesman:

Salary and bonus	$28,000
Transportation	7,500*
Expenses (food, lodging)	3,500†
Fringe benefits	4,000‡
Total per salesman	$43,000
Number of territories......................	58
Total direct selling expenses.................	$2,494,000
Number of regional sales managers...........	4
Estimated salary	40,000§
Sales management costs	$ 160,000
Total cost of salaried sales force	$2,654,000

* 15 cents per mile at 50,000 miles per year.
† $35 per day at 100 days travel per year, conservative, because government allows up to $50 per day for tax purposes.
‡ $20,000 base salary × 20% = $4,000.
§ $25,000 salary + $15,000 expenses and fringe.

regional sales managers. Masonne's controller, Mr. Holtz, estimated employee benefits at 20 percent of salary. Exhibit 8 incorporates Mr. Walker's revisions to Mr. Jamison's proposal.

Mr. Walker also felt that changing to a salaried sales force would cause staffing problems. Finding four regional managers would not be easy: existing reps would probably not apply for the positions. In fact, if the salary plan were introduced, Mr. Walker expected resignations from two thirds of the reps, because they were "not the kind of people to be told what they can earn." The thought of training a new sales force with a third of the original sales force intact worried Mr. Walker. Assuming that he found the regional managers, Mr. Walker wondered what management tools they would need to control the sales reps. Mr. Walker knew that most sales managers developed formal control systems with call reports and formal appraisal evaluations.

But only one alternative to the salaried sales force had yet been proposed: Mr. Walker had considered creating a new position, the subrepresentative. One subrep would report to four or five reps, helping them with retail displays, fabric racks, catalogs, and training. The position could be best filled by candidates with two years of retail experience in decorating. Compensation would be a straight salary of $10,000 per year.

CONCLUSION

Although Masonne's marketing executives agreed that selling tasks were changing, they argued about the best use of marketing funds. Mr. Shean was responsible for allocating the marketing budget among the departments of product development and design, styling and display, advertising, and sales. Thus, he had to decide whether to hire salaried sales reps, as Mr. Jamison proposed, or to retain the compensation system that Mr. Walker felt was best suited to current Masonne reps. In addition to considering the effects of his decision on Masonne's current sales and expenses, he had to determine whether 1978 was the best time for a major change in allocation, and to forecast the impact that his decision would have on the division's achieving its goal of doubling sales and profits every five years.

Case 19
Worthington Corporation

Late in 1961, Mr. Cyril Freeman, manager of advertising and sales promotion for the Worthington Corporation of Harrison, New Jersey, was considering recommending the dollar-contribution method as a means of evaluating the contribution of advertising to the total marketing effort. The method had recently been tried with one product group, and Mr. Freeman was wondering whether the method was feasible as a companywide practice.

COMPANY BACKGROUND

Since 1840 the Worthington Corporation had been a leading manufacturer of pumps and other industrial equipment. Among Worthington's leading products were compressors, steam turbines, engines, steam condensers, liquid meters, mechanical power transmission items, and industrial mixes. Subsidiaries produced commercial and residential heating and air conditioning equipment. Worthington's major customers were to be found in the chemical, construction, oil and gas, public works, and utilities industries. In 1961 net sales were expected to exceed $186 million, and net profits after taxes were expected to be about $5 million.

THE DOLLAR-CONTRIBUTION METHOD

The basic premise of the dollar-contribution method was that the level of sales depended on the total marketing effort—selling, promotion, and advertising. Assuming that management's appraisal of the market was realistic, the dollars spent on the total marketing effort determined the sales achieved: X marketing dollars would produce Y sales dollars. To determine the specific contribution made by advertising dollars, one would first set specific communications objectives for the advertising compaign, objectives that supported overall marketing objectives. By placing a dollar value on these communications objectives, executives could determine advertising's dollar contribution to the attainment of the dollar sales level of the quota.

Mr. Freeman believed that the dollar-contribution method would help Worthington to analyze and manage the entire selling task. For example, before communications objectives could be set, sales and advertising personnel would have to meet together to determine exactly what was involved in selling the product and how each step could be performed most efficiently. Once these personnel decided what part advertising could play in each of these steps, communications objectives could be set and dollar values could be assigned to them. Mr. Freeman believed that such discussions would enable sales and advertising people to understand each others' activities and problems. Furthermore, the method would ease interdepartmental communications, for both sales and advertising expenses would be justified in terms of the tasks that must be done to accomplish sales quotas. The advertising manager would now be able to refer directly to advertising's contributions to marketing tasks, rather than discussing media, circulation, schedules, and so forth—terms that Mr. Freeman felt were meaningless to executives in other departments.

A TRIAL RUN: THE WATER PUMP PRODUCT GROUP[1]

This product group comprised a select class of pumps for general water service in air conditioning and industrial processes. Almost all plants were prospective purchasers of the pumps, and Worthington was one of six major national suppliers. The pumps ranged in price to the user from $50 to $10,000.

Worthington marketed the pumps through franchises to 150 of the nation's 1,000 distributors for this type of product. Of these 150 distributors, 25 percent accounted for 80 percent of Worthington's sales in this line. Approximately 75 percent of the Worthington pump distributors also handled other Worthington products. Competition among manufacturers to get and retain good distributors was extremely keen, and turnover among these good distributors was very low.

Worthington had a sales force of 20 assigned to this product group. The total annual field cost for these 20 people was $400,000; the cost of fielding additional salesmen was judged to be about $15,000 per person per year.

Projecting Sales

All major product classifications were analyzed each year to determine the projected sales level or quota for the following year. To set these quotas,

---

[1] All data pertaining to product distribution and sales have been disguised.

staff economic analysts projected the next year's sales and then met with the sales managers for each product line, who had prepared projections based on key account analysis made by the line sales force. After the economists and sales managers reached agreement, they forwarded their projections to operating managers, who reviewed the projections' feasibility. Finally, senior management determined whether the projections were in line with corporate sales objectives.

The final 1962 sales quota for water pumps was set at $4 million. Estimated shop costs for production at this quota level would be $3.2 million. The total marketing budget (sales force, advertising, and promotion) was set at $550,000, with $400,000 of this amount committed to field costs of the sales force. Another $85,000 was allocated to *normal* advertising and sales promotion efforts. The remaining $65,000 represented *variable* advertising costs.

Dollar-contribution analysis was designed to determine whether the $65,000 should be spent on additional advertising, or whether the communications objectives could be achieved more effectively by, say, adding more salesmen.

Analyzing the Selling Task

The next step involved analyzing the selling process entailed in the distribution of this class of water pumps. Marketing management was responsible for arriving at common agreement within the marketing group as to what the selling process and specific selling tasks within that process were for the particular product or product group.

During the first few meetings in which Mr. Freeman introduced the idea to sales managers, their reactions were lukewarm. Mr. Freeman believed that this reception was only natural, since the method required extra time and work from sales managers—efforts that did not seem to offer immediate benefits. However, initial progress began to build interest because, according to Mr. Freeman, the method tended to clarify sales managers' own understanding of the problems and goals they faced. Also, the sales managers found they could begin to see the formerly "intangible" advertising as a genuine contribution to the quotas for which they were accountable. As sales managers began to see how they might profit by encouraging a team effort with the advertising people, they become increasingly involved and interested.

The results of this team effort in analyzing the selling process and identifying the specific selling tasks involved are given in Exhibit 1, column (A). The three major types of tasks in marketing water pumps were identified as activities performed in setting up franchises, activities that served and/or motivated distributors, and activities engaged in by distributors themselves. Subtasks were also identified. Distributor effort, for example, included contacting users, developing user interest and preference, and closing the sale.

Exhibit 1
Analysis of Selling Effort

(A)	(B)	(C)	(D)
		Variable Advertising Program's	Variable Advertising Program
	Percent Task Is of Total Marketing	Contribution (Agreed Percent	Contribution (Percent of
Specific Selling Task	Process	of Task)	Total Effort)
Setting up franchises (20%)			
Contact distributors .10% × 20 =	2	33%	0.66%
Develop company's image . . . . .35 × 20 =	7	25	1.75
Product-market education . . . . .40 × 20 =	8	25	2.00
Negotiate/close . . . . .15 × 20 =	3	0	0
Serving/motivating distributors (40%)			
Help in management procedures . . . . .30% × 40 =	12	0%	0
Aid inventory control . . . . .20 × 40 =	8	20	1.60
Enhance customer/market acceptance . . . . .10 × 40 =	4	75	3.00
Train in product sales . . . . .20 × 40 =	8	10	0.80
Aid in job closing . . . . .10 × 40 =	4	0	0
Joint customer service . . . . .10 × 40 =	4	0	0
Distributor's efforts (40%)			
Making user contact . . . . .30% × 40 =	12	20%	2.40
Developing user interest . . . . .20 × 40 =	8	10	0.80
Developing user preference . . . . .20 × 40 =	8	10	0.80
Making proposals . . . . .10 × 40 =	4	0	0
Closing . . . . .10 × 40 =	4	0	0
Serving accounts . . . . .10 × 40 =	4	20	0.80
Total sales process	100%		
Advertising efficiency contribution . .			14.61%

Program value = .145 × $4,000,000 = $580,000.

Alternate salesman investment = $65,000 ÷ $15,000 = 4⅓ salesmen × $150,000 sales per man = $650,000 minus 14.5 percent of $650,000, leaving $555,750 added revenue.

Source: Company executives.

Weighing Each Task

After agreeing on the specific selling tasks involved in water pump sales, marketing executives proceeded to secure agreement on the percentage of the marketing effort required for each task, assuming the total marketing effort to equal 100 percent. To reach this censensus, managers used their own judgments as well as market research.

For example, in the sale of large capital equipment, where continuing service and reliability were considered to be the key factors, sales managers knew from experience that their firm's reputation was a prime buying motivation. Reputation was important both in the initial steps of gaining inquiries and in the later stages of gaining preference during negotiation. On the other hand, managers believed that company reputation was relatively unimportant in selling fabricated metal products that might just as easily be purchased from local sources.

Marketing research, including awareness studies, preference studies, distributor coverage studies, and so forth, also helped managers define the jobs to be done. The time currently being spent in the field on the various sales tasks was also available in the form of sales representatives' itineraries and call reports. For example, a recent sales control study had revealed that, for some products, sales representatives spent little time identifying new sales prospects. Most leads of this kind originated in various promotional activities.

The results of the weighing analysis are given in Exhibit 1, column (B). Franchise development, for example, was viewed as requiring 20 percent of the total marketing effort. Contacting distributors was viewed as 10 percent of the job of developing franchises and, thus, as 2 percent of the total marketing process. Mr. Freeman believed that in later years managers could reach agreement on these estimates much more quickly.

Establishing Advertising and Promotional Goals

Mr. Freeman believed that only in auditing the accomplishment of specific advertising goals could managers assess industrial advertising's direct achievements. (This concept had been presented by Russell H. Colley in a book published by the Association of National Advertisers.[2]) For example, advertising objectives could be defined as:

Persuading X customers to visit Y dealers over a Z time period.

Establishing new-product awareness among X percent of the potential market within Y months.

Increasing penetration of a particular advertising message from X percent to Y percent in Z months.

Mr. Freeman proposed that the $65,000 discretionary amount in the total $550,000 marketing budget, be directed toward the goal of increasing distributors' inventories. Experience had shown Worthington executives that the distributor who stocks was the distributor who promotes. These local promotional programs were considered to be effective in nearly every major market. It was also apparent to Worthington executives that these promotional programs were an effective inducement to stocking when the value of the programs was made obvious to distributor management. Adequate distributor inventory not only increased the likelihood that the distributor could provide quicker service. Service was judged vital to distributor success, because pump buyers generally demanded immediate delivery upon ordering, and expected the distributor to carry a substantial inventory of spare parts in case of emergencies.

With the overall goal of increasing distributors' inventories, marketing executives developed three specific advertising objectives, after balancing

---

[2] *Defining Advertising Goals: For Measured Advertising Results* (New York, 1961).

what they hoped to achieve with what was possible with $65,000. The three goals were as follows:

1. For setting up franchises, make 30 percent of nonhandling distributors aware of the line's availability and benefits.
2. For serving and/or motivating distributors, increase the number of stocking distributors running promotional programs by 20 percent.
3. For influencing users, increase from 5 percent to 50 percent the number of prospects aware of a new distributor stock plan.

Distributors participating in this plan would carry a predetermined inventory level designed to provide quick customer delivery on almost any size order and avoid stock-outs. For carrying this inventory, the distributor received a discount schedule.

After a few meetings, advertising and sales managers came to agreement regarding the contribution that achieving the communications objectives would make to each step in the selling process. The results of this analysis are given in Exhibit 1, column (C). For example, the achievement of the stated communications objectives would account for 33 percent of the job of making distributor contacts, i.e., advertising would make the salesman's call one third more effective or reduce the personal calling-time requirements by one third. On the other hand, managers agreed that the achievement of these objectives would play no part in signing up new distributors. Setting up franchisers was strictly a personal selling activity supported by normal advertising and promotion expenditures.

Mr. Freeman believed, as a by-product of these negotiations, that the process of coming to agreement had value in allowing both parties to view more clearly the advantages and limitations of each other's marketing capabilities. For instance, it was generally recognized that, in the case of this class of pump, salesmen needed specific support in weeding out and recruiting new and better distributors. On the other hand, advertising executives made no claims that advertising added to efficiency in proposing for specific applications.

Assigning Advertising's Dollar Contribution

By applying these agreed-upon percentages to each task identified in the pump's selling process, Worthington executives established the percentage contribution that the variable advertising amount would make to the total marketing effort. Exhibit 1, column (D), sums each individual task contribution and gives the variable advertising budgets' total contribution to the selling process as 14.61 percent. This figure, rounded to 14.5 percent, became the key figure with which management was able to determine the *variable* advertising program's revenue contribution to sales.

Worthington executives believed that this figure was a conservative one. First, each of the components was conservatively estimated and reflected many individual agreements on those aspects of marketing to which a contribution could be made. For instance, managers estimated that the stated communications objectives of the variable advertising program would do a minimum of 25 percent of the job of product-market education, a discrete task involved in franchise development. This task was weighted as 8 percent of the total marketing process. Therefore, advertising's contribution to this part of the total job was a conservative 2 percent. Second, the 14.5 percent did not account for any random benefits of advertising not identified in the analysis of specific aims, benefits that might appear, say, in the form of goodwill or some other intangible.

Using 14.5 percent as the variable advertising program's contribution to the marketing effort and $4 million as the total expected sales for the product, executives determined that the sales revenue contribution from the program was $580,000.

Analyzing Alternatives

Executives had now determined that using the $65,000 variable funds for an advertising program aimed at increasing distributors' inventories would yield additional sales revenue of $580,000. But this advertising program was not the only possible use of the $65,000. An alternative plan was to hire more salesmen.

The cost of fielding additional salesmen to cover this product was judged to be $15,000 per year. The projected sales for each additional salesmen were $15,000 in the product line. The added revenue from additional salesmen was computed as follows. The $65,000 variable advertising and promotion fund would "buy" 4-1/3 salesmen ($65,000 ÷ $15,000 = 4-1/3). These 4-1/3 salesmen would produce $650,000 in sales (4-1/3 × $150,000 = $650,000). Subtracting the promotional support from the variable advertising program on these additional sales (14.5 percent of $650,000) leaves $555,750 added revenue from using salesmen *exclusively* to achieve the desired sales goal.

In this case, using the $65,000 on the variable advertising program in tandem with the existing sales force was slightly superior to using salesmen exclusively. They were influenced in their decision by the fact that the former alternative would bring higher per-salesman performance levels.

EXTENDING THE DOLLAR-CONTRIBUTION METHOD TO OTHER PRODUCT GROUPS

Before attempting to use the dollar-contribution method for evaluating advertising's contribution to other product groups in the Worthington line, Mr. Freeman wanted to be sure that it was applicable. For instance, he was aware that gaining agreement concerning advertising's contribution to the heavy capital equipment group would be difficult. The market for these goods was extremely selective and of low density. Selling was relatively easy and potential suppliers were usually few and well known to the prospects. Mr. Freeman believed that for this type of product advertising often represented a "commercial gesture of intent" by the supplier. In effect, the advertising firm was reassuring buyers that the firm would direct its resources, service, and facilities to the industry involved. The advertising firm was also trying to convince the buyer that the firm and its product were completely acceptable to the buyer's top management, and that the supplier was competitive in all respects. For this type of product, the degree to which advertising persuaded the buyer regarding these factors, *beyond* the salesman's capability to do so, would be a difficult point to settle. Mr. Freeman wondered whether judgments in cases like these could be further refined by research. He was concerned not only with the kinds of information that research could contribute but also with the problem of whether the costs of research could exceed its benefits.

Another problem in the application of the method to other product groups was that of finding a satisfactory alternative to advertising. Comparing advertising to more salesmen was, in most cases, impossible. Actually, in most product groups, field sales personnel requirements were quite rigid from program period to program period, and it would be unrealistic to assume that personnel levels could be raised or lowered. However, there might be some items in the sales budget that were not so rigid, and sales managers might consider varying these items depending upon the analysis of a possible better alternative return through a strengthened investment in advertising.

A third problem involved differences in the strengths of the sales force of the various product groups. In certain groups the sales force was obviously undermanned; in others, the sales force was well established and any additions or deletions in manpower would tend to be marginal. It seemed to Mr. Freeman that these conditions might tend to reduce the effectiveness of the method as an evaluative device. Advertising would seem to be viewed as acting in support of an undermanned sales force in one instance, and as an alternative to "marginal" additions in the other.

A fourth problem involved defining advertising's contribution, given marked differences in the nature of the various customer groups. In the pump market, the effect of an advertising program on an equipment house viewing Worthington pumps as a major source of sales volume was likely to be different from its effect on, say, a mill supply house for which these pumps were an incidental item. For the pumps line, these differences were fairly easy to deal with. But for product classes with a wide variety of customer groups with varying attitudes regarding Worthington products, setting communications objectives might be difficult indeed.

Index to Cases